Jean Mocquet, Nathaniel Pullen

Travels and Voyages into Africa, Asia, and America,

the East and West-Indies, Syria, Jerusalem, and the Holy-land

Jean Mocquet, Nathaniel Pullen

Travels and Voyages into Africa, Asia, and America,
the East and West-Indies, Syria, Jerusalem, and the Holy-land

ISBN/EAN: 9783337245504

Printed in Europe, USA, Canada, Australia, Japan

Cover: Foto ©Andreas Hilbeck / pixelio.de

More available books at **www.hansebooks.com**

TRAVELS AND VOYAGES

INTO
Africa, Asia, and *America,*
THE
East and *West-Indies;*
Syria, Jerusalem, and the
Holy-Land.

PERFORMED BY
MR. John Mocquet,
Keeper of the *Cabinet of Rarities,*
to the King of *France,* in the
Thuilleries.

Divided into Six BOOKS, and Enriched with SCULPTURES.

Translated from the French,
By NATHANIEL PULLEN, *Gent.*

LONDON:
Printed for *William Newton,* Bookseller, in *Little-Britain*; and *Joseph Shelton*; and *William Chandler,* Booksellers, at the *Peacock* in the *Poultry,* 1696.

TO THE
KING.

May it Pleaſe Your Majeſty,

ONE of the Principal Graces which it hath pleaſed Almighty God to ſhew me, in Preſerving me from ſo many Perils and Dangers that I have run through in Travelling

Epistle Dedicatory.

Travelling about the World, is this, To see my self at present at Your Majesty's Feet, offering, in all Humility and Obedience, This, my Writings, as the only Fruit which I have been able to Reap in my Long and Dangerous Travels. I know very well, that 'tis a thing which of its self is not worthy to be presented to Your Majesty. But should it please Your Majesty to consider, that the late King, Your Royal Father, of Glorious and Eternal Memory, did me formerly the Honour, to command me to undertake the most part of these Voyages, and to take pleasure in the Relations which I made to him thereof, at my Return; I dare promise my self, that Your Majesty (as you follow in all things the Generous Steps of the Greatest King, and Best Father that ever was)

Epistle Dedicatory.

was) *will not also disdain to receive with Your wonted Goodness and Sweetness, this little Testimony of my most humble and most devout Affection to Your Majesty's Service; the which may encourage me to cause Your Majesty one Day to see (God willing) something of more Value, and to hope that, according to Your Royal Design, Your Majesty will give me Means to continue and perfect the* Cabinet of Rarities *which, by Your Command, I have began to erect in Your Majesty's Palace of the* Thuilleries, *an Enterprize so laudable, that it merits to be reckoned amongst so many other Worthy Actions of Honour and Vertue, which render Your Majesty Glorious and Commendable for ever: And in the mean time I will continue all the rest of my Life to pray to God,*

A 3   *That*

Epistle Dedicatory.

That it would please him to augment more and more to Your Majesty, his Holy Graces and Benediction.

Your Majesty's

Most Humble, and
  Most Obedient Subject,
   and Servant,

John Mocquet.

A
PREFACE,
FOR THE
Underſtanding of *Circles*, *Zones*, *Parallels*, *Degrees* of *Longitude*, and *Latitude*, *Climates*, and other neceſſary Things, in the Deſcription of the Univerſe.

BEFORE we come to a particular Recital of the Six Voyages which I have made during 14 or 15 Years in divers Places of *Europe*, *Aſia*, *Africa*, and *America*, I think 'twill not be much amiſs (for the more clear Underſtanding thereof) to ſpeak briefly, by way of Preface, ſomething of the

Four

The Preface.

Four Parts of the World, and of certain Principles appertaining to the Sphere, and Geography, to the end that the Reader may the more easily apprehend such things as he shall find dispersed here and there in these my Writings; laying down for certain and necessary Maxims several things which I should otherways have been constrain'd, too often, to repeat; tho' but touching as it were upon what might be said of this Science, the more exact Research, and Knowledge of which, I leave to those who make Profession thereof, and who are more Learned therein than my self, who desire to know no more thereof than what may be necessary for me in the Narration of my Voyages.

Know then that God hath so disposed the Universe, that he hath joined the Earth and the Sea in one round Mass, whose Weight reposes in the Centre of the World, as being the lowest Place, serving for a most sure Retreat and convenient Habitation for Man and Beast, in Parts raised above the Waters, which have their limited Place in

Earth for Man and Beast.

The Preface.

in the Abysms and Depth of the Earth. Now these Waters encompass all the Earth, and separate it by an admirable Artifice into Three great and spacious Continents, or firm Lands, upon the which (according to the order and situation of the superior Parts of the World) the Cosmographers place Five principal Circles, which are the Equinoctial, the Two Tropicks of *Capricorn*, and the Two Polar-Circles, Artick, and Antartick. The first Circle is called Equinoctial, because the Sun coming underneath the Circle, (which happens Twice in the Year, about the 21st. of *March*, and the 24th. of *September*) causes, throughout the whole World, Day and Night to be of equal length. It is equally distant from the Two Poles, and divideth the Terrestrial Globe into Two Hemispheres, or equal Parts, one extending towards the North, and the other towards the South.

Three Continents.

Circle of the Sphere upon the Earth.

The Second Circle is the Tropick of Cancer, or Solstice of the Summer, because the Sun arriving there, causeth Summer to all the Countries on this side the Equinoctial, the which happens

The Preface.

happens at such time as the Sun enters into the first degree of *Cancer*, which is about the *22d. of *June*; and then we have the longest Days, and shortest Nights in the Year. The Circle is distant from the Equator 23 Degrees and a half towards the Border of the North.

*Stili novi.

The Third Circle is the Tropick of *Capricorn*, or Solstice of the Winter, where the Sun arriving, which is about the 23d. of *December*, causeth the shortest Days and longest Nights with us; for to the other Hemisphere of the South happens the contrary. It has the same Declension of the Equator towards the South as the other, to wit 23 Degrees.

The Fourth Circle, is the Circle Artick, and the Fifth, Antartick; each of them distant from its Pole 23 Degrees and a half.

Zones.

Now by these Four last Circles, all the Earth is divided into Five Zones, or Girdles, which encompass and cover the Face of the Earth, one of which is called Torrid or Burnt, two Temperate, and two Cold. The Torrid is situated betwixt the Two Tropicks,

The Preface.

picks, 45 Degrees in breadth; one of the Temperate, Septentrional betwixt the Tropick, and Cancer, and the Circle-Artick; the other, Meridional, betwixt the Tropick and Capricorn, and the Circle-Antartick, of 43 Degrees each. The two Cold, are one betwixt the Circle-Artick and its Pole, and the other betwixt the Circle-Antartick, and its other Pole, each of 23 Degrees.

The Torrid Zone, thus called by the Ancients, in regard of the Opinion which they had, that because of the Perpendicularity, and ordinary Neighbourhood of the Sun, all these Countries were uninhabitable, because of the excessive Heats, also that the cold Zones were so, because of the excessive Cold, caused by the great distance and lowness of this same Planet. But the Navigators of ours, and the precedent Ages, have by experience found all these Countries Habitable and Peopled; so that some of the most Wise and Learned amongst the Ancients, have left behind them in their Writings more Discourse according to Reason and Science, *Torrid Zone Inhabited.*

The Preface.

ence, than by Experience: For in the Torrid Zone, the Heat of the Day is gently temperated by the Cold, equal with the Night; and in the cold Zones, the Air is mitigated in Summer, by reason of the long Residence of the Sun in their Horizon; besides the Cold there is rendred the less insupportable, in regard there being very little or no Winds, and their Blasts very feeble and weak. 'Tis true, the Countries under the cold Zones are scarcely Inhabited, because the Earth does not there fructifie as in the Temperate. But as for those of the Torrid Zone, there are vast Places wonderfully Peopled, as well for the Commodity of the Waters, as for the Goodness and Fertility of the Countries, which bear Grain, or Rice, in abundance, like the Countries subject to the King *Monomotapa*, towards the Cape of *Good-Hope*, *Angoche*, and the Cape of *Currants*, and the Country of the *Abissines*, or *Prester-John*, which extends in Land from *Bombase* to the *Red-Sea*.

Upon the Eastern Coast you have also very spacious Islands, as those of St. *Law-*

The Preface.

St. *Lawrance*, *Zealand*, *Maldives*, *Sumatra*, the *Java's*, *Moluque's*, and others without Number, extream fertile, and abounding in whatsoever is delectable, and necessary for Human Life.

Towards the West, are the Lands of *New-Spain*, *Brasil*, and *Peru*, and others adjacent, near to the Equator, which are very good. All which clearly shews the Falshood of the Opinions of the Ancients concerning the Habitation of these Zones.

Now the Extent or Breadth of these Five Zones, from the Equinoctial to each Pole, is divided into Paralels, as their length from East to West into Meridians; from whence is taken the Longitudes, and Latitudes of divers Countries.

The Parallels are Circles equally distant one from the other, beginning at the Equator, and finishing at the Poles. The Meridians are Circles passing through the Poles, and crossing the Equator; or when the Sun is arrived, it causeth Noon to those who are above the Horizon, and Midnight to those who are underneath.

The

The Preface.

The Latitude of Regions is diſtinguiſhed by the Parallels from North to South, as the Longitude by the Meridians from Eaſt to Weſt: The Meridians of equal Extent, gather together from Two Poles; but the Parallels do not ſo, who are always equally diſtant one from the other, tho' ſometimes greater, or leſs, according to their Approach to the Equator or Poles.

According to the Extent of theſe Circles, are taken the Longitudes and Latitudes of divers Countries and Places of the Earth. The Latitude, or Hieght, is counted from the Equinoctial to the Poles, from one part to another, by 90 Degrees: And the Longitudes, beginning at the Meridian of the Fortunate Iſlands, or *Canaries*, go from Weſt to Eaſt 360 Degrees quite round the Earth; in which 'tis Remarkable, that the Regions under the ſame Degree or Latitude whatſoever, have in the ſame moment the like *Time, as thoſe who under divers degrees have Diverſity, and that in varying, in an Hour's time, by 15 Degrees, ſooner or later, according as you

Weather or Seaſon.

The Preface.

you are more East or West. Thus those who are under the same Degree of Latitude, tho' several of Longitude, have Day and Night equally, and the same Seasons on the one side the Equinoctial; for on the other, 'tis quite the contrary: like as if the Winter is in the Septentrional Part, you shall have the Summer in the Meridional, tho' in the same Latitude, as I have remark'd in the Kingdom of *Canary*, and *Goa*, in the *East-Indies*, where they have their Winter in *June*, *July*, and *August*, contrary to the same Latitude of our *Europe*: But this Winter consists only in Rains, and great Winds coming from the South; and this Rain is very hot, insomuch that the Winter in these Parts of *Goa*, is rather hotter than our Summer here, the Trees there being continually green, and bearing Fruit in all their Seasons, as Jaquebar, Anana's, Jangomes, Carambola's, Jambo's, and others; for all the Winter is hot and moist, and then the Sun seldom appears, being hid under thick Clouds, so that it renders the Days very dark. But the Places who have divers Latitudes

Days and Nights divers.

The Preface.

tudes have inequality of Days and Nights, more or less, according to their difference, and approaches, or distance from the Poles: The Day beginning from Sun-rising to the setting thereof.

In the Countries under the Equinoctial, they are equal with the Nights, of 22 Hours each; on the contrary, in those Places stretching towards the Poles, they lengthen as in the 30th. Degree of Latitude, the longest Day being 13 Hours 5 Minutes; under the 50 Degree, 'tis 16 Hours, 20 Minutes; under the 66 and half, or in the Artick-Circle, 'tis 24 Hours intire; under the 70. the Sun sets not, during 64 Days, and 14 Hours, as in those Parts of *Moscovia,* as I have heard a *Dutch* Captain say who has been there, that their longest Day, without Night, was from *June* to *July,* as in Winter they have Night proportionably; so that it is expedient for the Ships which come from those Countries to return in the Month of *August,* except they have a mind to be stopp'd by the Ice. The People who inhabit those Countries, make, during

The Preface.

during the Winter, little Holes in the Ice to take Sea-Wolves, tho' sometimes they are deceiv'd, and caught themselves, as I have been inform'd; so that Multitudes of People have been swallowed up, the Ice coming to break on a sudden, by reason the time or season of the Heat approaches sometimes sooner than ordinary, the which has caused these People to be more circumspect for the future.

Degrees and their Quantity.

'Tis also Remarkable, That the Degrees of Latitude are always every where equal, each Degree containing 15 *German* Leagues, or 17 and a half of *Spanish*, 25 of *French*, or 60 *Italian* Miles: But the Degrees of Longitude are equal with those of Latitude, under the Equinoctial only; and the more they decline therefrom, they diminish, until that under the Poles they are reduced into one Point: For under the Line, the Degree of Longitude contains 60 Miles, whenas under the 60 Degree of Latitude 'tis no more than Thirty, and under the Pole nothing at all. So that it shall

a happen

The Preface.

happen, that Two Ships being diſtant one from the other 150 Miles, if they ſail from the Equinoƈtial towards the Septentrion, being arrived under the 60 Degree, they ſhall be no more than 75 Miles diſtant, and under the 71 Degree, 31 Minutes, they ſhall approach to Fifty, and at laſt under the Pole ſhall meet.

The Pilots ought well to obſerve this, in regard of the Currents which are found in certain Parts; ſo that thinking to make one way, they take another: Alſo I adviſe 'em to take heed they be not deceiv'd by certain Cards, which commonly are falſe, except they have been experienc'd by good Pilots. This happen'd to us in our Voyage to the *Weſt-Indies*, parting from the River of *Cayenna*, where the Caribes are, to the Iſles of *Santa-Lucia*: For we were deceiv'd as well by the Currents, as the Cards we had with us, which were falſe, we finding but one which was ſure for thoſe Parts; for inſtead of going to the Iſlands aforeſaid, we paſſed along by
the

The Preface.

the Isle of *Tobaco*, and *Trinidad*, and cast Anchor at the *White-Island*, where we could find no Water, of which we were in great want. 'Twas no small Astonishment to me, how such infinite Multitudes of Cabrits, and wild Goats, (besides other Animals which are there,) could live without so much as a drop of Water: But the Divine Providence has otherways order'd it, (as I have above-touched) by the cool Nights, and the Dew, with which these Beasts refresh themselves.

From thence we went to *Margurite* Island, but we found no more Water there than we did at the other, and so to the Mouth of the River of *Cumana*, where the People of a *Dutch* Ship had told us we should find some, as we did at the entrance of the River. This shews the Necessity of having good Cards, and well rectified.

But to return to the Three Continents, or firm Lands, from the which all the Earth is separated by Waters: The first was by the Ancients divided into Three Parts, to wit, *Europe*, *Asia*,

The Preface.

fia, and *Africa*, all joining together. The second, unknown to the Ancients, and discover'd in our Days by *Christopher Columbus*, in the Year 1492, and by *Americus Vespusius*, 1495, is *America*, which for its vast Extent is divided into Two Parts, *Peru*, and *Mexico*. The Third is *Terra-Australis*, or *Magellanique*, thus called, because of *Ferdinand Magellan*, who first found it out in the Year 1519. 'Tis suppos'd to be very great, but for the most part uninhabited and desart. 'Tis also called *Terra del Fuego*, for the great quantity of Fire there seen, the which renders it infertile and uninhabited, there being several Mines of Sulphur which cause those Fires, as I saw in going to the *East-Indies*; for passing by the Isles of *Cape-Verd*, there is one of them called *Fuego*, because of the Fire there continually seen, and is very high: One Night we sailed round about her; and seeing the Flames in great abundance coming out of the Earth in all parts, we were not a little surpriz'd; and the next Day passing along by this same Island, with a very

The Preface.

a very boisterous Wind, and approaching somewhat nigh, the Wind drove the sulphurous Vapours just into our Faces, which were very unsupportable and stinking.

Europe, the first of the Three Continents, is the least in extent, and for her Fertility gives not place to the others; but for Arms, Laws, Policy, Religion, Sciences, Arts, and all sorts of Vertues, she surpasses them by far. And of the Provinces of *Europe*, *France* alone is the Principal, according to the Judgment of the Nations her Enemies, whether you consider the Goodness, Fertility, and Beauty of her Lands, the Excellency and temperature of the Air, Salubrity, and Abundance of her Waters, and Number of Inhabitants; or in regard of the Manners of her People, their Piety, Valour, Erudition, Justice, Discipline, Liberality, Freeness, Courtesie, Liberty, and all other Qualities Military and Civil. In short, the Renown of the *French* has been such, by their Conquest in the East, that

The Preface.

their Name remains there for an Eternal Memory: So that to this Day, throughout all *Asia*, and *Africa*, they call all those who come from *Europe*, by the Name of *Franghi*, let them be of what Country soever.

The Fertility of *France* is such, that she furnisheth abundantly, *Spain*, *Portugal*, *Italy*, and *Barbary*, not only with Corn, but several other Commodities; and I verily think, that every Year there goes from *Provence*, *Languedoc*, *Bretagne*, *Poitou*, *Xaintoign*, and *Normandy*, above Six thousand Ships laden with Corn, and other Merchandise. To *Lisbon* only, there comes above a Thousand, as well great as small: And I believe that the *Spaniards* and *Portugueses* could not furnish Corn for so many Voyages, were they not supplied therewith from *France* to make Biscuit; besides Sails, Cordage, Salt Flesh, and other necessary things to furnish their Ships.

The Principal Provinces of *Europe*, are, *France*, *Spain*, *Germany* High and Low, *Italy*, *Sclavonia*, *Greece*, *Hungary*,

The Preface.

gary, Poland, Danemark, Sweden, Muf-covy, and the Ifles of *England, Scotland, Ireland, Ifland, Groneland, Sicilia, Candia, Malta, Sardania, Corfe, Corfu, Majorica, Minorica,* and others of the *Archipelago.*

Afia, the fecond Part of our firft Afia. Continent, is of very great Extent, Riches, and Fertility, and ever very Renowned for having born the greateft Monarchies, and firft Empires, as of the *Affyrians, Babylonians, Perfians, Greeks, Parthians, Bactrians, Indians,* and others; and at this Day, the *Turks, Perfians, Arabians, Tartars, Mogols, Chinefes,* and other *Indians.* But above all, this Part is the moft efteemed, for the Creation of the firft Man, planted in the Terreftrial Paradice, Colonies and People coming from thence, and difperfed through the reft of the World, and moreover, for the Redemption of Mankind, and the Operation of our Salvation acted therein; befides, for having given Religion, Science, Arts, Laws, Policy, Arms, and Artifices, to all the o-

a 4 ther

The Preface.

ther Parts: In short, for its inestimable Riches, the Wisdom and Dexterity of its Inhabitants. Her most celebrated Provinces are the Countries of the Great *Turk,* of *Persia,* the Great *Mogul,* the Grand *Tartar*, *Arabia, China, Indostorn* of the *East-Indies*: *Guzarat, Cambaya, Malabar, Coromandel, Bengall, Pegu, Siam,* and the rest of the *Indies,* on this and the other side the *Ganges.* The Isles are innumerable, as *Zeilan, Sumatra,* the *Java's, Molucco's, Philipians, Japan, Maldaves,* and others.

Africa.

The last Part of this first Continent is *Africa,* separated from *Europe* by the Mediterranean-Sea, and from *Asia,* by the Isthmus of *Egypt,* and the *Red-Sea,* making as it were a Peninsula, encompass'd on all sides by the Sea, save by this Neck of Land, which is betwixt *Egypt,* and *Palestine.* Its principal Provinces are *Egypt, Barbary, Fez,* and *Morocco, Æthiopia,* or *Abyssine, Nubia, Lybia, Guinia, Congo, Monomotapa,* and others of the South: This Part is very good and fertile

The Preface.

fertile in some Places; but it contains several great and sandy Desarts without Water.

That part of *Africa*, unknown to the Ancients, and discover'd by the *Portuguese*, about the Year 1497. is called by the *Arabians*, *Zanzibar*, and extends from the Lakes where the *Nile* takes its Original, to the Cape of *Good-hope*, containing several good Countries bordering upon *Monomotapa*, as amongst others, *Cefala*, and *Cuama*, from whence is gotten great quantity of fine Gold; insomuch that it has been the Opinion of several, That those Countries of *Cefala*, and *Cuama*, was the *Ophir* where *Solomon* sent to fetch Gold; tho' others think 'twas rather *Malaca*, and other Places of the *East-Indies*, and some will have it to be *Peru* in the *West*.

The last Continent of the World is that Part which we call *America*, and which, as I have said, is divided into Two Principal Parts, *Mexico* in the North, and *Peru* in the South, separated by the Isthmus of *Panama*:

America.

There

The Preface.

There are several Provinces, and People of different Languages, Manners, and Fashions. The greatest City in those Northern Parts, is *Mexico*, or *Temistitan*, opulent in Riches, and all manner of Delights. Before she was subject to the *Spaniards*, she contain'd (as they say) above 70000 Houses, with an exceeding great and glorious Temple, where they sacrificed Men, Women, and Children, of all Ages and Sex, to their Idols, in cleaving them down the Breast, and plucking out their Hearts whilst they were beating, which they cast into the Faces of these Idols; and sometimes they thus open'd Women with Child, but especially Virgins, tho' how beautiful soever, were not exempt, and whom they used in a most shameful manner, in exposing that which Nature hath hid from the Eyes of all the World: For this their great Cruelty, and horrible Tyranny, they acquir'd a very bad Name amongst the People their Neighbours, who would never become their Friends, but by Force; and what was the most strange, they
spared

The Preface.

spared not their nearest Kindred for these abominable Sacrifices; and when any Man of Authority came to die, they interred with him their Slaves alive, to bear him Company in the other World: When they had offer'd in Sacrifice their Enemies, they cut the Bodies into pieces, and then roast them, to feast with their Friends therewith. The *Caribes*, another People towards the South, do the same, of which we will speak in its proper place.

Ferdinand Cortez, who conquer'd *Mexico*, had no small Trouble to make them quit this abominable Custom; also the Hatred which their Neighbours bore them, was cause of their total Destruction: For they rais'd such great Numbers for the Assistance of *Cortez*, that at last, by their Help, (after a great Slaughter of 'em,) he got the Victory, and took their City, to the extream Joy and Contentment of these neighbouring *Indians*, their ever sworn Enemies.

The Septentrional, or North Part of *America*, comprehends the Countries

The Preface.

tries of *Mexico*, or *New-Spain*, *Florida*, *Virginia*, *Canada*, *New-France*, *Estotiland*, the Countries of *Labrador*, and *Cortereal*, and several other Countries towards the North, to the Straights of *Anian*, who are not yet discover'd.

Towards the North of *New-Spain*, were several Countries discover'd by the *Spaniards*, in the Year 1583. as the Land of *Conquas*, *Passaguates*, *Tiquas*, *Tobofes*, *Jumans*, *Quires*, *Pattarabives*, *Cumanes*, *Quivora*, and others.

The Meridional, or South Part of *America*, contains several Provinces, as *Peru*, *Chile*, *Los Patagons*, *Brazile*, *Cariabane*, *Cumana*, *Dariena*, *Uraba*, *Castillia d'Oro*, *New-Granada*, and others; besides the Isles, as well in the North Sea, as *Cuba*, *Hispaniola*, and others, as those in the South-Sea, of *Solomon*, and others unknown.

Brazil has for Limits towards the North the great River of the *Amazons*, and towards the South, *Rio di la Plata*, or the River of Silver. This
Country

The Preface.

Country is very pleasant and agreeable, with a good Air and temperate, for the most part hot and moist, abounding in several sorts of wild Fruits, and in Raisins, Potato's, and Cassaves, of which the Inhabitants live. There are a great Number of terrestrial and watry Animals, which feed upon these Fruits, and Serpents of such a strange and monstrous sort, that the colour of the Skin only is enough to cause Horror and Amazement. They frequently eat the Armadilla, which is a Creature armed with a Coat, as also the Crocodile, and Gouana's, which is a sort of a Lizard with very long Feet. The Flesh of these are savoury enough, tho' sweetish and insipid. *Wonderful Serpents.*

The People of *Brazil* are great Enemies to the *Portuguese*; and when they can catch any of 'em, they eat them without Intermission; and what is most admirable, they know how to find out by the sandy and dirty Ways, the *Portuguese* above all other Nations whatsoever, and can discover them by their *Brazilians great Enemies to the Portuguese.*

The Preface.

their Tract, like as the Hunts-man does the wild Beasts.

Miserable End of a young Woman. They once took a *Portugal* Woman, young, and very beautiful, whom the *French*, who were there, could not save from being eaten, and which was done in a strange manner; for assembling a Company of them together, in a Ring, in the midst of whom was set this poor young Woman, then having stript her stark naked, not at all regarding her Modesty, they viewed her from Head to Foot ; and after having well consider'd her Delineaments, some commending one thing, and some another, they fell to howling and yelling like so many Devils; whereupon immediately, like a Company of hunger-starv'd Dogs, they fell upon this poor innocent Creature, and in less than two Minutes tore her into above a Thousand pieces, which they as suddenly swallow'd down. They are very Vindictive, never pardoning, but by force, and not of Goodwill. When the *French* arrive there, they give them their Daughters to lie withal,

The Preface.

withal, hoping they will give them something at their Departure.

The Third Continent is *Terra-Australis*, not yet discover'd, which is otherwise call'd the *Land of Fire*, of *Parrots*, and *New Guiney*. There, towards the calm Sea, and the Archipelago of St. *Lazarus*, are the Isles of *Solomon*, not yet fully discover'd.

Some Years since, a *Portugal* Captain, named *Pedro Fernandes di Quieros*, sailed round some Parts thereof, and tells Wonders of those Countries, how that they abound in Beauty and Goodness; insomuch that they resemble an Earthly Paradise. But we ought to wait for a more certain and ample Discovery. The Geographers, and *Portugal* Pilots tell us, That these Countries of *Terra-Australis* are greater than *Europe*, and part of *Asia*. This Captain *Pedro Fernandes*, found out there the Bays of St. *Philip*, and St. *James*, and the Port of *Vera Crux*, which, as they say, is capable of above a Thousand Ships, in the Altitude of Fifteen Degrees and a half.

JOHN MOCQUET.

THE
CONTENTS
Of this BOOK.

THE *First Book of the Travels and Voyages of* John Mocquet, *to* Libia, *the* Canaries, *and* Barbary   Page 1.

The Second Book of the Travels and Voyages to the West-Indies, *as into the River of the* Amazons, *the Country of the* Caripous, *and* Caribes, *and other Countries of the* West   p. 39

The Third Book of the Travels and Voyages to Morocco, *and other Places of* Africa   p. 139.

The Fourth Book of the Travels and Voyages to Æthiopia, Mozambique, Goa, *and other Places of* Africa, *and the* East-Indies   p. 197

The Fifth Book of the Travels and Voyages to Syria, Jerusalem, *and the* Holy-Land

The Sixth and Last Book of the Travels and Voyages to Spain, *with an Intention to pass farther, and what was the Hindrance thereof.*

THE
TRAVELS
AND
VOYAGES
OF
John Mocquet,
INTO
Lybia, the *Canaries,* and
BARBARY.

BOOK I.

Ccording to the desire I had, of a Long time, to Travel about the World, I had a mind to begin with *Africa,* having occasionally found a Ship bound for *Lybia.*

The Travels and Voyages Lib. I.

Parting from St. Malo 1601. Encounter with a Ship.

I parted then from St. *Malo* the 9th of *October*, 1601. and embarqued in the Ship called the *Serene*, Laden with *Salt*, and very well furnished with Victuals, and munition of War; we were 25. men in all, and having born to the *S-West*, and the wind being very favourable, we passed the *Cape* of St. *Vincent*, and being come up within view of the *Canary* Islands we met with a Ship and a *Patache*, whom we descried a far off, using their utmost to come up to us, the *Patache* came with a Light-wind to view us nearer, and to know who we were; but they were not so ill-advised as to come within the reach of our Cannon. At last after having viewed us well on all sides, and taking notice of the Port, and fashion of our Ship, they returned toward their Admiral, who was about 3 or 4. Leagues off us, telling him that our vessel was not so great as theirs; yet they did not know what sort of people we were, not having spoken with us. Their Admiral hearing this, sent them again with the *Patache* to watch us all night, with, a Lanthorn upon

upon the Maſt, coaſting us continually a good way off. But we, ſeeing our ſelves ſo cloſe purſued by theſe *Pirate* Ships; broke our boat to make plat-forms, ſo that we might change our Cannon from one ſide to the other; then having fitted our Net-deck, and made ready our Muſquets, with our Cannons and Patterero's, and hoiſted our Sails, with proviſion of wine upon the Deck, for the Sea-men to drink, to make them the more Couragious; we were reſolved all to die, rather than ſuffer our ſelves to be taken by theſe *Corſairs*. Thus having been round about us for two days and two nights, at laſt their Admiral arriving, with all his top-ſails, full ſail, he commanded us to yield; but we being deaf to that, and ready to let fly our whole broad-ſide; he cried out aloud that we ſhould not fire if we were wiſe, and that if we were a *French* Ship he would do us no harm, and that we ſhould only put out our boat; we made anſwer that our boat was broke, and he might put out his if he would; upon which he was a long time

time disputing the matter: But at last seeing us so resolute, and so well cover'd with our net-deck, he put out his Boat, and came aboard us, and seeing nothing but *Salt* in our ship, he returned again without doing us any harm for so smal a matter, besides seeing us so resolved to defend our selves to the last man, and that there was nothing to be gotten but blows, he left us. From thence we pursued our course: But upon our return, meeting with us again, he beat us soundly, and did us a great deal of damage, having three or four ships to our one.

Another Encounter. The 6th of *November* we perceived a Ship, and a P*atache* hid behind *Cape-blane*, making ful-sail towards us: But we, seeing our selves so near being surprised about four or five a clock in the afternoon, we Tack'd from him that we might have time to prepare our selves: But before we could run out our Cannon and trim our Net-deck, they came up with us, and commanded us to yeild, or they would sink us; upon which our Captain (not at all affrighted

frighted at these threatnings) commanded the Cannoniers to do their duty, which they did, saluting them very near, and they in the mean time answering us very briskly: At last, having given us several broad-sides *A Fight.* and Volies of small shot, which rained upon us like hail, the night came on, and the Moon shin'd a little. In the mean time we had several of our men wounded, but none mortally: The enemy had battered us, thinking to have taken us, but he was as soon repulsed as come; he seeing that, made on the other side, thinking our Cannon had been changed; but he was deceived; For we had there three Cannons ready, with Paterrero's full of stones, and nails, besides bullets. Coming then close one upon the other, we let fly these three Cannons, and Patereros, directly upon his Fore-castle, where there were near Eighty men ready to leap into our Ship; They seeing themselves cover'd all over with fire, by so many shot, we discharged upon them, and many of their

their men lay along upon the Deck, they fell to crying out, God the Lord my God, in *English*, then runing back, they fir'd a great shot which pierced our ship through and through, and broke the leg of a mariner, who in haft was running to the pump, because they cryed out that we were sinking, for we had already almost six foot water in the hold by a shot receiv'd in the beginning of the fight: our Carpenter was very nimble in stopping it. Hereupon these Pirates presently bore away, and we saw them no more. I believe they had lost a great many of their men, otherways they would never have left us, they were so animated against us, and having sworn to cast us all into the Sea. They must needs have had great want of Victuals, that being all they demanded of us. Having then escaped this great danger, our next business was to fit up our Rigging, cut almost to pieces, and our Sails torn on every side; Our Masts also

also were ready to tumble down, they were so battered with great shot. All that we could do was to recover *Cape-blane*, where we found *Cape-blane.* seven Ships Laden with Liquor, who seeing us Arrive near the *Muscle*, which is a little Creek, or Bay, before the entrance into the Haven, where we had cast Anchor.

The Seventh of *November*, about two a clock in the morning; two of these seven Ships, the greatest and the best armed, came and cast Anchor on each side of our ship, and the other five round about, beating their Drums, and sounding their Trumpets, which mightily disturbed us, at such time when we thought to have taken our rest: Then we began to deck our Canons, and Musquets, order our net-deck, and to hoist our sails: but they crying out to us to tell them from whence we were, we were a long time without giving them any answer, not knowing what sort of people they were, and were just going to tell them that we were *Spaniards*: But at last the Master, named *Hamand Clement*, cried out, that we were French,

French, which they would not believe, commanding us to put out our boat; But it was broke, as I have said before; so we answered that they might put out theirs, which they a long time refusing, threatned to fire at us on all sides: At last they resolved to come on board our Ship with their Arms, to know who we were, which having done, after they had known us, they sent their boat again on board their Ships, saluting us with several Cannons,

The next morning we entred into the Haven, where we found three *Lybian-Moors* on shore, who had run away from the people of these seven Ships, they not being able to catch them again in these deserts. These three *Moors* came freely enough on board our Ship, knowing again our Captain, who had formerly travelled into these parts: They told us that there was a *Portugal* Pinnace hard by *Cape-veille*, on the other side *Cape-blanc*; upon which our Captain was resolved to find them out by Land, which he did with a great deal

Moors of Lybia.

Cape-veille

deal of trouble; for in his return he was well scorched, and tauned with the Sun, in passing these deserts. He caused this Pinnace to come, and cast Anchor in the Moule of the Cape hard by us.

In the mean time I had a mind to go on shore to get some *Ostrich* eggs, by the means of the King of *Baze-Alforme*, which is a place hard by where we were. But walking about these sandy-deserts I was in danger to have been taken, and carried away captive by these *Moors*, who were holding Counsel thereupon, but escap'd the danger by casting my self into the Sea, and got into a boat that was coming towards Land: These *Barbarians* seeing this, fell presently together by the ears; and the King *Baze* endeavoured to appease them: And thus I escaped from these People, who without doubt had carried me away, and sold me at some place far distant from thence.

Baze-Alforme.

Great danger.

All this County of *Lybia*, within Thirty or Forty Leagues off *Cape-blanc*, is nothing but Sands and Deserts:

serts: and those of the Country are forced to seek for water a far off, which they carry in Goat-skins upon *Camels*; they get this water at the Fort of *Arguin*, which is about Seven or Eight Leagues from *Cape-blanc*, and is scituated in a little Island where there is some *Portugal*-Souldiers, and a Captain. They are great friends to the *Moors* of the Country, who are not quite black, but tauny, yet there is some amongst them black, and are all *Mahometans*. They Traffick in *Ostrich*-feathers, and Fish, which they call *Hallebranches*.

Arguin-Fort.

As for the rest, the *Ostriches* (which are there in abundance,) Lay their eggs in the sand, and there they bury them; so that it is a very hard matter to find them out, but when the wind blows, they are discovered. These eggs are very good to eat, and the *Blacks* live upon them for the most part.

Now about Five or Six days after, there Arrived a *French*-Pirate, who would have entred into the Haven, but we would not suffer him; He desired

desired of us to let him take this *Portugal*-Pinnace; but because she was under our Protection, we defended her.

Seven, or Eight days after, Arrived Five *Spanish*-Ships belonging to the Duke of *Adelantado*, which made us to bestir our selves a little, and to stand upon our Guard, and to hinder them from entring into the Haven, sending out the boat of the *Portugal* Pinnace to know who they were, that, if they were friends, they might hang out their white Colours, and we would let them enter into the Haven; which they did, and put some of their men in the said boat to come on board us, to let us know that they would do us no displeasure: Being all Arrived, and Anchored in the said Haven, we visited one another, after that each one returned on board his own Ship. Three days after, the *Spaniards* being Anchored round about us, at their ease, they command us to depart out of the Haven, telling us that it was not permitted to the *French* to take any Fish there; the which we were forced

Spanish-Ships.

Spanish ingratitude.

ced

ced to do, and took a *Moor* along with us to guide our Ship to *Cape-veille*. This *Moor* was called *Hiſſe*, one who very well knew this Coaſt, we not being far from the Fort of *Arguin*, where there were *Portugueſe*, and *Blacks*. We found this place very good for Fiſh, and having ſtaid there for ſome time, a *Spaniard* coming from the Fort of *Arguin* came towards us, deſiring us to give him ſome Nails, and wood which they had occaſion for, for their Ship, which was in the *Cape* from whence we were come. We gave him what he ask't; but this Traitor, came only to ſpy us, and to know what we were doing, and if we had our Lading, ſaying that they found no Fiſh in their Haven, and that they ſhould be forced to come and ſeek it on our ſide: And all this to deceive us, as they did.

Treachery of the Spaniards.   For about three, or four days after they came with three boats to force us, and they made uſe of this trick; that is, they put their Nets into their Boats, and hid their Arms underneath, then ſeeing that all our men were

were on Shore busie about the Fish, they sent two of their boats to take our men, and the other came on board our Ship as friends, and their Arms being hid we suspected nothing; we being but three on board, the Captain, the Carpenter, and my self, with one *Black*. The Captain commanded me to make ready a Collation for them; but they saved me that labour, by seising upon our Captain, and the Room where the Arms were. One of the Duke's Ship-boy's taking a naked sword in his hand, set himself against the Cabine-door, to hinder any of us from entering, then they weighed the Anchors, and set Sail, and made towards the *Mole*, where their Ships were: Being arrived there, they took away all our Arms, our Pouder, and our Sails; then putting again all our men into our Ship, to compleat the Lading of Fish, they kept good watch all the night, continually mistrusting us.

But *Christmas* being come, which was almost the time to depart from hence, to return with the Fish, against Lent. They took all our men out of
our

our Ship, and put them in theirs, placing *Spaniards* in ours, leaving some of our men there, to help about the Fish. Of three Ships that remained there, two set Sail, and ours made the third, to return into *Spain*. But being in the open Sea, holding the Master of our Ship in theirs they gave the command to the *Spanish*-Captain, which was in ours, and the Duke's Cabin-boy being left there for Master: the others then held their Course, and left us alone: But being about *Porto-Santo* near to the Isle of *Madera*, we were beaten with contrary winds in so much that we were forced to make towards the Isle, where having cast Anchor a good way off from the City of *Madera*, we had a mind to go on Shore to refresh our selves: But the *Portuguese* that lived there would not suffer us, saying we had the Plague, and therefore set Guards at all the Avenues. In so much that we were forced to get down behind the Rocks, where we had bread, and wine brought us for our money, which was from a wall let down to

Port-Santo, or Holy Ile. Madera.

us with a rope, yet not without great intreaty.

We remained Fifteen days in this misery, at the end of which the *Spanish* Ships our companions, which we had left in the Sea, Arrived in the said Isle with their Main-mast cut down by reason of the bad weather. And their General of the Ship made such a doe, by words, and remonstrances, that he obtained leave to enter into *Madera*; upon condition to take the habit of the City of *Madera*, he, and his servants; a little after, this General being somewhat indisposed, sent to seek me out in this place, where we were in Custody and took the habit of the City, after the *Spanish* fashion, which one of the Souldiers of the Castle had lent me; and so I entered *Madera* to visit this General, where I tarried untill the time of our Embarquement.

Whilest I was visited, and stripped by these people of the Gard-maor in changing my habit, I had forgotten my Purse, which I left in my pocket; But these Gallants had remembred to handle it, and took out the most part

of

of my money for me, before I perceived it, and had I not returned presently again to see after it, they had not left me so much as a blanck.

Design to save themselves. Now one night, as we were all with-drawn into our Ship, except the *Spanish* Captain, and the Pilote, our Captain took a resolution with Six of his men who were there to play the *Spaniards* a fine trick, before the Master, and Pilote came on board, and the Captain's Mate was ordered to lead the others to the bottom of the Ship, promising to make them drink some good wine, to which the *Spanish* Mariners, (who are always ready for their share of such a game, when they can have it on free-cost) would not have failed. We had also disposed our other men in order, some to Guard the Chamber of the Poop, where the Arms were, where I was appointed with one of our men, who had but one Leg, having lost the other in the last Fight: others to set Sail with the wind: And the more to facilitate our design, we weighed one Anchor,

Anchor, leaving the other *a pique*. But no so sooner had we made an end of weighing Anchor, than presently came the Captain, and the Pilote, with the other *Spanish* Mariners on board. The Pilot was wounded by a blow with a sword, having on Shore fought a *Spaniard* of one of the other Ships. Thier Arrival quite spoiled our design, and the next day the wind being good we set Sail.

As for the rest, this Ile of *Madera*, one of the *Canaries*, or fortunate of the Ancients, may have about Fourty Leagues in compass, and hath two Cities, of which the principal is also called *Madera*, with two Fortresses, in one of which, and the strongest, there are *Castilian* Soulders, and in the other *Portuguese*. *A description of the Isle and City of Madera,*

The City is seated in a Valley, and at the foot of a Mountain, from whence comes so much water, and sometimes in such abundance, that very often it causes inundations, which do much damage, carrying away Bridges, Houses, Churches, and other edifices. The City is about as big as St. *Denis*, but very populous, having a great number of slaves, who work upon the sugar without the City; and about all the rest of the Island, stand here and there May-houses of pleasure. The soil is very plentiful in all sorts of excellent fruits, and especially in Wines: The Air there is very sweet and temperate, and the pleasantest place in the World to live in; And 'tis no wonder if the Ancients esteemed this country to be the *Elisian fields*, and as an earthly Paradice.

Sugar-canes.

Amongst the rest the Earth there produces a great quantity of Sugar-canes very spungie which they of the country cut, and bruise in a Mill, then putting it into the Press, and the Liquor, squeesed out, is put to the fire where 'tis boiled over and over in vessels like those which the Dyers use, so that all the moisture may be wholly consumed; and so having refined it, they clap it into Earthen-moulds, where it is formed into Sugar-loaves, as 'tis brought us. The substance, or husk that remains is a redish, and blackish sugar, which

Sugar-loaves.

Lib. I.　*of* John Mocquet.　19

which they call Meleche, that is to say black.

I saw there the *French* Conful, Named *Jean de Chux*, who had married the Niece of *Don Chriftoval de More*, Vice Roy of *Portugal*: He is very rich, and curteous, and did me and my companions a great deal of favour: There are always a great many Factors; as *French Englifh Dutch*, and others, who are to Load the Ships that trade there, They make there a great quantity of excellent fweet meats, that are carried from thence as *Marmelades*, *quidnies*, Candid Lemmon, and feveral other curious Paftes.

But to return again to our departure; we were not gotten Thirty Leagues from the Ile, when we were overtaken with fuch a great tempeft, that we were forced to return back to *Madera*, which was the Twenty fifth of *January*, 1602. and did not go out again till the Ninth of *February*, and made fuch haft, that we Arrived at St. *Lucar de Baramede* in *Spain*, where being come, our Captain was prefently made Prifoner in the *Real*

C 2　　　　　　*des*

des Galleres, saying for these Reasons, that in some of the former Voyages he had sold Corn, and Arms to the Moors of *Barbary,* at *Cap-blanc* ; upon which they brought informations with the deposition of the Moors ; The *Adelandate* (not being willing to give Credit to the Moors) Let go our Captain with his Ship, but our Fish was all spoiled, which was a great Loss to us. We went fromthence to *Lisbon* to sell it, where only we sold part of it, but the Visitor of health being come on board our Ship, and finding it bad, commanded us to sell no more of it upon great penalty, so that we were forced to cast the rest into the Sea.

Voyges to Mazagan. About this time our Captain found an opportunity to Fraight his Ship to go to *Mazagan* in *Afrique,* to carry Corn, and biscquet to the *Portugal* Souldiers who are there in Garison to make war in *Barbary.* With this Lading we parted from *Lisbon,* the Twenty third of *April,* the next day after *Easter,* and that in all diligence to go succour these Poor people, who were ready to die with hunger;

Lib. I. *of* John Mocquet.

hunger; There had been before several Ships sent with Victuals but had been taken by the Pirates. Being Arrived there, we fired a Cannon to give them notice, to send us a Pilot to come nearer; they answered us with another shot, and sent the said Pilot; we approached as near as we possibly could, and cast Anchor about three or four Leagues from *Mazagan*, with that a great number of boats came on board to unlade us. It was a great pity to see these poor people how they were starved, and if these Victuals had not come so seasonably as they did, I believe they had been either dead, or otherways had been forced to have yielded themselves slaves to the *Barbarous-moors*. I could not hinder the children, nor the great ones themselves, from boring holes in the sacks where the biscquet were that they might eat, or rather allay their hunger. I did my utmost endeavour to keep them away, tho' I was very sorry to see them so faint, and look so dreadfully with hunger. My Captain had given me the charge of the biscquet, for to return him the same

Great hunger of the Spaniard.

weight

weight that he had delivered to me at *Lisbon*.

This being all unladed and put into the Magazines for that purpose, I saw the Gentlemen and Cavalliers coming to look every one for his weight of Biscuit, and measure of Corn, which is ordinarily allowed them by the King of *Spain*. One of these Cavalliers received and lodged me in his House; for there is no Inn nor resting place for Strangers.

I ordered the Business so, that our Captain and Master were lodged there also, causing Beds to be prepared for them to lie in.

As for me, I received a thousand Courtesies from this Cavallier, whom I cured of an Humour he had in his Eyes, which he finding remov'd, knew not how to treat me. For in this place was neither Physician nor Apothecary, but only one Surgeon, who was very well skill'd in the Latin Tongue, but wanted the knowledge of Medicines, and Experience.

The Corrigidor, or Judge of this place, invited me one day to Dine with this Surgeon, who discoursed
very

Lib. I. *of* John Mocquet. 23

very readily in Latin; yet for all that he could not give Eafe to a Patient that he had.

The moſt part of the People of the City came to ask for me at my Lodging to give them Phyſick, and made me great Offers; But I had not leiſure to give Satisfaction to all; foraſmuch as we were to return in a ſhort time, as we did not long after.

As for the reſt, this City of *Mazagan* is very ſtrong, and the Walls ſo thick, that ſix Cavalliers may walk a-breaſt round about 'em: The Houſes there are very low, and over-topped by the Walls. There is a great many Cannon, very large and long, and line almoſt all the Wall, but ill mounted: There may be about forty Cannoniers, with ſome 600 Soldiers, *viz.* 200 Horſe, and 400 Foot, the moſt part Married. They make Incurſions upon the Arabians, whom they take Priſoners, and drive away their Cattle. They have hard by them a City called *Azamor*, which makes hot War upon them, and not above two Leagues one from the other. Every morning there goes out 40 Horſe to diſcover what

Mazagan deſcribed.

Azamor.

C 4 they

they can see, and tarry out till noon: In the afternoon 40 others go out, who stay till night: And there are about six of these Cavalliers whom they call *Atalayes*, that is to say, the Watch, who are far distant one from the other, and keep Centinel every where; and when they discover any thing, they Post back; and then the City Watch, who sees them, strikes 2 or 3 blows upon a Bell; with that, the others presently mount their Horses, and run to the place of the signal. For in every place where these *Atalayes* are, there is a long Pole, like a Mast; and when they perceive any thing, they with a little Cord heave their sign on high, which is the signal to all those who Sally out of *Mazagan*. When they have a mind to make an Incursion, every one arms himself, each of 'em carrying Forage for their Horses, whom they give Corn to, out of the Allowance, and Pension, which is sent them from *Portugal*.

<small>Atalayes.</small>

<small>Caricols.</small> They Eat there abundance of *Caricols*, which are little Snails in Shells, who feed upon the Plants; and there the

the Plants are of an exceeding force and virtue.

The Bees there make White Honey, and of an excellent Taste: Their Hives are upon the Houses, which after the African manner are covered with Sotees, like to Cieling after the Moresque; and one may easily go from one House to another. *Honey of Africa.*

This City of *Mazagan* is nothing else but a Fortress, being about half a League in compass; and is inhabited by none but Men of War, who have every one their piece of Land round about the City, where they Sow Corn, as Barley, Pease, Beans, and other Grains; but very often the Moors come and cut it up in the night time, and spoil it. The rest of the Country is Uncultivated. *Country of Mazagan. Villanies of the Moors.*

The Moors do them a thousand Injuries, even to Poisoning a Well, which they have out of the City in a Garden, by casting in Carrion, with other filth and nastiness.

Within the City there is a full Cistern; and upon the *Ciloe*'s Festival-Day, the watch is set: It is very high and large, and is capable of holding above 20000 Pipes of Water.

I was near being left to tarry in this City. For the day before we were to set sail, our Captain and the Master came ashore for me; for I never budged from the City, minding nothing else but the Cure of these People. Now, as I was gone to walk along by the Sea-side, to gather some Sea-Crift, which is there in abundance, being returned to the City to take my rest, I was sent for in great haste to go see a Patient, upon which our Captain went away, and left me there all alone. Knowing this, I went presently towards the Sea-shore, but he was already far enough from thence, so I was forced to go back again to the City to wait till the next day: In the mean time the Ship finding the Wind good, set Sail; and a Soldier, who was a Centinel upon the Wall, knowing that I was still in the City, came presently to give me notice thereof; At which all astonished I run presently to the Wall to see if it was true, and being in great perplexity how to get out from thence, I went to the Captain of the Foot Soldiers to desire him to cause the Gate to be opened, which he did, and gave the Key to the Porter; but I muſt ſtay till the Cavalliers were ready to go out: This time ſeemed to me an Age. At laſt the Gate being opened, I deſired the Pilot-Moor to get me a Boat ready, to carry me on Board our Ship; and by good fortune I found ſome Soldiers who were going a Fiſhing, one of whom had brought us from *Portugal*. They did me that favour as to take me into their Boat: Had we wanted that little Wind, which was weak enough, I had been forced to have tarried there; for which I ſhould not have been much perplexed, had I but had my Cloaths, my Medicines, and my other Things; but I had unhappily been in my Doublet, without comfort, or any other thing. Theſe Soldiers then did their utmoſt to overtake the Ship, which was already got far off, beſides the Sea began to riſe, inſomuch that theſe Men would not go any further, telling, that if the Wind ſhould riſe but never ſo little, they ſhould not be able to recover Land by their utmoſt Efforts, but run the riſque of their Lives.

Here-

Hereupon they left of Rowing, and and held Council amongst themselves what was best to be done; and having resolved to return, they began again to handle their Oars; upon which, I being much vexed, endeavour'd to urge them by Prayers and Promises, that I would certainly Content them, to return again towards the Ship; and by strength of Oars we made our way so that we arrived there. This was no small fortune for me, considering in what trouble they live in there; Besides, the most part of the Portuguese there are such People who are carried thither by Force, being Condemned to be there for a certain time to make War upon the Moors; In short, they are almost all Criminals, otherwise none would be forced to go there.

Having then happily overtaken our Ship, our Captain for excuse, let me understand, that he could not possibly wait any longer for me than until it was day, and if I had not been on Shore, he had set sail the same night, knowing well that when I saw them under sail I would haft to overtake them.

them. But I believe the reason that moved him to go away so hastily without me, was rather to Cheat me of some Money he owed me, and which he payed me since, against his Will, telling me of his Losses; but I was not bound to participate in them, forasmuch as the Condition that I made with him was neither for Gain nor Loss. But I could not get any thing of him since then, but by an Arrest of the Parliament of *Britagne* in the year 1603.

At last we arrived at *St. Lucar de Baramede* the 26th of *May*, and being laden with Salt in the River of *Seville*, near the Salt-Houses, which are there along the Coast, with some Scutcheneal, such as Scarlet is Dyed withall, and about 30000 Crowns in silver, we set sail the first of *July* 1692. accompanied with a little Flemish Ship. The 15th of the same month we descried two great Ships, with their Pataches, making full Sail upon us, and we prepared our selves presently to receive them, ordering our Net-Decks, and running out our Guns, in number 12, with our Pattereroes and

Return to Africa.

Mus-

Muskets; then hoisting our Sails, and handling our Yards, we waited for them in so ready a posture. It was not long before they were upon us, *Sea Fight.* commanding us to yield, and lowr our Sails, and began to Salute us, each with a Broadside; in the mean time we answering them in the same Language: The Fight continued so all the day, without gaining the least advantage one upon the other: We had a great many Men wounded and burnt with the Fire that was kindled by some shots of Cannon; and besides, one of the great Guns burst into pieces, and the Breech of it broke through the two Decks, fell amongst the Salt, and had it not been for the resistance that it found there, it had broke quite through our Ship. In the mean time the small *Fight.* Shot rained upon us like Hail, and without ceasing, insomuch that our Ship was pierced through and through on every side, and our Sails torn to pieces, and all the rest in bad Equipage; but the night coming on, the Fight ceased, and our Enemies watched us all until the next morning, then they left us at liberty.

liberty. All the night we were consulting what we had beſt to do, whether to yield, or to defend our ſelves to the utmoſt extremity. Our Captain, who was of a great Courage, would not hearken to yielding: Hereupon we went on Board the Flemiſh Ship to know their pleaſure. This Flemiſh Ship at the firſt diſcharge of her Cannon, had burnt all her Powder, with which a great number of her Men were diſabled and deſtroyed. They had put their Powder in a piece of Sail, and a Match by chance touched it, which was the cauſe of this Diſaſter. I went on Board their Ship to ſee their Pilot, who was quite Roaſted, his Belly, Face, and Hands, mighty big and ſwoln; I brought him ſome Remedies. I was told that there was 4 or 5 others in a very bad condition, and ready to die: They were Burnt after a pitious and horrible manner. In the end, after we had well conſulted with them, it was reſolved to ſend a Boat on Board the Enemies, with a Man that underſtood their Language, for they were Engliſh; which was done accordingly: But they

Accident of Powder.

they would be pacified by no means whatsoever, saying, that they had suffered a great deal of loss, and that it was not their intention to do any harm to the French, that being expresly forbidden them by the Queen their Mistress: But that our Captain had given them ill Language, and that he himself must come on Board them, to excuse himself, which was done; And they came on Board us, with the Boats of their two Ships, searching in every corner, but they found nothing but Salt: If they had met with our Money, we should have been in a bad condition; for they had played us a trick of their Trade. At last, after we had made them some Presents of Victuals, they withdrew themselves. Their Mariners and Soldiers told us that they had resolved to have fallen upon us in the morning; and had Drank to one another, and Eaten all the little Refreshment they had, hoping to have more of us; but God by his Mercy delivered us from them.

No. 1,

Note, That one of these two Ships by whom we were so beaten, was the same that we met withall at the first, and who had so Chased us in going to *Cape-blanc*: We having then made him good chear, which was no small help to us at this time; and he told us, that after he had left us, he took a Ship laden with Sugar, which paid him well for the trouble we had given him.

In the mean time, being delivered from this danger, we made such haste that we came near to the Cape *de Finibus Terræ*: On this side of the Cape we found a German Ship of *Lubeck*, very great, and put out our Boat to go on board her, that we might have a little Biscquet, for ours began to grow very short, because of the contrary * Winds. We had some of them for our Money, and they were very honest Men: I went also in the Boat to have some Refreshments; but the Wind being high, the Sea began to rise, and the fore part of our Boat was broke, drawing so much Water that we could find no way to empty it; and the German Ship was already a League and a half off us, but they made a little

Return to France.

* *Weather.*

towards us, seeing us in the Sea: We had much ado to get into her, and I to find hold betwixt the Boat and the Ship, because the Sea was very high; but taking the end of a Rope, I was very nimble in mounting up, and had only one Leg a little bruised.

Arriving at St. Malo.
Great danger at Anchoring.

At last, we arrived at *St. Malo* the first of *August*: The next day our Ship was likely to have been lost in the Road, by a great Storm that came so unlooked for, that we had much ado to make the Men go on board, or otherways the Vessel had sunk at Anchor; And so this troublesome Voyage was finished, for which God be Praised.

The End of the First Book.

A Description of the following Cutts.

The First, *The* Lybians, *towards* Cape Blanc, *go in this posture in search of their Enemies.*

The Second, *The Form of the* Lybian's *Fighting when they Encounter.*

A Description of the following Cutts.

The Third, *The Moors of* Lybia *go thus about the Desarts with their Camels.*

The Fourth, *How the* Lybian *Women go along by the Sea-side to look for Fish, and Ostrich Eggs to Eat.*

THE TRAVELS AND VOYAGES

OF

John Mocquet,

INTO THE

WEST-INDIES:

As also,

In the River of the *Amazons*; The Country of the *Caripous* and *Caribes*; and other Nations and Isles of the West.

BOOK II.

AFter my return from *Africa*, I continued for some time in *France*, and knowing that the Sieur *de la Ravardiere* was going away for the *West-Indies*,

Embarking for the VVest-Indies.

Indies, I had a wonderful defire to fee thofe Countries: And for this caufe I entered my felf with the *Sieur,* and embarked in his Ship in the Haven of *Concale* the 12th of *Jan.* 1604. We went to *Choze,* (which is an Ifle five Leagues from *Concale*) there to wait for weather for us to put to Sea. We tarried there till the 24th of the fame month, not without having fuffered by great Winds, which gave us no fmall trouble, befides the lofs of our Boat; but we foon bought another, and at laft fet Sail, bearing South Eaft, and in a little time we paffed the Channel. And forafmuch as our Ship was new, not having as yet been proved in the Sea, we were forced to fuffer her to take her Courfe; not being able to bear up Sails; for fhe veer'd after fuch a manner, (her Top-Maft being high) that fhe was continually with one fide upon the Water, which was a great inconvenience: Neverthelefs, putting our truft in God, we proceeded on; and at the height of the *Cape de Finibus Terræ,* we found a Ship, and made full fail upon her to know what fhe was. Coming clofe up

Lib. II. *of* John Mocquet. 41

up to, and being prepared to attack her, and they also provided to receive us, we found out that it was a French Ship, the Captain of which came upon the Poop well armed, with his Sword in his Hand, crying out to us to Steer Leeward, or else he would fire at us; but we contesting a little thereupon, that we might find out and know of what part of *France* he might be: After having well considered him and known him for a right French Man, we came up Leewards of him, of which he was not a little Proud, thinking that we had been a Man of War, and durst not assault him; for he made signs with his Sword upon the Poop, that we had done well to come up so: But our design was not to make War upon our Nation; besides, that might have been enough to have broken our Voyage.

Holding then our Course, we had so favourable a Wind that we came near to the Isle of *Lancelot* the 6th of *February*; upon which day one of our Men fell over-board into the Sea, and it was impossible to save him, because we had a right Wind. We presently tack'd

A Disaster.

tack'd about upon him; but coming to the place, where he fell, we found nothing but his Breeches. All things that belong'd to him were presently put to Sale upon the Deck, and every one Bought what he had occasion for, as Coats, Linnen, and other Things, with which he was very well furnished: For he was of the Rank of the Nobility, and was named *Duvall*, of *Vire* in *Normandy*.

Coast of Barbary. This done, we steered our Course towards the Coast of *Barbary*, and the next day the 11th of the same month, we arrived near the Land to find out a Port, and cast Anchor in a Creek or Bay, putting out our Boat to go on shore: But coming there, we found nothing but Desarts, without any thing else; insomuch, that we returned again on Board the Ship to weigh Anchor, and to look out some other place more proper to stay in, and to fit up our Patache, scowring along this Coast all the rest of that day and the night following.

Rio del Oro. Presently after, we found out the Mouth of the River *Rio Del Oro*, where we sent our Boat to Sound the Depth

depth of it, and to see if we might enter in so far as a little Island of flat Sand, which those in the Boat had perceived. They found but 12 Foot of Water, and our Ship drew already as many, so that the Keel touched Ground; but we had no harm, because the River was Calm. Coming then to this Island, within the River of *Rio del Oro*, about five Leagues within from the Mouth, which is not taken notice of in the Map. We named the same, *Touch Island*, after the Sirname of our Commander, the Sieur *de la Ravardiere*, where we cast Anchor to tarry for some time. And the 15th of *February* we began to fit up our Patache, which was ready in our Ship, and only wanted Mounting and Chaulking.

Touch Island.

During this time we went daily to look for Shells, the finest in the world, and seemed as if they were enamel'd with Gold: As I put some of them into my Handkerchief, the Poison within, (which was like little Snails) stained it into a Purple colour; and perhaps it might be the same *Espece de Murex*, so celebrated by the Antients, and

Sea Purple.

and unknown at this time. We gathered a great quantity of them for their Beauty. We caught also with our Nets, as much Fish as we could well find use for.

Cormorants and their watch. This Island was full of *Cormorants*, of which we killed a great number with our Harquebus shot. Of these Birds there is always one that watches when the others take their rest, as 'tis said of the Cranes. We had much ado to come near them, and were forced to creep along the Ground to take them. But after they began to be a little frighted with the Harquebusses, they came no more as before.

We tarried near a month in this place without seeing any Man; but about five or six days before our departure, we perceived a Smoak in the Country, about three Leagues from us; which made us conjecture that *Blacks of Lybia.* there were some *Lybians* and Blacks come there, because towards the Coast, the Desarts of *Lybia* begin. These Blacks were come a great way out of the Country, to look towards the Coast to see if there was any Ship to Traffick for Ambergreece, and carried

ried their Water in Goat-Skins, cut out for that purpose. In the night time they creep into the Sand to Sleep, for fear of being smelt out by the Lions and Tygers, who are there in abundance.

It might be properly said, that these Men came out of Hell, they were so burnt, and dreadful to look upon: We sent then our Boat to know the cause of these Fires seen in the Country, and found three of these Lybians, (of which 2 came on board our Ship) and one of them told me, that he was the Kinsman of *Taquide Alforme* of *Cape Blanc*, of whom I enquir'd news, forasmuch as having heard of him in my former Voyage, towards *Cape Blanc*.

This was the time that they fasted their *Ramadan*, and would not Eat any thing till night. 'Tis a great pity to see these People, how poor and miserable they are, without Bread or any other Food. They Eat nothing but Ostrich Eggs, and some dried Fish, besides some Flesh of the same.

He that had stayed alone on Shore, was Son to one of these other two, and

and came to receive his Father's coming out of the Boat, proſtrating himſelf before him, and kiſſing his Hand: Then his Father gave him ſome of the Biſquet that we had given him, of which he was exceeding glad, for he was very Hungry, and had ſupped but badly in theſe Deſarts; for the moſt part inhabited by Wild Beaſts, which are continually there: And from our Ship we heard ſometimes in the night terrible Cries and Roaring.

In all this Coaſt we could not find any freſh Water; nor before in the River, where we ſent our Boat to look for ſome, but in vain, all the Country being Deſart, and quite Barren. This Iſland where we had caſt Anchor, was directly under the Tropick of *Cancer*.

Iſles of CapeVerd. Sal, Santiago, Fogo. Brava. Now having fitted up, and put out again our Patache to Sea, we ſet ſail the 10th of *March*, and having born South Weſt towards the Iſles of *Cape Verd*, we roved all along by the Iſles of *Sal*, *Santiago*, and *Fogo*, to go to Anchor at that of *Brava*, where we tarried until the 22th of the ſame month.

All

Lib.II.   *of* John Mocquet.   47

All thefe Iflands are much fubject to Storms and Boifterous Winds, as it happened to us at this Ifle of *Brava*, where we loft an Anchor, being oblig'd to weigh and drop Anchor fo frequently there, when the Wind would drive us fometimes towards Land, prefently again to the Sea. 'Tis fuppofed that thefe Winds are fhut up there in fome Gulf, as they come out at certain hours of the day. And what is more ftrange, is, that a League from thence, the Sea was calm, and without Wind; which made me believe that thefe Winds being fo fhut up, and come out with fuch violence, have not the force to penetrate far, being ftruck back, and repulfed by the Winds which come from the Sea.

We could not find out the Habitations of thefe Iflanders; who are Portuguefe, Meftices, and Blacks: The Ifland bears Tobacco, abundance of Mace, and other Fruits. The Country is very Mountainous, and there are fome Fig-Trees to be feen, with Mulbery-Trees, and others.

After

After we had well refreshed our selves with sweet Water, dried Fish, and other things, which the Islanders sold us, we weighed Anchor to Steer our Course, and had the Wind so favourable, that we arrived at the Mouth of the River of the *Amazons* on *Palm-Sunday*, about three hours before day. There are great Streams there about the Sea side, which run with a strange swiftness and horrible noise, carrying along with them Trees and Plants, which they pluck up by the Roots along the Coast.

We seeing our selves as soon as it was morning intangled amongst these roaring Streams and Currents, having scarce any Wind, they who were upon the Watch began to cry out, that we were all lost, thinking we had been upon the the Shelves. At this noise every one began to stir himself to look out for help; and I hearing this word *Lost*, mounted presently upon the Deck to see if there was any way to swim, and if we were near Land, having no other way to save our selves but by Swimming till day, hoping to have sight of Land, from which

River of the Amazons.

which according to our Heights we were not far off. Hereupon the Pilot well advis'd, took the Plummet in Hand, and found in Sounding 25 Fathom; whereof being very glad, he cried out, that we were in the River of the *Amazons*, which is almost one Degree on this side the Line. We made but little Sail in expectation of the day, that we might see Land, which we saw the next morning; and Sounding again, we found but nine Fathoms, and so lessening to three or four, and yet we saw no Land; which was a great trouble to us.

On Monday we descried Land, very low towards the South West, and by little and little we approached the Coast, to have knowledge of the Country, but with fear to run a-ground; for there the bottom is nothing but Mud, which we touched every moment.

As we were thus wandring about, by good chance we perceived a Canoe with 17 Indians, who came towards us, and went to our Patache which was before us; after that they came on board us: They were all naked,

River of the Amazons.

Encounter with Indians.

and

and Painted, as they go in thefe Countries, with their Crowns of Feathers; and told us that they came from War off the Cape of *Caypour*, one of the Capes near to the River of the *Amazons*, and they had fome Booty in their Canoe. Their Captain feemed to be a Man of good fafhion, yet he was ftark naked, and had only a Langoutin, which is a little piece of painted Cotton, to cover his Privities. He fpake with fuch a Grace, that he might have been taken for a Man of Counfel; for he fpake foftly, and gave a grace to all his Words and Geftures.

Country of Yapoco. After we had difcourfed with him about the Country, and where we fhould Anchor, he left us two Indians for Guides, who conducted us to the Land of *Tapaco*, in the Mouth of the River, or very near, and caufed us to fhelter our Ship in a private corner, fo that when the Tide went out, fhe ftuck upon the Mud; but the Tide coming in again raifed her up.

Arriving then in this Country of *Yapaco*, we left the River of the *Amazons* on the left Hand, on the other fide of which, towards the South, is

the

Lib. II.   *of* John Mocquet.   51

the great Country of *Brasil*, and on this side towards the North, are the *Caripons*, and *Caribes*.

Thirty or forty Leagues off from this great River, we found along the Coast a certain Rock, which had Veins of the colour of Slate, with some silver mixed amongst it, out of which I took a little Stone I since lost. We saw there also the marks of some English, or Dutch Ship, that had passed by that way.

We arrived there on Monday night, and afterwards on Tuesday morning, the 10th of *April*, desiring to know what profit we might make in this Country, we went on Shore to Exchange Hatchets, Bills, Knives, and Glass-Beads of several colours, with divers other such like things. *Arrival in the Land of Yapoco.*

We saw these Indians with two little pieces of Wood strike fire: I made the Experiment of it since to the late King *Henry the Great* at *Fontainbleau*, in the year 1605. All the Indians were run there from their Habitations; and had trimed up their Hammocks, or hanging Beds, made with Wreaths of Palm-Trees; and *Wood to strike Fire.*

E 2   were

were in great numbers, Men, Women, and Children, all as naked as when they came out of their Mothers Bellies; except some Beads with which they decked their Bodies; and in their Ears they had long pieces of Wood and round Stones. They had brought a thousand Trifles, as Gumbs, *Egrets Feathers*, and Parrots, Tobacco, and other Things which the Country afforded. I did my Duty in Exchanging, and took as much of their *Merchandize* as I possibly could. We made our Bargains without speaking, shewing by signs what we would have, or give.

Merchandize of the Country.

The King of this Country of *Tapoco*, named *Anacajoury*, was then making ready Cannoe's to go against the *Caribes*; This was the cause that we could not then make much Bartering in this place: For they were all busie at work, some at the Cannoes, others to make Arms for their Visage; and others to prepare Victuals, which was the Women's Province: we saw all those People mighty busie at that. Amongst others, they made a certain Wine, or Drink of Fruits, which inebriates

Wine of the Country.

britates like Beer or Citre: They chaw a certain Root, then Boil it, and after Strain it. There is another sort of it more thick, which is made of Fruits and Palms, as big as a Gall-Nut, they bruise only the Bark which is upon them; it's as yellow as an Orange; for they make nothing of the Nut; after that they Boil and Strain it. They have another sort, which might be taken for clear Milk, mixed with soft Cheese. I had a great mind to Taste of it, besides, being desired by them to Drink, I would not refuse, for fear they should have thought that I intended 'em any harm; insomuch that they were mightily pleased to see me Drink of it.

They do not love Melancholly and green Persons; and if you make sport with them in Jest, it must be in Laughing. I clapped them sometimes upon the Back with my Hand in Jest, but they would always return again the like in Laughing. They are very hardy and warlike, courteous and liberal, and have very cheerful Looks.

Nature and Manners of those Indians.

The *Caribes* are not so, for they would give us, as the saying is, not so much as a * Patatre; This is a Root like a Turnip, but longer, and of a red and yellow colour: It is of a very good taste, and they Eat it boiled or roasted upon the Coals; but if it is often Eat of, it is very Disrellishing and Windy.

Patato.

As for Fruits, they have several sorts of 'em, good to Eat, but wild and unknown to us, except the Ananana's, or Figs which are very long, and as big as a great Pudding. They have Plantanes, or Fig-Trees, which the Spaniards call Plantins. They make small thin Cakes of *Casava*, which is a Root that they Grate upon a Stone, or a piece of Wood made in the form of a File; not having any Mortar to bruise it in: Then they put it into a great Basket made of little Twigs, like Willows. These Roots also yield a juice which is poisonous. After having well pressed it, dried it, and sop'd it in Water, they make it into a Paste, spread it upon a great flat Stone that is upon the Fire, which gives it the form of a very thin Cake. When

Fruits.

Bread.

When it is done so, it may be kept three, or four years, or more, so it be laid in a dry place. I'tasted of it, but it did not relish as our Bread, and I believe that one would soon be weary of Eating it often. They make several other sorts of things to Eat, but very course and grosly, which is not very pleasant to those who are not accustomed vvith them.

 I saw them make their preparations in the Lodgings of their King *Anacajoury*, to Victual the Cannoes which were to go to the War; but they put all these Casaves, or Cakes, (which I spoke of) into a Pile in the middle of the House, and their Drink in Gourd Bottles, which hold more than a Pail. For these Gourd Bottles are of a wonderful greatness in comparison to ours.

 I saw at the House of this King, a *Caribe*-Slave, whom they made to work to get ready these Victuals for the War. This little Naval Army was about 35 Cannoes, with 25 or 30 men in each.

 But to return again to our arrival in this place of *Tapaco*; as soon as we were entered into this Country, the King

King Anacajoury.

King *Anacajoury* gave us two of his Nephews in Hostage, if by chance any of ours should there loose himself, or his way: The Grandchild of this King led me about the Woods; for all the Coast is covered with Trees, and there was some Indians with him. This little Boy was very brisk, and mighty witty for a Savage, and shewed me the Fruits, which were good to Eat, and which not. Amongst others, they have a Fruit called *Mancenille*, of the bigness of an Orange, very yellow, and beautiful to look upon; but yet so venomous, that they say, if it is put never so little to the Mouth, it kills immediately; and the Fish themselves, which are all along the Coast, who suck this Fruit, are carried by the Sea to Land: for the Tree which bears it is near to Sea, which comes up into these Woods, and drags along with it a thousand sorts of Fruits, as we saw in the River of the *Amazons*.

The Fish who suck this Fruit, peel and loose their Scales: Whosoever Eats of this Fish loose all their Epiderme, or Upper-Skin, like the Lepers

Mancenille Fruit.

pers who Eat the Flesh of Vipers. As soon as any one finds himself seiz'd with such an accident, they presently conjecture they have Eat of the Poison of *Mancenille,* as the Spaniards have named it, who inhabit these *Indies.*

This King's Grand-Child shewed me several Herbs which they make use of, and one amongst others which serves them for an Antidote when they are struck with Poisoned Arrows. *Antidote against Poison.* I took some of the Leaves of this Herb to compound an Unguent, which is an excellent remedy for Wounds, and other Sores. I would also have plucked up some of the Root, but this little Boy would not suffer it: And besides, the Indians who were with him, seemed to be very angry he had shewed me this Plant, which they prised and esteemed above all others. I would not insist any more thereupon, for fear his Grand-Father should be displeased with me.

After I had gathered a great quantity of Plants, Fruits, and other Rarities, I returned on board the Ship to lock them up.

On

On Tuesday the 11th of *April*, I went to their Habitations to see if I could get any more Curiosities, taking some Knives, and other Pedlars-Ware, to exchange with them. Our Pilot being with me, we went into a Cabin, where there were a great number of Indians, Men and Women; and there were amongst the rest some about 17 or 18 years of Age, pounding in a Mortar made of a hollow piece of Wood, with a long Stick. I also took a Stick to help her to Pound, of which she was very glad, seeing I understood the manner of Pounding after their way: And though she was Stark-Naked, she cared not for my being over-against her. After that, she gathered us some Potato's, and besides those, gave us other Things to Eat, and all with an admirable Grace and Civility.

Innocent nakedness of these People.

I believe these *Caripous* are of all the Indians the most sweet and mild in Behaviour: They are very curious of Honour, Ambitious to do Kindness to those who visit them: The Women, Girls, and Children, came very freely on board our Ship, without any shew of shame for their Nakedness,

ness, but were continually drawing their Legs close, like Half-Moons. There was a little Indian brought me some Balls of Tobacco, with a little Case made of the Bark of a Tree, as wide as a Pocket, and as round as a Ring: It's that which the Men make use of to bind up their Privy-Parts; they can easily change them, or take them away when they please. I took two or three of them for curiosity, seeing 'em so ingeniously made. All the Indians round about having heard the discharge of Cannon, came presently from every quarter that was nigh, to exchange their Goods with our Knives, Hatchets, and other small Ware.

When the Cannon had fired, the noise of it continued near a quarter of an hour in these rough Woods, so that all the Country, Mountains, and Vallies, were filled with the Eccho's, which answered one another with a wonderful noise, which might be heard as I believe, above 25 Leagues from thence.

As for the rest, these *Caripous* People are great Enemies to the *Ca-* *ribes*, who make mortal War one upon

Caribes.

The Caribes eat the Caripous, but the Caripous do not eat them.

upon the other *. This little Grandson of the King of *Tapaco*'s, shewed me by signs, how the *Caribes* had great Teeth, and Biting his Arm, made me to understand that they Eat them when they happen to take them in War. The Hatred betwixt them is so great, that it is impossible ever to reconcile them; nevertheless I have heard say since, by a Mariner of *Havre de Grace*, that they had made some sort of a Reconciliation betwixt 'em.

Being then amongst these Savages, I saw one day amongst others, the Captain of the Cannoes, whom we found at the first: He made me great Demonstrations of Friendship by his Gestures, saying, that he would bring me from his Country, (far from thence) several choice Things, and amongst others, some little pretty Parrots, speaking their Language. Yet I waited not so much in expectation of his Promises, as to neglect to provide my self elsewhere. My first thing was a little Parrot as big as a Sparrow, with a long Tail, and very Tame, which would with a wonderful Pleasure pick the

Parrots.

the Hair of the Beard, so that it could scarce be felt. I gave a little Knife in exchange for it. This Captain who had promised me so many Rarities, came to offer me amongst other Things, a Truss of Serpents, which were as Fat as a great Conger, and the Skin so speckled with yellow, grey, blue, and other colours, that I had no great mind to try how they relish'd, though some living on them, make great Feasts together: They are prepared in Leaves, and roasted. I also took notice that these *Caripous* live better than these *Caribes*; for they know how to make Cakes with Mace, which are very good, and have other things to Eat, agreeable enough to the Country where they live.

Serpents good to eat.

These People Eat also another sort of Serpents, like Adders, of a strange greatness and length. This Country of *Tapoco* is above 120 Leagues from the Country of *Toupinambous*, which is towards the River *Maragnon*, or *Brasil*: And those of *Tapoco* are of the same colour and swarthy Complexion with the others, but they are

are far finer, more lively, and pleasant.

Speaking of this Captain, I will relate in this place a strange and remarkable thing of these People, that the Nephew of *Anacajoury* told me, to whom the Soveraign Command of this Country belongeth, and because of his Youth, his Uncle governed until such time as he should be of Age to Rule. He told me, That they did Eat neither Flesh nor Fish until they had killed some of their Enemies; and when they had killed any one of them in War, they observed this Ceremony, which should not be otherways agreeable to our French Captains. They make a Link of Palm in which they put him whom they design for Captain, who before he may Eat either Flesh or Fish, must undergo therein the Exercise of their Weapons; Then causing all the greatest Captains of the Country to come, who with the King of the place, make one after another, a Harrangue or Speech to this new one, telling him, that he must be couragious, hardy, and nimble in Battel, and never give

Strange Ceremonies to make Captains.

Ground

Lib. II. *of* John Mocquet.

Ground but upon great occasion, and with Judgment undergo all the hardships of War, be they never so great; and love the Virtue, Honour, and Reputation of a good and just Captain. When they have finished this Discourse, they take a great Switch in Hand, wherewith every one gives him three great Blows, with all their force, so that the Body is all over Black and Bloody, upon which Blisters may be seen to rise as big as ones Finger; and so one after another make him the same Discourse, repeating so many Blows with the Switch; which lasts a full Month, 3 or 4 times a Week. In the mean time this poor Patient in all that time Eats nothing but Casaves and Potates, until he has had all his Ornaments of Virtue. And then they make a great Fire, putting thereon Green Leaves to make it Smoak, and also to hinder the force of the Flame; Then they have an *Amica*, or Hanging Bed after their manner, in which they put this new Captain, crowning him with Leaves; and there he must endure all the Heat and Smoak untill he Swoon's away, and

and seeing he scarce Breaths, they let the Bed down, and taking plenty of fresh Water, they cast it upon him, untill he comes again to himself, as from Death to Life. All this being done, he is Honoured as a great Captain, and then they go a Cruising along the Coasts to meet their Enemies: After being upon their return to their Habitations, they make still Remonstrances to this new Captain, and give him each one, three Blows; and from thence forth he may Eat Flesh. Sometime after that, they take another turn in the Sea with their Cannoes; and if they find any of their Enemies, they fail not to return to perfect this Captain, to whom they give three Blows more, and then he may Eat Fish; and so he is created and admitted into the Office, to bear Command over the others. But that is not done but to those who have well behaved themselves in Battle, knocking down many Enemies.

I leave it to you, if our Men of War (who come to this Honour most commonly by the Purse, than Virtue) would Buy that Honour at so dear a Rate

Rate as these poor Savages do: Yet what I wonder at most of all, is, that the Indian who suffers these Blows with a Switch, is neither to stir, nor cry out in the least, but only to shrink up his Shoulders if he please. *Admirable patience of these Indians.*

As for my part, I saw almost the like in my return: For we had in our Ship three Indians, whom we brought into *France*, two *Caribes*, Brothers, and one *Caripou*, Nephew to the King of *Tapoco*.

Now one of these Brother *Caribes*, the least named *Atoupa*, (we being in the River of *Cayenne*, where the *Caribes* are) said, He would go into *France*, but he thought the Ship was *France*, and called it so; but when we were to go away, he strove with all his force to leap into the Sea, to save himself on Land; And we being at Anchor in the River, to hinder him we gave him in custody to the *Caripou Tapoco*, their sworn Enemy; so that at every step that *Atoupa* took, *Tapoco* took another, following him up and down every where in the Ship, and bid us let him alone, and if at any time he were so bold as to cast him- *Atoupa.*

F self

self into the Sea, he also would be presently after him, and make him Dive his Head to the bottom, to Drink to his Friends. This little *Caribe Atoupa*, not being above 14 or 15 years of Age, one day took a resolution to Drown or Kill himself, as he could best have occasion; and had cast himself into the Sea had not he, who, ever had an eye upon him, catched hold of his Legs. When we were in the main Sea, his Brother held him continually Embraced, and in the night he tied him, but he was often found untied; and seeing that he could find no expedient to Drown or Kill himself, (for he was not suffered to get to any Knives, wherewith he might do himself a mischief) one day finding a piece of sharp pointed Wood, he struck *Tapoco* such a blow therewith upon the Throat, that it sliced away the Skin from one side of his Neck; which our General hearing of, caused him to be brought upon the Deck, and with a Whip made of Pack-thread, tied to a Stick, to be severely Whipp'd, but he seemed as if he had not been touched, only shrinking up his Shoulders a little, without either crying out, or speaking one word; which seemed very strange to me, seeing him so marked with the Stripes he had received so severely.

But to return again to our Traffick in this Country of *Tapoco*, having made Exchange of all the Merchandize that could be found there, we took a resolution to go to the River of *Cayenne*, where the *Caribes* are: But before our departure, the King of *Tapoco* came on board our Ship, with his Wife, his Sister, and his Mother, with the Indian *Tapoeo* whom we carried away with us, who was his Nephew, his Sister's Son, in whose room the King *Anacajoury* governed, untill his Majority, which would be in a short time. This Nephew told me, that he had almost received all the Orders of Captain, having undergone the same that all the others do who would attain to that Degree; and that he had been upon an Incursion, and had already Eaten Flesh, but not Fish, which was his last Ornament for the heighth of Honour. His Uncle, and his Mother put him into our Hands, and earnestly

Cayenne River.

Spanish Cruelty.

nestly desired us by no means to suffer him to fall into the hands of the *Caribes*, their Enemies, nor the Spaniards, having heard of the Cruelty that they had exercised against those of their Country, and of the bad usage they had done to those of *Jucatan*, *Zempallan*, *Tlaxcallan*, *Panuco*, *Teconantepec*, and *Mexico*.

This King also desired our assistance against the *Caribes*, and that he would go with us, with his Naval-Army, which was ready prepared, as I have said before; and that all the Booty that was taken should be ours: But our General having a mind to Traffick fairly with these *Caribes*, would not yield to his demand, only he promised to keep his Nephew safe, and that he would not assist the *Caribes* against him. This Nephew who went along with us, was drawn on by an Indian, Son to the King of the Island of *Trinidad*, that the English had taken by Subtillity, and who served us for an Interpreter. It was the *Millord-Ralle* who carried him away in a Voyage; yet he did not understand so well the Language of the *Caripous*, being at so great

great a distance from them; besides, it is a Language very particular, and different also from that of the *Caribes*, who have much ado to understand it, though they are not above 30 Leagues one from the other. Now this Indian Interpreter, having a mind to Marry one of the Daughters of *Anacajoury*, and already treated with the Father about it, had caused his Cloaths and other Things to be brought on Shore, telling this King that he would make War upon the *Caribes* with him, because they had Eaten one of his Brothers; Of which our General being advertised, commanded him not to stir, seeing he was so necessary to us for the Language. He seeing himself detained by force, never rested untill he had persuaded *Yapoco*, this young Boy that we kept for Hostage, with one of his Brothers, telling him such pleasant Things of *France* and *England*, that neither his Mother, nor his Uncle could disswade him; so he came into *France* with us, where, upon his arrival he was set to turn the Spit, at which he was so offended, that he went away from *Cancale* to *St. Malo's*;

without saying a word, but was thence fetched again: This was in the year 1604.

History of the Indian Yapoco.

Since, in the year 1613, upon my return from my Voyages to *Paris*, living in the *Tuilleries*, as Keeper of the Cabinet of Rarities to the King, the Sieur *de Raſilly* came back from those Parts of *Braſil*, and hearing that he had brought along with him some *Braſilians*, to present to the King and the Queen Regent, I went one morning to the Capuchins, were they were, as well to see them, as to hear News of the Sieur *de la Ravardiere*, Lieutenant to Monſieur *de Raſilly*, who had tarried behind at *Maragnon*, to go to the River of the *Amazons*: But I was no sooner entered into the Chamber where these *Braſillian Toupinambeax* were, when I perceived *Yapaco*, who knowing me, came presently to me and caught me about the Neck to embrace me, telling me all his Fortunes, and how he was returned to *Braſil*, within almost 200 Leagues of his own Country of *Yapoco*, where he could not go; and that he went to

Maragnan *Marguan*, a little Iſland of *Braſil*;
Then

Then he embarked in a little Ship with the Segnior *du Bos*, a Gentleman of *Bretaigne*, who was come from the Voyage that I made with Monsieur *de la Ravardiere*; but having been taken by the Pirates towards *England*, he found means afterwards to return into *France*, and went to find out Madam *de la Ravardiere* in *Poictou*, where he had been before, the other Voyage, and told her News of her Husband, who tarried behind at *Brasil*. It happened that one day, a Hog falling into the Castle Ditch, this Lady commanded her Servants, and among the rest *Yapoco*, to help to draw him out; but he, though born in the Country of the Savages, disdaining a piece of work so vile and base, told her plainly, that he would not do it; upon which, the Lady giving him some harsh Language, he out of Anger went away without a farewel, and came streight to *Rochelle*, where he found some *Hablois*, who brought him to the *Havre*, and from thence he went to *Paris*.

When I had thus met with him, and Careſſed him, I carried him to my Lodging, where I treated him as well as I could: After that, I took him to the King, who deſired to ſee him: I cauſed him to Kneel before the King, who commanded me to ſpeak to him in his own Language, for I underſtood a little of it; Then he ordered ſome Money to be given him.

After that, he was carried to the *Havre*, where Madam *de la Ravardiere* ſent for him by her Servants, and ſince I heard no more News of him: Such was the Fortune of this young *Tapoco*.

Good Nature of the Caripous. But to return to theſe People, Savage as they are, they are great Friends to Honour, and of all that which is juſt and true, which they reverence from their Infancy, abhorring all wicked Men and Cheats, as much as they are Friends to the good and vertuous. They do not Love a Coward, or a Pultron, but Honour ſuch as are Valiant and Couragious.

But ſince we are ſtill near the River of the *Amazons*, before we part from thence, it will not be much amiſs to ſay

say something of it from what I was able to learn in those Parts.

Some have taken the River of the *Amazons*, or *Oregliane*, for that of *Maragnan*; but others will make two of them, and say, that their Mouths are distant some hundred Leagues; that of *Maragan* making the limits of *Brasil* on the Northen Coast, as the River of Plate, or Silver, makes the other Bounds on the South. All these Rivers come from the Mountains of *Peru*, the highest, and of the difficultest access of any others in the whole World.

The River of the *Amazons* is very broad in its Mouth, some 50 Leagues or thereabouts from one Shore to the other, and contains several great Islands.

River of the Amazons.

The Sea there runs at the hours of the Tide, being very swift in its Ebbing and Flowing, and carries along with it many Trees and Plants it plucks up by the Roots, all along the Coasts, which are like great Forests; for there the Coast being low, the Sea easily enters far up into the Country. The colour of this River inclines to a

dark

dark grey: We found the Water of it Sweet 30 Leagues within the Sea. Within this River, about 30 or 40 Leagues up, are some Islands where these Warlike Women, the *Amazons* inhabit, who make War upon those of the Continent of the Coast of *Brasil*; and on the other side, where the Indians inhabit, towards the Cape of *Voyanpouc*, are their Friends and constant Confederates. These Women for Propagation, have to do every year with the said Indians in the month of *April*, and give them notice when they desire to have them come to see them, all the Days and Hours of that month, and do not suffer the said Indians to enter into their Islands more strong than themselves, setting some to guard the entrance, whilst others pass away their time, exchanging always these guards, by their turn, and so imploying all this Month of Love in the soft Caresses of Joy and Delight. At the end of the year, when their Confederates return to them; if they have Conceived in the mean time, they keep the Females, and give the Males to the Men, not keeping

ing them above a year; And 'tis probable that these Sons which they give to these Indians, may afterwards have to do with their Sisters and near Kins-Women; For they have a Custom always to seek out the Children of those they have had to do with. Now, though these Indians should be all Married in the Continent, these *Amazons* serve them only for Friends, and make Presents to one another for a sign of Mutual Love and Good Will. As to that which some say, that they wear but one Breast, and Burn off the other, according to the manner of the ancient *Amazons*, who inhabited towards the *Thanais* and *Thermodon*, they are nothing but Fables. 'Tis true, that these Women do on purpose lose the Milk of one Breast that they may the better draw the Bow; and so perhaps this saying of the Ancients is to be understood.

The Son of the King of *Yapoco*, amongst other Things, told me, That these Women wear the Hair of their Privy-Parts very long, Combing them like their Heads, and that they are of a very great stature; adding also,
that

that he had been in their Country with his Uncle *Anacajoury.*

We could not go to see them, as we desired, because the Streams there are too violent for Vessels, and especially for our Ship and Patache, who drew in already abundance of Water: For the Streams run towards the Coast, and 'tis impossible to go there except it be with a Boat and Oars, or with the Indians Cannoes, which draw but one Foot of Water.

Behold what I was able to learn of these *Amazons* ; which makes me not to give credit to all that we find written of those antient Women, so famous. 'Tis said that there are still some of them in *Africa,* towards the Cape of *Good Hope,* in the Kingdom of *Monomotapa.*

All the Country on the Left Hand, at the entrance into the River of the *Amazons*, is comprehended in the great Province of *Brasil,* first discovered by *Alvarez Cabral,* a Portugal Captain, in the year 1500, and by *John Vincent* and *Arias Pinco,* who in the year 1509. discovered the great River *Maragnan,* reckoned the biggest

in

in the World. Since, *Americus Vespuceus*, and others, made a fuller discovery of those Countries. In the year 1542, the French Captain *Oregliane*, sent by *Gonzale-Pizarro* the Spaniard, found out the River which comes from the Province *Atunquixo*, thirty Leagues from the South Sea. He parted from *Peru*, and followed this River, descending above 400 Leagues in a streight Line to its Mouth, and more than 1700 with the turnings and windings, finding many Peopled Islands.

He was eight months in this Navigation, with a thousand Perils and Incommodities; and reported, that he had found (upon a certain Rivulet here) Women Archers, which are of the *Amazons*: The Spaniards had Wars with them.

Before this, *Columbus* in his second Voyage had discovered these *Amazons* in an Isle, which the Indians call *Madannina* or *Martinina*. This Captain *Oregliane* gave his name to this great River of the *Amazons*, which he took for *Maragnan*, as the modern Navigators seem to agree: And indeed, they who
were

were in the year 1612. in the Country of the *Toupinambous*, and in the Isle of *Maragnan*, report, That there is no River there of this Name, but only a Creek or Bay, in which is this Isle of *Maragnan*: This Name hath perhaps been the cause that this River towards *Oregliane*, or that of the *Amazons*, hath been taken for another River of *Maragnan*, though they are one and the same.

Parting from Yapoco.

But to return to our departure from the Country of *Tapoco*, to go towards the *Caribes* Man-Eaters, we departed from thence on *Easter-Day*, the 15th of *April* in the year 1604. bearing along the Coast, and our Ship running a-ground when the Tide went out, we were forced to strike Sail, and cast Anchor until the Sea floated us again. We run all along the Coast, which is very pleasant, and filled with an infinite number of green Trees, which render all these places very sweet and agreeable.

Cayenne.

We had no sooner approached the River of *Cayenne*, than we perceived a Cannoe, which came on board our Ship, and there was in it, one named *Yago*,

Yago, Brother to *Camaria*, King of the Caribes. Caribes, who having spied the Nephew of *Anacajoury* whom we had in our Ship, was mightily surprised at first, not knowing what to think of our coming with this *Tapoco* their Sworn Enemy. Nevertheless, he failed not to guide us in this River of *Cayenne*, which is very pleasant, and convenient for Ships to abide in, being 5 or 6 Fathoms deep, in some places more, add others less. This *Yago* told us, That he knew well enough the King of *Tapoco* was preparing himself to come and visit them, and that they expected him within 3 or 4 days, as their *Toupan* or Devil had told them; which was true: For while we continued there for some days, at the end of 'em our General sent some of his Men into the Country, with *Camaria* their King; one of my Servants also went along with them, to procure me some of the most curious and rare Things he could find. Being come to a place where *Camaria* conducted them, 5 or 6 Leagues from thence, they found out, that *Anacajoury* had been there, with his Naval-Army,

and

and had wasted and burnt the Country, and carried away a great number of the Inhabitants from this Coast, and saw also how they served their Enemies, who had been killed upon the place.

Cannibals or Man-Eaters. They Eating them Roasted, an Indian Woman offered a roasted Hand to our General, but he angrily refused it.

Our General had already been amongst them in the first Voyage, but having seen some of their Cruelties, would go there no more, yet he sent some of his men, as I have said before:

My Servant being returned, told me, they made great lamentations at *Camaria* for the loss they had suffered; and that *Camaria* thereupon was troubled in such a manner, that it was impossible to appease him; yet he comforted them as well as he could, promising to order the Business so as to get into his Hands *Tapoco* the King *Anacajoury*'s Nephew, to make a Solemn Feast of him; and that they should e're long have Revenge upon their Enemies, whom they would with

joy

Joy Feast upon at their Pleasure. There was an Indian Woman, who, knowing my Servant was a Surgeon, entreated him to Cure her of a blow of a Sword, she had received upon her Head: But he perceiving that the Skull was split, and the Brains to be seen, told her freely he could give her no help. There were several others wounded, to whom he did what help he was able.

Whilst he was amongst them, he told me, that one Night retiring with them into their Cabbins, (made of Branches of Palms) he saw the Ceremonies observed to their Husbands and Friends who had been killed in the fight.

First, An Indian Woman, sitting upon her *Amica*, or Hanging-Bed, began a Song, very pleasant and agreeable, which continued a long time. That done, she came to reckon up the Exploits of her Dead Husband, how he had Loved her, been Valiant against his Enemies, excellent in Drawing the Bow, able to undergo all the Hardships of War, and a thousand other Gallantries and Perfections, of

Ceremonies of the Dead.

G which

which she gave a particular account. After that, one of these Indians raised himself from his *Amica*, and went to desire the others to lament; whereupon they presently fell to Howling so strangely, that one would have thought them to be out of their Wits. These Lamentations ended, they rose up to make Merry with the Flesh of their Enemies, with some Lizards and Crocodiles intermix'd, and all roasted together, thus Feasting upon the Graves of their Husbands and dead Friends, thinking themselves thus to have obliged them. Thus much, my Servant told me, he had taken notice of concerning their Ceremonies to their departed Friends.

In the mean time we Equipped our Boat, the 18th of *April*, to go to find out the end of the River of *Cayenne*, and know from whence it comes, and takes its head. We had with us two *Indians*, to shew us some Brasil, whereof they make their Bows, and having taken with us a Barrel of Liquor, and some Bisquet for Victuals, we spent all the rest of the day and the night in rowing along the Coast, which

Coast of the River of Cayenne and Voyage upon it.

is

nt; and there are a thou-
orts of Birds making such
t is a very dreadful thing

every place a great num-
like unto a sort of Gnats,
ry troublesome, and tor-
nightily both night and
ecially in the night time.
orning we arrived at the
River, seeing a violent
descended from a Moun-
alley, where it is below
then comes to pass upon
flat and broad, and from
down as into a hollow
h groweth wider by lit-
, until it casteth it self
; the Tide comes up to
here it beginneth to fall.
no great matter in this
ept several sorts of strange
nd Indian-Hens of ano-
an those of our *Europe*:
s carry their young, and
fly away, seeing us, but
ame. These Hens have
on their Heads which are
very beautiful, and like

to thofe of a Heron. We carried fome of them to our Ship, but we could not preferve them all until we came into *France*.

In fhort, we found all this Coaft Defart, and being returned on Board, we told what we had feen in this Voyage: Our General fent us again to difcover another River, which feparates it felf from that of *Cayenne*, and runs towards the South-Eaft.

We prepared our Boat, with fome Indians, thinking it had not been very far off, or elfe not well underftanding our Interpreters, infomuch that we took not Victuals enough with us, only I furnifhed my felf with fome Bifquet, and gave of it to one of our Indians, who was very glad of this Provifion that I had made.

Having then Rowed a good way up into this River, we found nothing but Branches of Trees, which covered in a manner all the paffage, fo that we were forced ever and anon to lie all along in the Boat, to pafs underneath thefe Branches of Trees, which were laded with Oyfters. At laft we came to a certain place where there

there were Trees cut down by the People of some Ships that had been there before us. These were exceeding great, and the Heart very red like unto Brasil, yet it was not so as I have experienced it.   *Red-Wood.*

Moreover, the Indian whom I had given the Bisquet to, did not mind to follow our Men, but sought for something to live upon, and came again presently towards me, shewing me by Signs, he had found something good for us, and went to find out the Wooden-Bowl of the Boat, which served only to cast out the Water; so led only me along with him, a good way into the Wood, to a Tree cut down, which was hollow, and had in it a Bee-Hive, the most excellent, clear, sweet and agreeable that could be imagined. This Honey was of a Jelly, like Oil, and exceeding clear, of a greenish colour, and enclosed in Bags, like those great Purses the Merchants use, wherein there is several little Leather ones. There the Honey is environ'd with a Membrane or Skin, which is the *Crisis*, very clear: When this little Skin is broke, the Honey comes

comes out of this only, and not the others; so the Indian broke one after another, throwing the Honey into the Bowl, which he gave me to drink of as a choice Liquor.

Having taken some of it in this manner, he went to look for Water to mix with it, to the end that we might have the more of it, as also to quench our Thirst the better.

In the mean time our Companions were in another place, on the other side of this Wood, seeking for the Brasil-Trees. I saved some of this Honey in the Bowl, not having elsewhere to put it: But our Thirsty People returning from this Wood, and taking the Bowl to Drink, mixed Water with the Honey, and so drank it up; which caused me to Quarrel with our Carpenter who had done it on purpose, like a Man of his Country, where they are born to Envy and Malice. I bore the loss of this Honey, so excellent, as patiently as possibly I could, because our Lieutenant was there, who had not a mind to do what this bold Carpenter did, but had

Lib. II.   *of* John Mocquet   87
had taken Water with his Hand out of the River to Drink.

I could never fince find any more of this fweet Liquor, by whatever Signs I could make to the King of the *Caribes*, to caufe him to underftand what it was; for he did not know the name of it. But what I wondered at moft, was, that this Indian could fo eafily find out this Honey in thefe Woods, feperating himfelf from the others for that reafon. If I could have faved only 3 or 4 Ounces of it, I would not have parted with it for any thing whatfomever, but would precioufly have preferved it, to make a Prefent thereof to the late King my dear Mafter; as I gave him fome of that which I brought from *Africa*, which he found of an excellent Tafte, and caufed me to lay it carefully up in his Trunk, as they do in the fame Country from whence I had brought it. This Honey of *Africa* was as white as Snow, clear, and of an excellent good Tafte; alfo the King confeffed, that he had never before feen any fo excellent: But that was but courfe Honey in comparifon to

Honey of Africa.

G 4   this

this of the Country of the *Caribes*. The Bees which make this Honey in the *West-Indians*, are of a pale and yellowish colour, little and harmless, and are not troublesome at all, as I found out in the place whence I took this Honey, which was like to a most precious Balm, and I believe, that as the Honey of *Africa* is excellent for Healing of Wounds, so this of the *Indies* quite exceeds it every way, as in its consistence, taste, smell and colour.

Another Voyage to the Caribes.

Being then returned from this River, where we could discover nothing to serve our turn, our General was resolved to send me vvith the King of the *Caribes*, to go to their Habitations, and look in the Woods, to see if vve could there find a certain Tree, *Aloes Wood.* vvhich is a sort of Wood of Aloes, called by them *Aparubou*, for vve had found of it in the Country of *Tapoco*. For this effect, I parted the 29th of *April*, vvith *Cam ria*, the King of the *Caribes*, vvho had left in Hostage for me 7 or 8 of his Indians, and Embarked in a Cannoe, with vvhich vve entered into a little River, vvhich

runs

runs about two Leagues up into the Country, and was very narrow, the Branches of Trees quite covering it, so that we had a thousand Inconveniencies, and much ado to lie flat down in the Boat to avoid 'em. The Indians being stark Naked did not matter it so much; for if these Branches had made them tumble into the River, they knew so well how to Swim, that they would not have much needed to fear: That which did us the most harm, was, that some of these Branches were laden with certain Oysters, little, and of the colour *Oysters.* of Pearls, of a very good Taste; for I was willing to try, opening some before these Indians, who wondered mightily to see me open 'em so easily, not knowing how to do it.

We went thus Rowing along to find out their Dwellings, that at last coming to the end of the River, we went on Shore, and about a League and a half from thence, we saw one of their Habitations, and the *Caribes* came about us, offering to their King, Fruit, and other Things to Eat, with which he also presented me. After that,

that, we left this Habitation and continued our way towards that of *Camaria*: When we were come to the foot of a Mountain, this King fell a crying out as loud as he could, and desired me also to do the like, which I did; and I believe that it was, to call home all those who were about the Woods, because thereupon they presently returned to the Habitation; for I saw them run from all parts to their place, which was in a Valley, where being come, I found a great number of *Caribes*, Men and Women; amongst the others, the Wife of *Camaria*, who was making an Amica or Bed of Cotton. All these Indians, Men and Women, naked as they were, came running to see me and my Companion, a young Carpenter of our Ship, who was under a mortal apprehension that they would Eat him, desiring me mightily to give them something of that which I had brought to exchange with them: Then I commanded them to make *Ovato Courende*, which is to say, a good Fire, because we had been Wet with the Rain, by the way, which the Indians did not much matter, being not

Habitation of the King of the Caribes.

not much troubled to dry their own Cloaths: They presently made me a a Fire, it being very late at night, so that we were pretty well dried in this great Hall where all these Indians were; and thus we Supped with the King and his Wife, in the sight of all the others: They made mighty much of us with their Savage Victuals. I had brought a Bottle of Wine and some Bisquet with me, which was no small help to us, after so many Fatigues by the way, troublesome with Water and Woods, where sometimes the Indians were forced to carry me upon their Backs in certain places that were very hollow.

After Supper, the King caused us to retire into his House, where he ordered two Amica's or Beds to be hung up for me and my Companion. They had put my Bed so, that it joyned to the King's, and my Companion's a little higher; and that of the Queen's was on the same side with the King's; and all the night there was Guards which kept a Fire near the King and me. Our poor Carpenter did nothing else but tremble all the night long, think-

Amacas or Hanging Beds.

thinking every moment they were coming to Eat us.

King Camaria.

The King *Camaria* in the mean time began to discourse with me of the King of *Tapoco*, whom he said he did not fear, and who had come up into one of his Rivers, where he had killed a great number of his People; but that he desired mightily, (if it was possible) to have in his Clutches, his Nephew *Tapoco*, who was in our Ship, and that I should speak thereof to our General, and use my utmost Policy and Endeavour to have him delivered up, that he might be Eaten, saying that he would send for all his Subjects and his Friends to be at this Feast of the *Caripou*.

As for my part, when he talked to me after this manner, I would not contradict him, but gave him the hearing, and promised, if I could, to do all he desired: And he told me that he would willingly give all he had to have this poor *Tapoco*, and that I would take care to have him delivered up, which I durst not refuse him.

I thought this Night very long, seeing also that the Queen, Wife of
Cama-

Camaria did not sleep. I rose up two or three times to go out of the House, continually suspecting the Malice and Cruelty of these *Anthropaphages*, and Eaters of Human Flesh: Besides that, I perceived in the middle of this House, a Toad of the strange and most horrible bigness that ever I saw; and I believe that it was rather some Devil than a Toad, because *Camaria* often spoke with the Devil, to know what their Enemies were doing.

<small>Anthropophages, or Cannibals.</small>

<small>Wonderful Toad.</small>

<small>Caribes speak with the Devil.</small>

As soon as it was day, I presently rose up to know what we had to do, and *Camaria* shewed me his Throat, which was very much out of order by a Cold that he had.

I carried him with me into the Woods to seek for Herbs fit for his Disease, and used my utmost to procure some Honey to compose a Remedy for him; but he could neither understand me, or comprehend what I demanded of him. At last, having Breakfasted, we went along with some Indians to look for Wood of Aloes. This is a Tree of an extraordinary bigness, bearing Leaves like a Fig-Tree, but a little greener: The Tree contains in its

its Heart a black Wood, very oiley, sharp, and of a very good Odour; And a Tree as big as a Tunn shall have in its Heart but a very little quantity of this black Wood. This Tree is very hard, and where it is black, 'twill sink to the bottom of Water like a Stone. We laded thereof about 35 Tuns, which are 70000 pound weight or thereabouts. We laded Store of 2 or 3 other sorts of Wood, one resembling a Red-Sandal, and the other a Cittern, and partly of the same Odour. It is of a very sweet Scent when first cut, but by succession of time it comes to lose its Odour. I have learnt that this black Wood is certainly a sort of Wood of Aloes, but not so sweet-scented as that of the *East Indies*, because it comes so far upon the Sea, receiving thereby a certain Saltish quality. But at such time as I was at *Goa*, being in an Ensarail where the Idolaters Work, I there saw some Wood of Aloes of the River of *Ganges*, which was sweet, and had almost the same qualities as that of the West, as I since found out by curious Experience. The Gentiles told me that

Virtue of the Wood of Aloes.

that this Wood was very excellent and odoriferous, and neither Rotten nor Worm-eaten, and was chiefly a good Remedy for the Head-Ach, or the Ague. For the Head-Ach, you must rub this Wood against a flat Marble, agitating it with Rose-Water, or common; then rub the Forehead therewith. And for the Ague, drink Water thus agitated, taking 2 or 3 Ounces. This Virtue is not found in that Wood of Aloes which is brought us, because it is quite Rotten and Worm-eaten, having in it no other Virtue but for the Perfumes, and very little for Medicine; So that I advise all curious Apothecaries to chuse for the good and right Wood of Aloes, which is sharp, joined with a certain bitterness. As for the colour, the best is that which is black, enclined to grey with Veins, very hard and ponderous, rendering a sweet scent in the burning, and above all very Gummy. These are the marks of the best as far as I could take notice of in my Travels. I know very well that the price thereof is a little high, and that is the reason why it is so seldom

True Wood of Aloes.

seldom kept in Shops, where they have instead thereof the Sandal-Cittern, which is of a quite contrary Faculty and Vertue: And so likewise of the Turbit *, of which they chuse more of that which is white, light and falling to Powder in the breaking, (than the grey) which is of a sweet scent, gummy and heavy, which is the good and right, as I have seen at *Goa*, where they gather it. The Indians themselves never make use of any other sort than the grey inclining to white; but one Dram of that will make more in effect than three of the other; and I believe that this white is not the right Turbit, never having seen any such in the *Indies*, but that it rather comes from *Persia*, because 'tis brought from *Aleppo* and *Alexandria* by the Caravans which come from *Babilon*. Thus much can I say at present of the right Turbit. As for the rest, the Indians call this Wood of Aloes *Aupariebon*.

* *Which is a Root.*

We gathered then together, in the River of *Cayenne*, ſtore of this Wood of Aloes, which was very good and excellent: but the quantity that hath been found thereof, greater than has been hitherto ſeen, hath been the cauſe that it is not ſo much eſteemed as formerly; yet nevertheleſs the able and learned Apothecaries of *Tours*, *Poitiers*, *Angiers*, *Rochelle*, and other Cities, have bought it of me at ten, fifteen, and twenty Sols the Ounce. I believe that if this Wood of Aloes of the Weſt was dryed and cut twenty or thirty years, like that of the *Ganges*, where the beſt grows, that it would very much reſemble it in Virtue, Colour, and Odour: But in regard I brought it green as it was, the ignorant Apothecaries thought it was not the right Wood of Aloes.

But to return to this River of *Cayenne*, there is, in the middle of it, a little Iſland, about 100 Paces in compaſs, where a great number of Birds, from all parts thereabouts, come to take

take their rest at night; and amongst others, some of those beautiful Birds have Carnation Feathers quite to the Bill: and having a mind to carry some of them alive with me into *France*, I strewed Bird-lime all over this little Island, (for I had brought 9 or 10 Pounds of it from *France*) and the next day some of our Men went there, who found a great number of them taken; But as the ill fortune would have it, they tarried not till I could see them, (for I was then in the Ship) but Eat them all up, like Gluttons as they were, which I was mightily vexed at.

These Birds are of the bigness of a Crane, and are at first of a Dove colour, then in growing, change by little and little into a Carnation: The Indians make their Garments of them, and Crowns of Feathers for their Heads: And it is a fine sight to see them thus array'd, painting also their Bodies with * a reddish colour, which is that they use to Paint themselves withall: This is made of a little Seed inclosed in a Vessel of the Fashion of

* Zinzolin, or Red the colour of the Indians.

Alques

Alquequangi, a little Plant which grows commonly in the Vinyards; They are called *Coqu:lourdes*, and are filled full with thefe little red Seeds, wherewith they Paint themfelves.

In the mean time, we fet thefe *Caribes* to work, and employed them in looking out the Wood of Aloes, and gave them a Hatchet or Bill for a piece or two of this Wood; and when they had prepared a piece, they came to give me notice of it, to know if it was neat, and peeled of from the white Wood which is round about it, and hath in it neither Force nor Virtue.

They fet feveral Men to trail a piece of this Wood to the Sea fide; for it is very heavy: Then they chofe which they liked beft, a Hatchet or a Bill, to exchange for their Wood. I faw one of thefe *Caribes*, who was mightily puzzel'd, and in great doubt, which of the two he fhould chufe, and was a long time confidering and paufing with himfelf which would be the moft neceffary for him; at laft, after

after having well confidered and bethought himfelf, he took the Hatchet, feeing he who gave it him began to be angry for his ftanding fo long about it. They brought us alfo, to Sell, an abundance of Fruits, as Anano's and Plantins, which are long Figs, and as big as a Cervela, with Patato's, and other Things good to Eat; Alfo fome Crocodiles, and a fort of an Animal, armed with a Coat, which the Spaniards call, *Armadil'e*. I made the Diffection of a Crocodile, and Eat fome of it's Flefh, which is pretty good, only it is a little fweet and unfavory, though I had well Salted and Spiced it.

Cervelas.

Armadille

I had alfo in exchange, of them, another fort of a Creature, which is a kind of an Ape or Marmot, but more Arch and Roguifh, and with a very long Tail.

Apis.

The Indians fay that this Beaft carries her young ones upon her Back when fhe has caft them out of her Belly, and goes jumping from Tree to Tree with them upon her Reins and when any one of them is ready to fall, she holds them up with her Tail.

This Animal makes such a noise about the Woods, that when they are together tho' never so few, you would say there were a hundred Hogs a killing.

That which I bought was Dead, and cost me a little Horn: It was a Female, having two Teats in the Stomach like a Woman. The Indians had taken it with the Bow, and it had a stroke with an Arrow in the Belly, and carried one of her young ones upon her Back; which they brought us to Sell for a Hatchet. This little one, being in our Ship, howled after such manner, that it made us all quite Deaf; it died afterward, for it would not Eat.

There happened to be a Monkey at that time in our Ship, and this Creature catching fast hold about its middle, griped it so hard, that the poor Monkey could not shake it off, running about the Cordage from one side to another, and endeavouring with his Paws to make her fall, but in vain.

We had another Animal, the strangest that can be imagined; for it had a very long Beard, the Head set up very high, and the Legs very long, with three Paws behind and two before: It kept it self continually in a Ball, not being able to stand upon its Legs. We tied a Rope cross the Ship, and then put this Beast upon it, but she continued always in a round, like a Ball. That which was given it to Eat, she took in her Paw like a Monkey, and so put it in her Mouth. We had many strange Creatures, which it would be too long and tedious, to give a particular account of.

I return then to some Manners and Fashions that I have observed amongst these *Caribes*. A little before our departure from this River of *Cayenne*, we saw one day these *Ca-* *Manner of* *ribes* leading a new Bride about the *the Caribes* Woods with a very great noise, and *in their* pursued and killed all that they found *Marriages.* about the Forest: Then they came to the Sea side to see our Vessels.

These

Lib. II.   *of* John Mocquet.   103

These are People of a very good Stature, and Plump. They sat down upon the Bank of the River to view our Ship at their leisure: This Bride was there, all alone, with a company of these Savages, and having continued there some time to see us, with Admiration, she again rose up; then the others conducted her about the Woods as before: Thus they lead about their Wives, their Kindred, and Friends. As I kept Watch one night upon the Deck, I saw these *Caribes* upon a high Mountain keeping also Watch, and Sounding with a Horn very loud; then all the other Habitations answered, in the same manner, every hour of the night: After that they made a clear Fire, which they presently put out again. They do all this that they might be thought not to Sleep; for they mightily fear their Enemies the *Caripous*.

Now our Ship being laden with as many Commodities as we were well able to procure, and being ready to set Sail, I took a Resolution, the 17th of *May*, to go once again towards their Habitations with some

Another Voyage of the Author.

H 4   small

small Ware, as Knives, Combs, and other Things; and gave all these to an Indian, to carry in a little Basket, who was wonderfully pleased to follow me; but he, being subtile and sly, would not march before me, saying, that it did not belong to him to go first; which made me not a little wonder that this Indian could know what Honour was due to another; But, the Rascal did it, that he might the more easily put his Hand into my Basket and sharp something out; I perceived it happily, turning my self about, and so caught him in the very act; upon which I shewed him gently that *that* was neither handsome nor well done: He excused himself as well as he could and then went before me until he found in the Wood a little Way or Path, on the right Hand, which went straight to his Habitation, and then he returned me my Basket, not being able to retain him for all I could do; I gave him a Comb, for his Labour, of which he was very glad. I do not know but that he had cast something aside of what he had taken out of my Basket.

I proceeded on my way untill I came to a high Mountain where there were, a great number of *Caribes*, with their Wives and Children: There by chance I found the Indian, our Interpreter, who helped me mightily in making my Bargains, for what I wanted, as well for Parrots as other kind of Animals. Having exchanged what I defir'd thefe Indians led me into another Habitation, where I faw, *Tapoira*, the Brother *Caribe* of *Atupa* who was in our Ship: He was upon the top of one of their Houfes of Palm, and as foon as he perceiv'd me, he caft himfelf down, and came to embrace me, remembring that *I* had given him a Hatchet when he had broke his own in our Service.

<small>Yapoira.</small>

He fpoke to me of his Brother *Atoupa* and that his Mother had no more than this little Boy who was all her Comfort; That the *Caripous* had killed all his Brothers and Sifters, and that, if our General would let him return to his Mother, he himfelf was content to go with us into *France*. *I* told that he fhould go along with me, to make his Remonftrances, which

he

he did : *I* asked him for some Water, which they call *Tonna*, and presently he caused his Wife to bring me some, who was of an extraordinary sweet Nature, and very handsome, though she was stark Naked: Having drank, they caused me to enter into a great Hall made of Palms, where they keep themselves in the day time, with their Amaca's, to hold Counsel concerning the Affairs of War. Then they led me into a certain House where there was a great many Women and Girls stark naked; and put some Patato's upon the Fire for me to Eat: and having made some exchange, as well for Mace and Patato's, as Gums, which is a black Bitume which they Chaulk their Cannoes with, *I* laded 2 or 3 Indians, and so we returned, towards the Port, to our Ship. I had a great deal of trouble in returning back because these Savages led me through the Wood where there was a great many Waters to pass; besides it rained, and was very bad Weather. After we had gone 2 or 3 Leagues of this bad way, we came to the end of a little River, and found a Cannoe on Land

Gums.

Land that wanted only to be set a Float, but we had no Oars; yet these Indians looked so long amongst the Herbs that at last they found out some that were hid. These Oars are very little, and like to a Battle-dore which they beat Hemp withall.

Being thus Embark'd, we Rowed so hard that we soon arrived at our Ship, where they waited for me with great earnestness, not knowing where I should be kept out so late, and they were to have set sail the next morning, as we did.

But before we come out of this Country, I will not forget, that amongst other Rarities that grow there, there are certain Gums to be found, called *Copal*, and *Anime*, and certain Bitum, or black Gum, very Odoriferous when it is put upon the Fire; It is also good for the Rhume, by receiving the Smoak of it; the same is also the *Anime*, which is a Gum, yellow and transparent, like the Gums of *Arabia*, and is found in great Tears.

As for the *Copal*, it hath not this quality, but it serves for * Apost-humes, to ripen and heal them, so they

Animes Gums.

*Swellings.

they come from a cold Cause and Phlegm. For, as for those which come from Heat and Blood, the *Copal* is not so proper to apply, being it is hot. This *Copal* is a White Gum, enclining to gray: The Tree which bears it is like to a Lawrel in its Leaves, but 'tis bigger in the Trunk, and hath also young ones. I picked out some of this Gum, by making an Incision in the Tree; then the next morning, or two days after, I found the Gum pure and clear upon the slit. The *Anime* is gotten after the same manner, and its Tree also resembles the other. As for the Bitum, or black Gum; it comes from a place where there are Springs of Water, and it is gathered, mixed with Earth at the foot of certain Trees amongst Green Moss. The Indians make use of it, instead of Pitch, to Chalk their Cannoes.

Language of the Caribes.

As for the Language of these People, I will only say, that it is of several sorts; and that of the *Caripous* is something different from that which the *Caribes* speak, and have much ado to understand other, although they are
not

not far distant. These *Caribes* were mighty desirous to know, of us, what it was that we Worshipped in Heaven; whether it was the Sun, which they call *Occayou*, or the Moon, which they name *Nona*, the Stars *Cherica*, Heaven *Capa*, the Clouds *Canopa*; as for the Fire, they call it *Ovato*, Water *Tonna*, the Sea *Parano*, the Woods *Vropa*, the Mouth *Pota*, the Eyes *Onou*, and the Hair *Omchay*.

Now as for the Religion of all these People of *Brasil*, and amongst others the *Caripous* and *Caribes*, they live without Faith and Law, and without any certain Belief of a Divinity, true or false; not Worshipping Idols, nor any thing whatsoever: only they believe some kind of an Immortality of the Soul. They speak much of a God, which they call *Toupan*, which is some Devil with whom they have Familiarity, and exercise several sorts of Divination and Witchcraft: And I remember we were told that when *Camaria*, King of the *Caribes*, had a mind to know any thing concerning their Wars against their Enemies, he made made a hole in the Ground, pronouncing

Religion of these People.

Caribes deal with the Devil Toupan.

nouncing some certain Words, and then came something up with a horrible thundering noise, which spake to him, and instructed him, giving him notice what their Enemies were doing at that time. And indeed, when *Camaria* and his Brother *Yago* came on board our Ship, they told us, that they knew very well, that their Enemy *Anacajoury*, King of the *Caripous*, was preparing himself to come to attack them; that which he could not have known so readily but by such means.

Yapoco.   But to return to the *Caripou-Yapoco*, of whom I have spoken before, that *Camaria* King of the *Caribes* had instantly desired me (being at his Habitation) to order the business so with our General that he might have him in his power, to Eat him in Revenge of the mischief that his Uncle *Anacajoury* had done them before: When I was returned back to our Ship, I spoke to the General about it, who told me, that I did very well to promise, but he would take care to avoid such Wickedness: Thus *Camaria* was promised to have *Yapoco* given him, of which he was mighty Joyful, and sent

about

about all his Country, to all his Friends and Confederates that they should prepare themselves to come to this Feast. The next morning hoising our Sails, and weighing Anchor to go away, presently comes *Camaria* with a great many Indians to have *Tapoco*, who being refused him in good earnest, went away so affronted and vexed that I had not a mind to return to be his Guest; for I believe they would have done the same to me they designed to do to the poor *Tapoco*. This *Camaria* had but one Eye, and was mighty Crafty and Treacherous.

As for *Tapoira*, the Brother of *Atoupa* the *Caribe*, who had tarried all night in our Ship as I have said before: *Atoupa* did all that ever he could to persuade us to let go his Brother; but seeing he could not obtain that of our General, he said that he would also willingly go with us into *France*, and that he would either kill or drown himself rather than leave him. The General told him that he was content, and that he should come betimes in the morning, and whilst he was in such a good Humour. This being thus

thus resolved upon, as soon as we began to set sail, we saw the Mother of these two *Caribes*, who came towards us in a Cannoe, crying and howling after the most pittiful manner that could be imagined; She brought along with her the Bow and Arrows, the Paintings and the Amica, of *Tapoira*, which is all their Wealth. *Tapoira* was mighty sorry to see his Mother keep such a mourning for him, and desired our General to give her a Hatchet, to appease her a little, which was done; yet she returned again thus Disconsolate.

Departure from the Country of the Caribes.
Santa-Lucia.
Tabaco Isle.
Isle de la Trinadad

After that we set sail the 18th of *May*, and passed by a little Island, very pleasant, near to the Coast of the *Caribes*, holding our Course to go to the Isle of *Santea-Lucia*, but we were deceived by the Currents which come from the South-East, having made (according to the Estimation of our Pilot) in one night, above seventy Leagues, without scarce any Wind. We went to touch at the Isle of *Tabuco*, which remained Northwards of us. Then, leaving the Isle *de-la-Trinadad* towards the South, we discovered the

Lib. II. *of* John Mocquet.

the Testigues of the Isle *Blanche*, which Blanche-
are 5 or 6 Peninsula's, very near to one Isl.
another, and passed through the middle
of them, then seeing Land of some places
above: We were a long time considering if it was Land, or thick Clouds,
because it was very low; and thereupon several Wagers were laid, whether it was Land or not: At last,
bearing directly towards it, we found
out that it was really Land, but unknown to us, since deceived by the
Currents.

As we approached it, we saw Animals, running in great Companies *Wild-*
along the Coast: Some of us not know- *Goats,*
ing what they were, said at first they
were Bands or Cavalliers; but these
Cavalliers proved to be Wild-Goats,
of which this Isle is full: Taking
down then our Sails very low we
went as near to this Island as we could,
our Patache going continually before
to discover if there were any Rocks,
as indeed we had gone directly upon
one had not the Patache given us notice thereof with a signal at the end of
a Pike, and took the way that she
shewed us, leaving this Rock about

a little Stones caſt off us: It was not covered with above a Foot or two of Water, ſo that we going ſo ſwift with a light Gale of Wind, had without doubt ſplit, and been all loſt in ſuch a place without help or ſuccour; and beſides, it being in the night; but God by his mercy preſerved us therefrom; and being there was not much clear Water to be ſeen, we could not find the bottom to Anchor, but at laſt we found but 30 Fathoms of Water, where we caſt Anchor for this night.

Voyage into the Iſle. The next morning the 29th of *May* we cauſed our Boat to be Equipped to go on Shore, and to ſeek ſome Water: Our Men after Breakfaſt, went thus away, with their Muskets and Pikes, without the leaſt drop of Water along with them; but they payed dear for it: For after having gone a good way up into this Iſland, with the heat of the Sun and running after the Goats, they were ſo wonderful dry and thirſty, that, they thought, they ſhould all have Died for want of a little Water; and returning again with great Trouble and Fatigue, they were forced to carry the weakeſt upon their Shoulders:

Lib. II. *of* John Mocquet.

ders: They brought along with them a great many Pelicans, and coming confusedly one after another very weak and discomforted, and not minding any thing but Drinking; and then our General's Brother of Friendship coming on board our Ship, said aloud, that they looked for Pearls, but he had rather have a Barrel of Water, than of Pearls, for the great Thirst that he had endured with the rest.

The next morning we went (sixteen Men) to discover the other side of the Island, and if there was any Water; and coming on Land we saw before us a great number of Wild-goats, who came running along the Sea side, and began to enter into a Valley, where we with Harquebuss and Musket killed five or six upon the place. These Creatures, not being used to be Hunted after this manner, made a horrible noise and bellowing; and though they were Shot quit through the Body, yet they did not fall for that, but fled away with a light pace. We left there a Man to order these we had killed. I never thought then to look for the Besoart-Stone, which these Beasts

The Author visites the Isle.

Besoart-Stone.

Beasts carry in their Ventricle, but to follow the others about this Isle to find out Water, and some curious Things.

We went thus three or four Leagues without finding any Water, at which our Companions were mightily astonished, and deceived as well as those the day before: For we had nothing at all to quench our Thirst, amidst such excessive heat of the Sun: As for me, I had carried in my Pocket a Coco's or Palm-Nut, full of Liquor, which was no small help to me at this time, and I believe without that, I should had much ado to have returned. Our Carpenter was forced to stay behind, earnestly desiring me to tarry with him; But it was not my intention to lie in these Desarts; besides, the Ship was to set Sail the next morning, which gave me the more courage to return the same day. After having thus rambled about, and run from one side to the other, at last we came under a great Tree, where we sat down in the Shade to take our rest. And as it is certain that there is no better Remedy to quench the Thirst than Sleeping, all our Men who were a little harrassed and fatigued, as much with Thirst, as by the way, and having run after the * *Cabrettes,* fell presently a Sleep: But I not being at all sleepy, laid down upon my Back, with my Face upwards to suck in the Air; and upon this I espied a great Lizard, full and very high, the Tail very long, and about the bigness of a Cat; I presently rose up without awakening our Men, and having taken a Pike, I gave the branch of the Tree therewith such a blow, that there tumbled down two of them, which the Indians call *Gouyana's*. I run after them trailing along my Pike, which broke in two pieces, and made such haste that I overtook one which was creeping under a Rock, and I took it by the Tail, plucking it with all my force; but it being very strong, stretched it self in such a manner against me, having very long Paws, that it saved its Body, but the Tail remained in my Hands, and was alive above three hours after, continually moving. As soon as our Men were awake, I gave them an account of what had happened,

* *A sort of Spanish Kid.*

Hunting of the Lizards

Guyana's or Lizards.

pened, and made so many Courses about this Island, that I caught two of these Lizards, whereof I made very good chear, for the Flesh thereof is pretty good; I kept their Skins to carry away with me. This Creature is of a very hard Life, for after having taken, and leaving them for Dead, yet they from time to time come to move and start up, so that carrying them in a Napkin, I thought to let them fall every moment. After we had reposed our selves a little under this Tree, we took our way towards the other side of the Sea, finding a little beaten Path which went towards these *Cabrettes*, thinking that it was the way, where they went to look for Water to Drink; but after having gone about a League of this way, we found in a flat ground, a great place where these *Cabrettes* came to take their rest, for the place was mightily beaten. We saw there another Path which went from this place; and hoping that it would lead us to some Water, we found it brought us to the Sea-side, where we saw some Sea-Water upon a Rock, which was high

high and flat; it made us glad, thinking it had been fresh, but tasting of it we found the contrary, and that it was nothing but the Waves of the Sea which broke against this Rock, where there always remains some little of it, besides the Sun had Congeled it into Salt exceeding clear and pure. Seeing then that we found no Water, it behoved us (tho' with great regret) to take again the way to our Ship, each one seeking the nearest he could, for we went confusedly, striving who might arrive first to quench his Thirst; but the allowance we had was not sufficient, not being more than a little Cupfull of Drink, which was sower Citter, with two parts Water, but some had provided Liquor for themselves.

I rrived the third at the Ship, and Bathed my Body in the Sea to refresh my self, sopping also a little Bisket in the Sea to Eat, and swallowing some Mouth-fulls thereof. The rest of our Men were tarried behind, and being come there with the Fleming and Scotchman, we called the Boat: But the Ship being above a League and a half

half from Land, which was a great hinderance to us; for the Boat would not carry us back without the others, who were still far enough off, and kept one another up by the Arms; But at last I perfuaded the Mariners to carry me on Board, where, as foon as I came, I went to vifit my Cheft and my Bottle, and remained full three days without being able to quench my Thirft: The reft of our Men returned very late, and were wonderful weary and fatigued; But the poor Carpenter tarried behind to keep company with the Cabrettes, Lizards, and Parrots, who were there in abundance, and very beautiful. Our General feeing that he was wanting, faid, he would not part from the Road until he had News of him; and fent Seamen all the Night, with the Trumpet to Sound all about the Ifland to call him, but all to no purpofe, for he was far enough from thence. The morning being come, his Seamen was commanded to take a Shovel, with other Mariners who knew pretty nigh the place where they had left him, and went thus feeking about thefe Defarts, (for

Adventures of the Carpenter.

(for it is a flat Island having very few Trees:) At last they found him trailing along his Musket as well as he could; for he was very Sick, and being come to the Ship, he was taken with a Fever, accompanied with a Frenzie, continuing 3 or 4 days, and did nothing but cry out for Drink, and it was almost impossible to satisfie him: He told us afterwards how he had lain under a Tree quite full of Parrots, which he could easily take with his Hand; and that the *Cabrettes* came to smell upon him in the night time; but that he never stirred from his Musket which he always kept close by him: The moisture of the night had a little quenched his Thirst; He was also forced to Drink his own Water.

Being parted from this Isle the first of *June*, to go to the *Margueritta*, as we were under Sail very late at night, we descry'd two Ships coming full sail upon us. We had sunk our Patache in this Desart Island. We got the Wind a little upon them, and being very near one to the other, their Trumpets began to Sound, and ours to anſwer them. As we were prepared to receive them, having put out our Cannons, and ready to come to handy Strokes, the Wind being very favourable for us, and the night very dark, they would not come on board without having firſt known who we were. We got the Wind of them as much as we could, and in the end, during the dark and ſtormy night, we eſcaped, and made towards the Iſle of *Margueritta*, where we arrived the next day towards the Evening, and caſt Anchor near to a little Habitation on the Eaſt-ſide: Then we ſent our Boat on Land, with Arms, to diſcover the place: They found Fire ſtill in the Houſes, but no Body within, all being fled into the Woods at the ſight of us. We found a Cannoe, which came from Fiſhing of Pearls, not having any thing in it but Shells. The Maſter's Mate was ſent to a riſing Ground in the Iſland, to ſee if he could diſcover any thing: He eſpied 3 or 4 Blacks, who run away into the * Thorn-Buſhes as ſoon as they ſaw him, and it was impoſſible to find them out, tho' very diligent ſearch was made:

margin: Margueritta Iſland.

made: We had a great mind to take some one of the Islanders to shew us the place where they Fish for Pearls, which is in certain places along by the Isle; but it was impossible to find any one of them.

The third of *June* in the night time we had so violent a Tempest, that our Ship was in danger to have run aground, but leaving an Anchor in the Sea to save the Ship, we were preserved from this imminent danger.

The fourth day of the same month, seeing we could not find any sweet Water, we weighed our Anchors and bore towards *Cumana*, and arriving 2 or 3 Leagues on this side, we perceiv'd a Fleming Ship in a Bay or Gulf, lading with Bay-Salt, which is there in abundance: We cast Anchor on the Starboard-side of her, and put out our Boat into the Sea to Board them, and so to ask them where we might find some fresh Water. After having saluted us with their Cannon, they told us, that bearing towards the River of *Cumana* we should find some, and that we should by the way meet their Shalop, which they had sent there;

[margin: Cumana.]

which

which we did accordingly, but the Men therein would come near us by no means, they were so afraid needlesly. We continued our Course towards *Cumana*, where coming near the River, we espied along the Coast two Ships at Anchor, not knowing what they should be. Nevertheless we proceeded on, for it was necessary to have Water, and could not live without Drinking. We found that of these two Ships the one was a Fleming, and the other English: The Fleming Traffick'd there underhand with those of *Cumana*, where the Spaniards are; And the English Patache came there to seek some fresh Water for their Admiral, whom she had left along by the *Margueritta*

After several Guns for Salutation, the English came on Board our Ship, Feasting our English Pilot and 5 or 6 others of their Countrymen which we had in our Ship.

Our Trumpeter shewed me their Pilot, and told me, that he some years before being in an English Vessel, as they were upon the Coasts of the *West-Indies*, towards *St. John de Love*, (the first

Marginal notes: Extream Thirst. Rencounter with the English. Strange History of an English Pilot.

first place of the *Indies* to go to *Mexico*, where the Spaniards are, then their Sworn Enemies) a great Storm overtook them, which cast them upon the Coast, where they were all lost, except this Pilot, who saved himself by Swiming to Land, carrying with him a little Sea-Compass, and went thus wandring about to return by Land to the *Newfound* Countries: Upon that, he had found an Indian-Woman, of whom he was Enamoured, making her fine Promises by Signs, that he would Marry her; which she believed, and conducted him through these Desarts; where she shewed him the Fruit and Roots good to Eat, and served him for an Interpreter amongst the Indians, which he found, she telling them that it was her Husband. After having been thus 2 or 3 years continually wandering about, and that for above 800 Leagues, without any other Comfort but this Woman: At last they arrived at the *Newfoundland*, guiding himself by his Compass: They had a Child together; and found there an English Ship a Fishing: He was very glad to see himself escaped

from

from so many Dangers, and gave these English an account of all his Adventures: They took him on Board their Vessel to make him good chear; but being ashamed to take along with him this Indian-Woman thus Naked, he left her on Land, without regarding her any more: But she seeing her self thus forsaken by him, whom she had so dearly Loved, and for whose sake she had abandonned her Country and Friends, and had so well guided and accompanied him through such places, where he would, without her, have been dead a thousand times.

Strange and Cruel Acts of an Indian Woman.

After having made some Lamentation, full of Rage and Anger, she took her Child, and tearing it into two pieces, she cast the one half towards him into the Sea, as if she would say, that belonged to him, and was his part of it; and the other she carried away with her, returning back to the Mercy of Fortune, and full of Mourning and Discontent.

The Seamen who took this Pilot into their Boat, seeing this horrible and cruel Spectacle, asked him, why he had left this Woman; but he pretended

tended she was a Savage, and that he did not now heed her; which was an extream Ingratitude and Wickedness in him: Hearing this, I could not look upon him, but always with Horrour and great Detestation.

After then that we had Feasted one another, the English Convoyed us to get some Water: All the night long, I went to Drink in full Streams, to compense the former Thirst I endur'd, filling the empty Vessels of my Chest for the time to come. In the morning before we set Sail, two Spaniards, with an Indian-Woman, came from *Cumana*, on Board, to exchange Pearls with some of our Merchandize, but we had nothing fit for them: We weighed then our Anchors, and took our Course the 5th of *June*, and repassing along by the Isle of *Margueritta*, and the White Island, we went to get out of the Channel by the *Virginies*: But having seen there a great Ship at Anchor, we could not imagine what she should be, whether English or Spanish; we passed close by her, without perceiving any one upon the
Deck,

Water found.

Virginia.

Deck; And bearing a little further, we perceived a great Ship, in form of a Galley, coming full sail upon us. We kept our selves to the Wind as much as we could, nevertheless we were prepared to receive them; but the night coming on, when they were near us, and at such time when we thought to come to handy-Blows, this great Ship that we had left at Anchor made a Fire on Land, which made them leave of Chasing us. We bore all night along by *Portorico*, and the next day, at night, the 12th of *July* passed all the Island: We saw our selves at break of day out of the Channel, and very joyful that we were in the Main-Sea, holding our Course about the height of the Isle of *Bermuda*. We had tarried a long time without making any way, because of the Calms: And visiting our Bread, and finding it very short, we were forced to come to parting, and my part fell to about 8 or 10 pound, as well good as mouldy; But having a great many Parrots to feed, I was in perplexity what to do, being this Animal is very Gluttonous.

Portorico.

Bermude-Isle.

last, I was resolved to
diest, and Rost him, which
at him up before I came
e Bisquet. In the mean
the Wind was not fa-
us, we began already to *Extream*
l; that if this Weather *Council.*
ly longer, we should be
o cast Lots, who should
panion. We had in our
Indians, who would have
st: But in the midst of
ities, it pleased the Di-
ss to visit us a little after
ay, and to send us a fair
h carried us to the Isle *de*
of the *Asores*, where we
Refreshment; but not
have as much as we de-
ssed the Coast in waiting
l; but as it came good
we quitted the Isle, and
our Course as far as *Con-*
ne, where we arrived the
ust 1604. for which all
lory be to the Most High.

d *of the Second Book.*

A Description of the following Cutts.

First, *The manner of the Fights, betwixt the* Caribes *and the* Caripous.

Secondly, *The Indian Woman go thus about the Woods looking Fruits to Eat.*

K 2

A Description of the following Cutts.

The First, *How the* Caripous *are Euiqpped going to War against the* Caribes.
How the Caribes *take Fish.*

The First, *The manner of the Dances of the* Caribes.
Amazons *going to the Wars.*

A Defcripiion of the following Cutts.

The Firſt, *The manner of the Cannoes, or Boats, of the* Caripous, *and other Indians.*

The Second, *How the* Caribes *Roaſt, and Eat the Fleſh of their Enemies.*

A Description of the following Cutts.

The First, *How the* Caribes *Eat the Flesh of the* Caripous, *and Feast together therewith.*

The Second, Amaca's, *or Hanging-Beds of the* Caripous.

THE TRAVELS
AND
VOYAGES
OF
John Mocquet,
INTO
MOROCCO,
And other Places of *AFRICA.*

BOOK III.

THE Voyage that I had made the former year to the *West-Indies,* had left me such a desire to see also the rest of the World, that I was resolved to go to the *East-Indies,* if I found any fit opportunity: For this effect, I parted from *Paris* the 12th of *April* 1605. and taking

my

my way ſtraight to *Britagne*, I went to Embark at *St. Lezer*, (*St. Nazare*) in a Ship of *Poligain*, where we were not above twenty Perſons in all.

We were at the beginning of this Voyage ſo beaten with contrary Winds, that we were forced to the Coaſt of *Galice*, a little below Cape *de Vere*. Having continued there for ſome time, we ſet ſail with the Wind, and arrived at *Lisbon* in *Portugal*, at ſuch time as they were Rejoycing for the Birth of an Infant of *Spain*; which was a very fine ſight. For after having a long time run the Bulls, according to their manner of Paſtime, where there was a great many Horſes maimed, and Cavalliers overturned to the Ground, they laded a Bull with Crackers, but there was ſuch a great number of them on him, that he fell down under the Burthen; and they were forced to fetch a ſtrong Ox to carry them, and yet he ſtoop'd under ſo heavy a Load: Theſe Crackers were faſtened one to another, ſo that they covered all the Body of this Ox; then there was others tied to his Horns. When the Feaſt was ended, fire was
pu

Rejoycing at Lisbon.

?amed.

put to thefe Crackers, and then you would have faid, that the Ox flew in the Air, with fuch an Impetuofity, which looked like Lightning; for Ten Thoufand Muskets would not have made fo great a noife, each Cracker anfwering one another, fo that the Ox remained quite roafted.

I made fome ftay at *Lisbon*, upon the hopes that I fhould, (as I have faid) find paffage to the *Eaft-Indies*, if the Fleet had gone there that year: But as it was ready to part, the Dutch Fleet came to caft Anchor about the Bar of *Lisbon*, where they ftayed a long time, waiting for the faid Fleet; but the Portuguefe were not fo foolifh as to venture out. After that, Don *Louis Fajardo*, General of the Army, knowing that the Hollanders were now retired, riged out a Fleet of 35 fail to follow after; and went a good way out into the Sea, fending a little Ship before, called the *Pearl*, (taken from the *Rochellers*) to difcover 'em; But this Veffel meeting with the Hollanders, was taken by them, and all the reft returned to the Haven of *Lisbon* without doing any thing.

Dutch Army towards Lisbon.

Having

Having then lost this occasion of passing to the *East-Indies* at that time, I was resolved to go to *Barbary*, and for this Cause Embarked at *Cascais*, in a Vessel belonging to Captain *Poulet* of *Rochelle*.

Voyage into Barbary.

We bore South East, and passed along by *Azamor*, near to the City of *Lions*, which is a place ruined, having still very high Towers. On Wednesday the 8th day of the month, we cast Anchor in the Road of *Saffy*, where I tarried some time without going on Shore at all: But *Cidi-Hamet-Talbe*, or Secretary to the King of *Morocco*, *Mulei-Boufairs* being come to *Saffy* with his *Almahalle*, or little Army, to conduct the Caravan which was come to *Morocco*, and to reconduct the other, which was going there, he fell Sick; and having heard that there was a *Tabibe*, or a Physitian on board our Ship, he sent some Moors immediately to fetch me. I went with them on Land, not knowing what they would do with me; and coming there upon the Port, I found this *Cidi-Hamet* sitting with a great number of Moors along the Walls

Saffy.

Almahalle.

Walls of the Castle; and as soon as he saw me, he rose up, and taking me by the Hand, led me into his Camp, which was without *Saffy*, into his Tent, being very fine, and curiously Embroidered with Figures, after the Moresque. There I found a Jew, which served for Interpreter in the *Gemique*, (which is Spanish or corrupted Portuguese) which I understood; and having discoursed with me about his Disease, I resolved upon that which I thought best for his Cure; and for this cause went on board our Ship to look for Drugs fit for this purpose.

In short, I Purged him so, that I caused him to Vomit up Worms like little Serpents; which made me not a little admire, for they were so very great, and long, that it was almost impossible to imagine that such odious and horrible things could be in Human Bodies: Since that, he was very well and was my great Friend; and he and his *Alcades* shewed me all the kindness imaginable: He gave me a Horse to go to *Morocco*, making very much of me by the way.

Thus

Thus we parted from *Saffy* to go to *Morocco*, the 28th of *August*, and went to pitch the *Almahalle* near to the *Adouars* or Tents of the *Arabs*, and went to see them with some Moors their Enemies. These *Arabians* caused us to enter into their Tents; then they put some Carpets very thick and hairy upon the Ground for us to sit upon, and brought us some Camels Milk to Drink, with I don't know what other things: After that, we retired in the night to the Camp of the Moors, which was not very far from thence.

The next morning we raised our Tents, and went to pitch the *Almahalle*, at the *Duguele*, were there is Water. The *Arabians* had made there a great many large and deep Ditches, which they call *Matamores*, in such manner that it is a very dreadful thing to look to the bottom of them: 'Tis there they find Water; in some of which there is some, in others none: And these *Arabs* come to look there for VVater, above 4 or 5 Leagues round about. From the *Puquelle* they come with their Camels, which they

they lade with this VVater, in *Oudres*, or Goat Skins. And when they have Reaped their Corn, they raise their *Adouars*, or Tents, and go away to some other place far distant from thence, leaving this Ground to lie waste a long time: Then afterwards, they return there again, laying their Houses and Husbandry, VVives and Children, upon their Camels, like as the antient *Nomades*, and the *Tartar Hordes*, at this day, and go altogether in a Company, by *Cabilles* or Generations; so that if any one comes to strike one of their Generation, they think themselves all thereby injured, and presently Revenge it. There are some of these *Cabilles* who joyn themselves together to make VVar upon other *Cabilles* that are not their Friends: There are sometimes above Twelve thousand of a *Cabille* or Parentage: For they Marry one another like Cousins, and thus conserve the Memory of themselves. The most Ancient, and VVisest amongst them, they make Chief, and Obey him in all Things, and every where, as their own Father, with a wonder-

Arabians, and their manner of Living.

ful

ful Respect, as I have seen in their *Alcayde-Abdassis*, Captain of one of these *Cabilles*, which conducted us from *Morocco* to *Saffy*, to hinder those of his *Cabille* from doing us any prejudice, for he had taken us in his Custody upon his Head, having so promised it to the King of *Morocco*; forasmuch as his People held a good part of the way betwixt *Morocco* and *Saffy*.

But to return to our Voyage; the morning being come, we raised the Tents, and in waiting till the Camels were Laded, the *Cavaliers, Moors* and *Arabians* exercised themselves at the Lance: And there was, amongst others, a young *Alcayde*, who took his Course with his Lance against me, crying out to me in his Language, *Bara, bara, aben senari*, which is to say, Guard thy self, thou Son of a Christian: I spurr'd then my Horse, which was a *Barbe*, very nimble, having two Pistols at my Saddle-bow, I ran at the Re-incountre with this *Cavalier*; but my Horse being strong in the Mouth, was very near Precipitating me to the bottom of these *Matamores*, or Pits of Water,

Senari Christian.

Matamores.

Water, which I have spoken of; for the Mouth of them are hid amongst the Grass, and they are there in great numbers: But seeing my self almost upon the brink, and my Horse going to leap to the other side (which he could never have done without loosing us both:) I reined him so to the purpose, that if the *Alcayde*, which exercised with me, had not also stopped, seeing me so near this Precipice, I had infallibly tumbled therein, but never come out again entirely; considering their great and horrible Depth.

When I saw my self delivered from this danger, I praised God, and retired as far as I could from thence, leaving these *Moors* to exercise by themselves, not knowing so well as they, where these *Matamores* are, so dangerous to those who are not aware of them.

After that we Travelled all the rest of this Day, and endured extream Heats until toward Evening, then we pitched our Tents along by some Water, where all these *Arabs* cast themselves to wash, and refresh 'em, at which I was not a little vexed, for

I had a great mind to drink of this Water, all muddy and dirty as it was, and besides a little saltish, yet I was forced to Drink thereof. We pitched then in these Deserts, and the next day, early in the Morning we departed, Travelling all the Day in the Heat of the *Sun*, the greatest that can be possibly imagined, in these Fields Scorched and Burnt, because of the Hot Winds which blew after such a manner, that we were ready to Die with Thirst: At last, we came into a Desert, where we were forced to look for Water a far off. There was there the *Adouars* of the *Arabians*, who helped us to some Refreshments of Water and Camels Milk, which is not very sweet, but of a strange tast to those who are not accustomed to it; but necessity makes every thing to seem Good, as I have often experienced in all my Voyages.

The next morning going on our way, we perceived several *Arabs* with their Camels laden with Corn, who came to joyn with us, to go to *Morocco*.

Departs without Waters.

Adouars.

We met also great Numbers of *Arabians* on Horse-back with their Launces, who came about us to salute their chief *Abdaffis*, and others of their kindred who were in our Company; I saw them come with great Humility to kiss the Hands of their General *Abdaffis* who had Govern'd them a long time.

I went always in their Company, leaving the other Troops behind, for the desire I had, by following them, to get some Water of the *Arabs* their Friends, whom we found encamped in a Valley of the Desarts; for we went continually with so excessive a Heat, that I durst not so much as lift up my Eyes. Going thus, we met at the bottom of a Mountain some *Arabian* Shepherds, who kept Flocks of Sheep, Goats, and Camels: We went with a number of Cavalliers towards them, to know where we might find some Water, but they would not shew us: Hereupon one of these *Arabs*, who came along with us, commanded one of these Shephards to give him his Stick; and having it in his Hands, began to beat

Water dear beat these poor Wretches with such fury, that I was very sorry to see it, although I was also very Thirsty. This Savage Treatment made the Shepherds shew us where their *Adouars* were, about a League from thence; where we went with all diligence, and found there one of these *Arabs*, who came to fetch Water far from thence, in a Goat-Skin. This Water was very Salt and hot; yet every one of these Cavalliers cast themselves thereupon, for it was very little for so many Men. I obliged them so, with Money, that I obtained some of one of these *Arabs* where we were come. Truly it seemed, that they bereaved these poor Wretches of their Lives in taking away their Water they come to look for so far, and besides there is but little to be found, the Weather being so excessive hot; for all their *Matamores* were dried up at that time.

Having a little refreshed our selves, we went to rejoyn the Camp of the *Aimahake*, and pitched our Tents near the River *Tenfif*, a little days Journey from *Morocco*. We met a great many

Tenfif River.

many *Arabians* all on Horseback, with their Launces, who came about us, to Salute their General *Abdassis*, and others of their Friends, who were in our Company.

I saw them again come with great Humility to Kiss the Hands of this their Chief, *Abdassis*, as before. There we quenched our Thirst a little with this Water; though it was very hot. All the Land in these Countries is various, some part good, and others bad, but for the most part Incultivated, except that which is near some Water, which they Till. This River *Tensif* Breeds the most excellent Trouts of any in the World, being very little, and their Flesh red, but of an excellent Taste, and are mightily esteemed at *Morocco*.

The next morning, going a little further, we discovered *Morocco*, in a great Campagne; and this City seems to be situated near to Mount *Atlas*, though it is above 7 Leagues distant: VVe found by the way some Christians, who came about us.

Morocco.

Atlas Mountain.

These are People that Traffick there, and when they hear that any other Christians come with the *Cafile*, they are very glad, and meet them by the way: They bring with them a little Mule laden with Victuals. Now the most part of the Christians of this *Cafile* were English, Prisoners, with Irons upon their Feet, and had been Arrested at *Saffy*, upon the account of an *Alcayde* named *Abdelacinthe*, who was a Portuguese by Nation, but a Renegado: And for his Capacity and Worth, he had given him the Command of the *Cafile* who returned from *Morocco* to *Saffy*, with about 500 Soldiers under his Charge.

English Prisoners at Morocco.

Now it happened by chance, that *Antonio de Soldaigne*, and *Petro Cæsar*, Portuguese Gentlemen, had been both taken at *Tangier* in *Africa*, and brought to *Morocco*, and being there detained Captives 13 or 14 years, until such time that they were Released by the Sieur de l'Isle, a Physitian, and at that time Agent there for King *Henry the Great*. As these two Portugueses were returning in liberty, this *Alcayde*, *Abdelacinthe*, had Negociated with them

Abdelacinthe, &c.

them to save himself in their Vessel wherein they were to Embark. For this cause, he went to Pitch his *Almahalle* towards the place where they come to take Water for the Ships, near to the Cape of *Cantin*; and being there one night, he told his Men, that he had caused a Moorish-Woman to be brought him, with whom he desired to speak in Secret, a good way off from the Camp, and took none along with him but a Slave of his: When he was near to the Sea-side, he fired a Fuzee, which was the signal that he had given to those of the Ship. As soon as they heard this, presently the People of Boat (who were hid in the Bushes) came to seize upon his Person, and took him, and carried him away in their Vessel, by which means he saved himself. The Slave fled to the *Almahalle*, to give them notice of the taking of his Master, at which they were mightily astonished, and presently retired to *Saffy*: But as the People of an English Boat at the same time were come on Shore for some things they had then occasion for, they were Arrested, and had Irons clapt

Cape of Cantin.

clapt upon their Feet, as I saw them in the Castle of *Saffy*, in very poor Equipage, and were since carried to *Morocco*, where the Merchants paid for them, I don't know how many Ounces of Gold, which was very near the Ransom of the *Alcayde Abdalacinthe* who had escap'd: For those Kings will not loose any thing, it being the Custom at *Marocco*, that when a Slave runs away, all the others as-

Cautioning of the Slaves at Morocco.

semble together and pay for him, cautioning one another to go freely about the City without Irons; which is meant of the poorer sort: But as for the Rich, they are put into the *Si-*

Sifane.

fane, which is the Kings great Prison, where they are well guarded, as these two Portuguese Gentlemen were of whom I have already spoken.

To return to the Christians of *Morocco*, who met us by the way, they made us very good chear, in a Garden, along by a pleasant Water running some two Leagues from *Mo-*

Arrival at Morocco.

rocco. The *Almahalle* entered not into *Morocco* this day, but I left it where it was pitched, and went to lie within the City, in the House of the Christi-ans,

ans, paying for my entrance to the *Talbe* or Regifter; This was the 2d of *September* 1606. As foon as I was arrived, I failed not to go vifit the Sieur *de l'Ifle*, Phyfitian, who was lodged in a very fine Houfe in the *Juderie*, or Jews-Place. The Sieur *de l'Ifle* was a long time near to the Perfon of the King of *Morocco*, in Quality of an Agent, for our King *Henry the Great*; And there had been fince fent the Sieur *Hubert*, the King's Phyfitian, in the room of the Sieur *de l'Ifle*; Then both went into *France*, but fince that, the faid Sieur *de l'Ifle* returned there again. The Sieur *Hubert* lived about a year at *Morocco*, practifing Phyfick near the King, and there following his principal defign, that is, the Learning the *Arabick* Tongue; fo that fince he rendered himfelf very expert therein, as he hath made publick Profeffion thereof at *Paris* it felf, with great Solemnity: He contented himfelf to depart out of this Country more laden with Science and *Arabick* Books, than with Riches, or any Commodities, in which the Sieur *de l'Ifle* was more happy than he.

Be-

Being then in the *Juderie*, I was there conducted by a Jew, who Cozened me of some Rials, giving me falsly to understand, that I was to pay some at the Door of this place, where we were to enter; and indeed he brought one, who came to demand it, and I was forced to Content them.

Juderie of Morocco. This *Juderie*, or Jews-Place, is above a good League from the *Douane*, where the Christians inhabit; and near the King's Palace; and is like a City by it self, encompassed with good Walls, having but one Gate guarded by the Moors: It may be as big as *Meaux*. There the Jews inhabit, to the number of above 4000, and pay Tribute: There is also some Christians; And in this place also live the Agents and Ambassadors of strange Princes: As for the rest of the Christians Trafficking, and others, they live in the *Douane*.

Description of the City of Morocco. The City of *Morocco* is very great, and is much bigger than that at *Paris* which is called the City; being wonderful populous, containing above 400000 Inhabitants, of all sorts of Religions; and such Streets, that for the great multitude of People you can scarce

scarce pass along. The most part of the ordinary Houses there are low, little, and but badly built, with Earth and Lime: But the Houses of the *Alcaydes*, Lords, and other Persons of Quality, are great and high, built with Stone, environed with Walls, with a high Tower in the middle, to go take the fresh Air, and a great many little Windows and Wickets: The upper-parts of the Houses are flat and in Co-tees. The King's Palace is built with little Stones, like in-laid work; and a great many Pillars of Marble, Fountains, and other Ornaments. Their Mosques in great number, well built with Marble, and covered on the top with Lead. There are a great many Halls, or Vaults, where the Merchants are, and amongst others, those which Sell the *Alhec*, or Clothes, like Brokers. There is also several Colleges where they teach Law. There is no River which passes by the City of *Morocco*, but a great many Water-Ditches, and Channels on Land to guide the Waters which come in abundance from the Mountains of *Atlas*, partly from the Springs, and partly from the melted Snow;

Water.

and make this Water run here and there for their Gardens and Fountains. They have also Wells and Cisterns: They serve themselves dexterously with this Water to sprinkle their Gardens and Land. Without the City, about the Fields, are a great number of Gardens, with all sorts of Fruits, and Vineyards, with Water; and a little Habitation to go recreate themselves: They keep their Slaves at work: All the Ground is very good and fertile, and the Seed presently ripens. The Mountains are on every side of the City, except on that towards *Saffy*, which is level. There are the Mountains of *Draz* towards *Lybia*, from whence comes the good Dates. There are no Trees in the Fields, except some Palms: All the Trees are in the Gardens, which are like unto Orchards.

Justice. As for Justice; there is in *Morocco* but one only Judge, which they call *Haquin*, who does ready Justice most commonly upon the place; and hath continually his *Citeres*, or Sergeants, on Foot, armed with Cudgels, and *Alfanges*, or Cimmeters; and as occasion requires, when it appears to be some

nenotorious Offence, they Behead also upon the very place; for they who are offended, cry *Quoavac, quovac,* c. to the help of the King, in demanding Justice. The King, besides his ordinary Taxes, which he sends to gather about the Country by his Guards, and in the Mount *Atlas* by force of Arms, he takes also upon all Merchandizes and Traffick the Tenth part. The Women of *Morocco* are very beautiful and white; the others, who are of Quality, and who stir not much abroad, are more Tann'd and Sun-Burnt. Every one hath 2 or 3 Wives, and as many Concubines as they can keep, and give to these Concubines so much by the day, 2 or 3 *Tomins* to live upon; each *Tomin* worth half a Rial. The King hath four Wives, and Concubines without number, whom he keeps in his *Seraglio,* or Palace; and when he hath a mind to lie with any of them, he causes them all to come before him stark Naked; then he chooses her which pleaseshim best, for that time.

The Moors have but few Houshold Goods, except some Alcatifs, or Carpets, upon which they Eat, and Lie, and have

have some Covers, and sleep very low: Very few have Couches and Linnen: The Jews have such Beds as we use.

Victuals.   As for Victuals, they are good and cheap, and all, whether Flesh, Fish, Fruits and other things to Eat, are sold by weight, and the Pound. As for Flesh, 'tis Beef, Mutton, Poultry, Venison, which comes from the Mountains: Some Fish, as the excellen Trouts which come from the Mountains of *Atlas*, and from the River *Tensif*: The Wines there are excellent, and wonderful strong, of which the Moors do not Drink, but only the Grapes. When a Moor makes himself drunk, at any Jews or Christians who sell the Wine, the Judge comes to Stave all the Vessels of Wine which are upon the Ground, and besides lays an Avarice, or fine upon the Master Vintner. I will content my self to have said this little of several other things, which I could describe concerning this City and Country of *Morocco*, since they are so well known to every one; only, I will add to this, that about 6 Leagues from *Morocco*, near to *Atlas*, is a City called *Angoumet*,

met, where are still to be seen a great many ruinous Buildings of the *Roman*, and Antique Letters * half worn out: The City is little, and nothing but Ruins. The Moors say, that there is Interred some Holy Personage of the Antients, and for this Reason will not suffer the Christians to enter: And besides, in the Mountains of *Atlas* are certain People, which they call *Brebbes*, who cut their Cheeks in the manner of a Cross, and have a Language by themselves, besides the *Arabick*, and are very strong in these Mountains: They pay Tribute to the King of *Morocco*, who sends Forces to raise it. There is some signs that these People should be the relicts of the antient *Africans*, Inhabitants of the Country before the *Arabian Saracens* entered there; and that they retired there for security, being also in some manner Christians; but since, the society and imperiousness of the *Arabians* have corrupted them.

As for the rest, when I arrived at *Morocco* the Affairs of the Country were thus; That *Muley-Boufairs* the then King of *Morocco*, one of the Sons

War betwixt the Cherifs of Morocco.

of *Muley-Hamet* had War with his Brother *Muley-Chec*, and *Muley-Abdalla* his Nephew, and with *Muley Zidan* his other Brother: For all these three Brothers made cruel War upon one another for the Kingdom of *Morocco*. Now this *Muley-Boufairs*, trusting wholly upon his *Baffa-Joda*, lost all: For *Muley-Abdalla*, the Son of *Muley-Chec* King of *Fez*, won a Battle of his Uncle *Boufairs*, who fled in the night time to the Mountains of *Atlas*, in the House of the *Alcayde* of *Afur*, which is an exceeding strong Castle: But the *Brebbes* Robbed him, and did him a great deal of mischief before he could get conveniently there. After that, he sent some of the *Alcaydes* his great Favourites to go fetch his Wives and his Daughter, who brought along with them all his Treasure, but they were Robb'd before day, near to *Anzoumet*, in a place where they had sat down to take a little rest from the fatigue of the way. The *Brebaes* had his Wives and Daughters at their pleasure, and carried his Daughter to *Muley-Abdalla*, because he desired her to Wife, though she was his Cousin.

Alcayde of Afur.

The

The *Alcaydes* or Conductors of these Women, seeing themselves thus Rob'd, and without any means to recover their loss, did enter themselves into an *Asoy* or Mosque to the *Alforme*, or Sanctuary, of a Saint *Marabou*: But *Muley-Abdalla* hearing of it, sent to fetch them out, with the *Marabou* also, who earnestly desired *Abdalla* to give them their Lives, which he promised to do; But before they arrived at his *Micouart*, or Palace, he commanded all their Heads to be chopped off, which he sent to his Father at *Fez*, who was not so well pleased thereat as he expected, because he had deceived the *Marabou*. This was the State of the Affairs of these Princes.

African Faith.

Now, as I passed one day about the *Alcasaue*, which is the King's House, I saw a Cannon cast of a wonderful bigness; and being surprised at the greatness of the size, I was told that it had been made for a certain *Alcayde*, a great Favourite, who had a mind to betray a King of *Morocco*: But the King having discovered the Treason, by the means of one of his Letters; Hereupon, one day, without making

Story of an Alcayde.

M 2 shew

shew of any thing, demanded (by way of queſtion) of this *Alcayde*, if there was a Servant dearly Beloved of his Maſter, and neverthelefs who fought to Kill, what ſuch a Servant would deſerve; The *Alcayde* preſently anſwered, that he deſerved to be put alive into a Cannon, and to be ſhot out like a Ball; to which the King replied, That he himſelf deſerved the ſame Puniſhment; and there-upon ſhewing him the Letter writ by his own Hand, the other remained all aſtoniſhed and benummed; and then the King ordered this Cannon to be made, in which he commanded to be put this *Alcayde*, to fire him out as he himſelf had fore-judged by his own Mouth, according as the Treaſon deſerved.

Juſtice of a Traytor.

In the City of *Morocco*, there are a great number of Chriſtian Captives, as well Men as Women, who are brought there to be ſold from all Parts of *Barbary*: Now it happened upon a time that a Chriſtian Maid, being Slave in a great Houſe of the City, inſtructed a young Woman of the ſame Houſe in the Chriſtian Religion;

Hiſtory of a Chriſtian Maid and her Martyrdom.

gion, teaching her secretly her Belief, insomuch that this Damsel engrafted so well the Law of the True God in her Heart, that it was impossible for her former Teachers to make her learn any more of the *Alcoran*, or Law of *Mahomet*, and kept her self constant in the Religion of the Slave, without going any more to the Mosque. The King being informed thereof, sent for this New Convert to come before him, and Threatning her, that if she would not renounce the Law of the Christians, he would put her to Death, She generously answered, that she did not fear Death; and that all the Torments of the World should not make her quit the Belief she had acquir'd. The King seeing this, commanded her to be put into the Hands of the *Faquin*, or great Judge, to be put to Death: But she being resolved not to make any shew that she feared Death, and about to be executed, the King asked her again if she would not be Converted to their Law again: But, she answered, that their Law signified nothing in reference to Salvation; and that she would Die for

the

the Love of him who had suffered Death for us. When this barbarous King saw that all these Prayers and Remonstrances were in vain, he endeavoured once more to divert her from this Resolution, promising to Marry her to one of his highest Court Favourites; But she mocked the more at all his Promises; at which, the King being enraged, commanded her to be Beheaded, which was done accordingly. And thus Christianly, and constantly, this innocent and vertuous Damsel suffered Martyrdom.

Kings-Palace.

Now as I curiously visited this City of *Morocco*, I entered one day into the *Micouart*, or Palace of the King, and saw in the first Court extraordinary fine Buildings *A-la-Moresque*, with Fountains, and a great many Orange and Lemon-Trees, laden with Fruit; But at the second Court, where I also entered, were little Galleries sustained with Pillars of White Marble, so well cut, and contrived, that the best Workmen would admire the Workmanship thereof; and upon the Ground were a great number of Vessels of Marble, full of clear and

and fresh Water, where I saw the Moors wash themselves before their going to Rehearse their *Sala* or Prayers; But as soon as they espied me, they began to cry out, and run after me, which made me mend my pace in good earnest to get presently from thence. I saw in another Garden, a very fine Fish Pond of Stone Work, where the Moors Bath themselves, and found there some Moorish Women who were washing their *lquisayes* or Vails, after that they had washed their Bodies.

After this I went to see the Lions, which were shut up in a great ruinous House, open at the top, and to be mounted one pair of Stairs; and saw there many remarkable things, but one more particularly, which was concerning a Dog, who had formerly been cast to the Lions for their Food; for one of the Lions (and the oldest of all the others who feared him) took this Dog that had been cast in under his Paws, as if he would have devoured him; but having a mind to play a little with him before, it happened that this Dog flattering the Lion,

Lions. And the History of a Lion and a Dog.

M 4 as

as knowing his Strength, began to scratch him gently with his Teeth upon a Scab which the Lion had upon his Throat; at which, the Lion took such pleasure, that he not only suffered the Dog patiently so to do, but also defended him from the others: So that when I saw him, he had been then seven years with these Lions, as the Christian Slave told me who look'd after them; and told me also, that when they gave the Lions any thing to Eat, the Dog fed with them, and would sometimes snatch the Meat from their very Chops; And when the Lions would fight together for their Food, the Dog did all he could to part them, and when he saw he could not do it, by a Natural Instinct he began to howl after such a manner, that the Lions (who fear the cry of Dogs) presently would part themselves, and agree together.

This example of Animals shews that we ought to be humble and obedient towards those who are greater than our selves, and how noble and generous the Lion is amongst other Beasts.

At my going from these Lions, I *Horses.* went to see the Kings Horses, who were in Stalls after their manner, and were fat, and extraordinary well Dress'd and clean Skin'd. They are Christian Slaves who look after them, and have a great, and lesser Stable also, well ordered that it is impossible for any to be better: They are all *Barb*-Horses, the finest in the World. After having walked enough about the City for this time, I returned back to the *Douane*, which is the place where the Christians are oblig'd to retire themselves, a good League from the *Alcasave*, or Palace Royal, which is near the *Juderie*.

I was there told a very pleasant *History of* History of a King of *Morocco*, who *a Son of the King of* having upon a time sent one of his *Morocco.* Sons with an Army to conquer the Kingdom of *Gago*, from whence comes the finest Gold. This young Prince having passed all the Desarts of *Lybia* with great Trouble and Fatigue, which both he and his Army there endured; as he approached the Country of *Gago*, this King, informed of his coming, went to meet him with a

great

great Army of Blacks, and invested and encompassed him about, so that he could get neither backward nor forward; and besides, he was oppressed with two great Extremities, Hunger and Thirst; insomuch, that the most part of his Men were Sick, and knew not what to do in such an extremity: For, to continue there, they must all Die with Hunger, or yield themselves Victims to their Enemies Malice; and to return, or to pass on, they must give Battel; and his Men were so weak, as well by the fatigue of the way, by the Desart, as for want of Victuals. Now as this Prince of *Morocco* was in this perplexity in his Tent, it happened that two of his Soldiers were playing at Chess in their Tent, and one of them found himself so much engaged, that he could not make his King go either backward or forward, he being under Check; upon which his Companion, Laughing, said, he was like their Prince, who could neither advance nor retire without exposing himself to great danger: As he was saying these Words, it happened that one of the Prince's Favourites

rites, paffing by chance near this Tent, overheard them, and went prefently away to give his Mafter an account of this Difcourfe, who, hearing it, fent at that inftant to fetch thefe two Soldiers before him, who were mightily aftonifhed; and having enquired feveral things of them, and particularly of that which they had done and faid; At laft, feeing themfelves urged, they confeffed the truth, and proftrating themfelves upon the Ground, they begged his Pardon, which the Prince did eafily confent to, and demanded of him, who had faid thus, what he would advife him to do in fuch an extremity: The Soldier wifely anfwered, that if he would take his Advice, he fhould not only fave himfelf and his Men, but fhould alfo come of with great Honour, if the thing which he had contrived in his Mind took effect. The Prince Commanded him to fay boldly what he would; upon which the Soldier proceeded, and faid, that the King of *Gago* had a Beautiful Daughter to Marry, and that he, who was a young Prince, and wanted a Wife, fhould fend Ambaf-
fadors

sadors to this King to let him understand that he was not come into his Country with intention to make War upon him, but only to demand his Daughter in Marriage, of whom he had heard many Perfections and excellent Qualities reported. The Prince found this Counsel so good, and so much to the purpose, that he presently dispatches Ambassadors to this King, upon this account, who were very well received, according to their Ambassage, and the Peace made accordingly; The Marriage was agreed upon by this means, and Consummated with great Triumphing *A-la-Moresque.* The Prince receiv'd from his Father-in-Law, the King of *Gago*, several curious and rich Presents, amongst others three Balls of Gold, hollow within, weighing in all 750 pounds, and are all three of a wonderful bigness, but proportionably one a little less than the other, and are to be seen to this day in the *Alcasave*, or Palace at *Morocco*, upon the top of a high Tower, being all three fastened upon a Bar, the greatest at the bottom, and so mounting, the least at top: When the Sun shines they cast

cast a Reflex at a great distance, as I observed in my coming to *Morocco*: In the Wars they have fired several shots of Musquet at them, but without any prejudice. Thus the Counsel of this Soldier took happy effect, and since that time, the Kingdom of *Gago*, (of which this Daughter was Heiress) fell to the Kings of *Morocco*, who send there to fetch their Gold. After having returned from my Voyage, one day as I was at Dinner with the late King *Henry the Great*, who had taken Physick that day, and was in his morning Gown in his Closet, I was desiring his Majesty to grant me liberty to go to the *East-Indies*, he thereupon came to speak of the play at Chess, and how that two of the Grandees of his Court had been two days and two nights at playing a Game at Chess; upon which, the King discovering the cunning and subtility of this play, I took the boldness to relate to him this History of the Prince of *Morocco*, at which he was mightily pleased, and thought the Soldier's invention very much to be applauded: In short, all these Moors are great players

Game of Chess amongst the Moors.

players at Chess, as I have observed amongst them. For at such time as I went to the *Juderie*, I found almost all those who kept the Door a playing at this Game, at which they are very subtile; and it is mighty diverting to them, in regard of their Melancholly Humour; which renders them very ingenious, and great lovers of sharp and subtile Tricks; as there was one day one of them, who made shew of Friendship to another, and gave him great store of Fruit upon a Carpet to Eat: But the other, who was thus Honoured, told him gently, give me not so much Meat, but thy Heart rather; which was to say Good-Will and Affection, for he well knew that he wished him no good in his Mind. This Story is said to be of the *Alcayde Mummin*.

The Authors return.

After having continued for some time at *Morocco*, seeing that the Caravan was preparing to go away for *Saffy*, I endeavoured to obtain my

Haquin.

Letter of Free passage of the *Haquin*, who is the great Justice there, to the end that I might safely Embark, without any Let or Hindrance by those of *Saffy*;

Saffy. I payed then for my Entrance ond going out to the *Talbes* of the *Douane*, who keep the Door, which is a right that every Christian who comes to *Morocco* is obliged to pay; And truly 'tis impossible ever to have done enough to satisfie these sort of People.

<small>Talbes.</small>

I parted then from *Morocco* the 22th of *October*, and went to pitch the *Al-mahalle* some 4 or 5 Leagues distant, in a Campagne, along by Mount *Atlas*; and being there, there were 3 or 4 Companies of us who went into the *Adouars*, or Tents of the Arabians, to furnish our selves with Fowls, Eggs, and other Victuals. But when we came there we perceived a great number of Cavalliers of the same Nation, running after one another, who drove away their Camels and other Beasts. The Wives of these Arabians took the Saddles of their Husbands Horses upon their Heads, and run to the place where their Horses were feeding: The Husbands, who were hard by at work, presently mounted on Horseback, and flew like lightning after their Enemies, with their Launces and other Instruments;

ments; and I believe that at laſt they recovered their own. Theſe Women adviſed us to return with all ſpeed to our Camp, for fear that theſe Arabs, their Enemies, ſhould carry us away Captives; which we did, ſeeing all in an uproar and confuſion, and the noiſe which they made amongſt themſelves: For it is a ſtrange thing to ſee theſe People, who are all of the ſame Law and Nation, to make ſo frequent War upon one another.

War a-mongſt the Arabians.

But, amongſt themſelves, they obſerve this Rule and Diſcipline, that when the time comes for them to Sow their Land or to Reap their Corn, they make Peace; After that, they begin again to their Wars when their Corn is beaten, and laid up in their *Matamores* or Ditches in the Field, where they put it, then cover it with Planks, and above that with Earth, after ſuch a manner that they can Till and Sow upon it: They lay up their Grain thus in the night, that none may ſee them, no not their very Wives nor their Children: Afterwards, if they happen to have occaſion for any quantity of Corn, either to Sow, or to to carry to sell at *Morosco*, they go and take it forth of this Magazine. This Corn is kept very well in the Ground, where it keeps dry a long time.

The 23th of the same month we went to pitch the *Almahalle* close by Mount *Atlas*, in a level ground, in which place I went to look for some Plants and Herbs, and as I returned again into the Camp, the *Alcayde Abdassis*, Captain of a Cabille of *Arabians*, perceived me, and called me to him, asking me what Herbs these were that I carried, and what I intended to do with them; after I had satisfied his Demands, I withdrew into our Tent: About 4 or 5 a clock in the evening, going out to walk and to take the fresh Air, I met again with the *Alcayde*, who was also walking about to visit his Camp; and having called me, took me by the Hand, and led me without the Camp, giving me account of several things of the Wars of *Africa*, and concerning the Battle of Don *Sebastian*, King of *Portugal*, at which time he was a young Man, it being 35 years since: He told me amongst other things, how the Christians at that time were

History of the Battle of Don Sebastian of Portugal.

were resolved to extirpate
that they who were befo[re]
amongst themselves,(tho o[ne]
had made Peace together,
that they might the better d[efend them]
selves against the Christian[s]
to meet the Christians t[o the]
City of *Tangier*, which b[elongs to]
the Portugals; That the[y re]
solved to venter Battle wi[th Se]
bastian, who was accompa[nied by a]
Moorish King, who was a[kins]
man to the Kings of *Moro*[cco, and]
was said to be the lawful [heir,]
that the others had Usur[ped his]
Prerogative. As these t[wo Armies]
were in Battalia near by [each other,]
the Christians made no sh[ew of charg]
ing the first, but kept then[selves on]
the Defensive; they on t[he contrary]
were all in the Action, co[ntinually]
ercising themselves at the [one]
against another; and see[ing the]
Christians did not stir, t[hey fu]
riously to attack them; [but being]
been beat back at the beg[inning,]
betook themselves to flig[ht; the]
Christians pursued them, [in such or]
der and confusion, that thi[s]

Lib. III.   *of* John Mocquet.

selves too sure of Victory, the Moors thereupon Rallying upon these disorderly pursuers, easily broke them: And thus Don *Sebastian* lost the Battle, where he was killed upon the place, with two other Kings; and they had a great number of Prisoners, who were carried to *Morocco*.

He told me also of *Muley Hamet Maluco*, or *Abdelmelech*, one of the Kings which had won the Battle, who died of Sickness in his Litter, after having given good Orders to all. When they who were about him perceived he was Dead, they concealed his Death for fear of discouraging the Soldiers, who had the better; and used this Artifice, that is, they put forth his Hand as if he had been still alive: He himself had found out this trick, and had ordered them to make use of it after his Death.

Abdassis having related to me thus much, told me also of *Muley-Boufairs*, the then King of *Morocco*, and how that he gave himself wholly over to his Wives and Concubines, and trusted too much upon a Bassa, named *Joda*, and was likely to loose the Battle, which he design'd to engage in when

[margin: Muley Maluco, or Abdemelech.]

[margin: Muley Boufairs, King of Morocco.]

we parted from *Morocco*; and that all his delight was in *Comer, Couscoussou, Auquam*; that is, eating of a certain Confection made up into Sugar-Plums; but he found himself deceived; for he lost the Battle, as I have said already, and was Deposed from his Kingdom, and fled away to Mount *Atlas* about the month of *November* 1606. according as our *Noster-Damus* had predicted in his Centuries, as I have been shewed since: *Abdassis* told me also thereupon, that the Soldiers are mightily discouraged when the King comes not to Battle in Person; And when he is Couragious, or a Coward, his Soldiers become the same.

Good advice for Kings.

As for the *Couscoussou* of which I have made mention, and which I have Tasted several times, it is Meal made up and Kneaded into the fashion of Sugar-Plums or Comfits, with Water, in a Frying-pan; then put it in an Earthen Vessel full of holes at the bottom, like a Cullender; after that, it is put in a Pot upon a hot Fire, and the Vapour boils it; then they pour Broth thereupon, and eat it by great bits like Balls: It is of a very good Taste, which nourishes

Couscoussou.

rishes and fattens the Body to Admi ration. *I* have often Eat thereof, it being prepared for me by the Moorish and Jewish Women: Their Corn is very fit for it, because it is very dry; ours, which is more moist, would not be so good, except it were first well dried.

    After this Discourse of the *Alcayde*, we withdrew our selves into our Tents until the next morning that we began again to take Journey, and had that day very bad way by steep and inaccessible Mountains, not being able to keep any Order for the insupportable Heat; as for fresh Water we had none. I was mounted upon a Mule, and was forced frequently to get down to beat it away on foot, which was no small trouble for me, in that I had near 6000 Crowns about me, as well in Lignots, as in Tybre, that is Powder, as it comes from *Gago*, and also in Money, which are Sequins of the Country: I had a great deal of trouble to remount; for it did not behove me to stay behind, for fear of the *Arabs*, and of those of our Caravan themselves.

    Having passed all the hardships of this Journey, we came to pitch at the

Duquele,

Duquele. *Duquèle*, where these *Matamores* are, of which I have so much spoken. Here came several *Arabians* on Horseback, mounted in order with their Launces, to salute *Abdaffis* their Chief, and Captain of their *Cabille*, every one bringing him Presents; then after having kissed his Hands, they returned again to their *Adouars*, who were gone above 2 or 3 Leagues from thence. The next day, the 2d of *October*, we went to lie at *Saffy*, and as we approached there, passing through some Woods of Broom, very high, there was two Moorish Cavalliers, who took me out of the right way, making me go with them cross these Brooms, which were so high that one could scarce see another in the middle of them. I was upon my Mule, and coming near to an old Well, they got down, bidding me also to do the like: I thought there had been there some Fountain to refresh our selves; but seeing that they had a mind to make me get down only to entice me into this Well, I immediately turned my Mule about towards the great Highway, with all the speed I possibly could, and thus narrowly escaped

Danger of the Author.

caped from their Hands: Their design was, (as I believe) to make me quit the Gold and Silver which I carried, and then to cut my Throat, and to cast me in some Ditch: But I had a good Inspiration when I was just upon the point of descending; and as my good Angel would have it, the great Road, through which the Caravan passed was not far from thence, which did facilitate my safety: My too much Diligence, and the great desire that I had to advance to get to *Saffy* the first, had been the cause of this Accident. At last, by the Grace of God, I arrived happily at *Saffy*: After having a little refreshed my self, I took care for my Embarkment, and caused my Materials to be visited by the *Talbes*, and payed them their due.

The next day, when I thought to Embark, causing my things to be carried to the Port, the *Talbes* came and demanded of me the Letter and Passport from the *Haquin* of *Morocco*, and having given it them, they told me it signified nothing to the purpose, because *Muley-Boufairs* was no longer King of *Morocco*, and that it behoved me

Muley Abdalla King of Morocco.

me to have another from *Muley-Abdalla*, who was then King of *Morocco*, under his Father *Muley-Chec*, who was at *Fez*: I was very much afflicted at this Retardment, which made me loose the convenience of a Ship, that was bound for *France*. Nevertheless, being forced to have patience, it behoved me to send a *Trotier* or Messenger to *Morocco* with our Letter to have another, which could not be done without a great deal of Trouble and Expences: But my ill fortune was, that this Letter being come, I must be forced to wait there near 2 months, upon the account of a Dutch Ship, which was not to set sail till *January* 1607.

Revolutions at Morocco.

This change of Affairs at *Morocco* happened after my departure from the City: For *Muley-Boufairs* King of *Morocco*, having lost the Battle against his Nephew *Abdalla*, fled away into the Mountains, where he was Robb'd, as I have said, and *Abdalla* was then in peaceable possession of *Morocco*; But during the Peace, *Abdalla* having discovered that the other hatched some Treason to dispossess him, he Stabb'd him with his own Hands, after having reproached him with his Perfidie: But after that, *Zidan* his Uncle, with the help of a *Santon*, or *Marabou*, hath chased away *Abdalla*, and made himself King of *Morocco*: Afterwards he himself was chased away by the *Santon*; and it was said that they were ready to engage in Battle together, and since I have heard that the *Santon* had been taken by *Ziden*, who had put him to Death by Sawing him down through the middle, with two pieces of Wood: Since that, he and his Nephew *Abdalla* had agreed together, and by the Agreement, the Kingdoms of *Fez* and *Sus* fell to *Abdalla*, and that of *Morocco* to *Zidan*.

As for the *Marabous* or *Santons*, they are very dangerous amongst these People, by reason that the pretext of Devotion and Sanctity of their Law, as in all others, is a great means to Commotions against the State, as it is often seen, and of fresh memory in him, who within this 100 years hath founded this last Family, which does Rule there at this day.

Santons dangerous.

As for *Muley-Chec*, who was at *Morocco*, he went into *Spain*, out of a desire fire to become Christian, and indeed he delivered the strong place of *Arache* into the hands of the King of *Spain*, who for this gave him a Pension, and promised to restore him, with an Army, to the Kingdoms of *Fez* and *Morocco*: But those of *Fez* would not hearken to that, not agreeing with the Spaniards; And *Abdalla* his Son returned to *Fez*, who also hindered him, insomuch, that the *Chec* has been since constrain'd to go back again of his own accord, without gaining any thing of the Spaniards save the loss of putting such a place into their Hands.

Saffy and its Description.

But to return to the Abode that I was forced to make at *Saffy*, I employed my self in the mean time in viewing this City, and the Parts thereabouts: 'Tis a little City situated upon the brink of the Sea, which has no convenient Haven but only a Road, and flat Shore, and has formerly been possessed by the *Portugals*: It may be as big as *Corbeil*, and very well Walled, being inhabited by all sorts of People, as Jews, Moors, and Christians, and hath a *Douane*.

Being there, I observed amongst other things, the manner of their Marriages, which

which are performed with this Ceremony. They put the Bride upon a Mule, well furnished, and surrounded with a Hoop like a Cage, covered with a Carpet, after the Turkish manner: Scarcely can any see this Woman thus shut up, but she can see the whole company through a transparent Vail: At the top of this is a Scarf: They walk her in this Equipage round about the City, and cause to follow after several Mules laden with Baggage of that which the Bride has given her in Marriage: Then follow the Men and Women, mounted also upon Mules. Both the Men and Women make a strange and ridiculous noise as they pass along, with their Mouths and Tongues. Amongst these are double Drums, *A-la-Moresque*. After having finished this walk, they go to Dinner, then they return to the place. And if it is the Wife of a Cavallier, or Man of War, all his Friends assemble there on Horseback, who exercise themselves at justing, continuing 2 or 3 hours before the Bride; then after that every one withdraws: As for the rest, if the Husband does not find his Wife a Maid, he Divorces her, and sends her back with

Manner of the Marriages.

with all that she brought; and for this they cause the Drawers of the Bride to be carried about the City, all stained in Blood, to testifie that she was a Virgin. The Jews cry, and observe the same thing.

Burials. As for what concerns the Dead, they have Burying-Places and Sepulchers, where they go to Weep and Lament upon the Graves of their departed Friends, especially the Women, who fail not to go there every *Friday*, and the days of their Festivals. The Jews do the same, as I have observed in *Syria*, where they use a certain Vessel pierced with holes at the bottom, and make their Tears run down from thence, right upon the Sepulcher, which is environed with all kind of Flowers.

Moors Slaves to their King. I will add to this, that all the Moors are nothing else but Captives & Slaves of their King; for they dare not so much as stir out of the Country and Kingdom, without his express Licence and Command, as I have taken notice of several times at *Saffy*. I remember one day, a young Man, a Moor, having by chance cast himself into a Boat of the Christians, out of curiosity, or to play

Lib. III.   *of* John Mocquet.   189

play and Fish, the *Haquin* seeing him, caused him to be taken by his Serjeants, then to be laid upon the Ground and cruelly Bastinadoed.

Whilst I was at *Saffy*, waiting for my departure, I went about the Fields and Desarts to look for Plants and delicate Flowers to carry to the King. I gathered a great many of them, which I laid up, and having caused Biscuit to be made for my Voyage, with other Refreshments, we set sail the 24th of *Jan*. 1607. and having contrary Winds towards the South Line: Having been driven from one side to the other, we arrived in the end near the Coast of *England*, in very tempestuous weather, having been so beaten by contrary Winds, we knew not well how far we had to any Land, in regard that we were scarce able to take the heighth of the Sun or Stars; But thereupon seeing a Ship coming, much about the bigness of ours, streight to us, we lowred our Sails to tarry for her, making signs for her to come up, which they did, telling us, that the South Line was very near us, and what Wind was best for us to take: We were very glad at this news, and

Departure for France.

South-line.

and a little after we saw the South-Line; but the Weather was very tempestuous, and I believe that without this advice we should have gone near to have lost our selves on the Rocks, which are low and in great numbers.

Being entered into the Channel, we descried a Ship, making full sail upon us, and believing that it was a Fleming, we prepared our selves to receive her, but the night coming on, which was very Stormy, we lost her, bearing more to the N.E. The next morning we saw the *Isle of Wight*, imagining it was the Land of *England:* But approaching nearer, we found out our mistake, and Coasting it a little, we perceiv'd the Land of *England*, which lay to the N. E. of us, and went to cast Anchor in a Bay, which advanced into the Land, and where there was a little Village: Those of the place seeing us Anchor there, came on board us, and told us, that when the Sea went out we should be a-ground, and that it behoved us to set sail in all haste to go to a Port not far from thence; so they helped and conducted us to the said Port, near the * Poulle,

Wight-Island.

* Portsmouth.

in

in a Creek, not far from a Tower, where we were at Harbour: But the night being come, we had the ſtrangeſt and moſt horrible Storm that had been heard of of a long time; inſomuch that we were forced to caſt 3 or 4 Anchors, which were all little enough to hold our Ship.

Horrible Tempeſt.

This happened on *Shrove-Tueſday*, the 27th of *Feb.* and in this Storm two Ships were loſt near the *Iſle of Wight*, the one a Fleming, who was lading, and the other a French, who ſeeing themſelves near being loſt, put out the Boat to ſave themſelves, leaving nothing in the Ship ſave a Cat: But theſe People approaching near Land, a Wave came which overturned the Boat, and they were all loſt.

The Ship in the mean time went with a right Winds towards *Plimouth*, a Town and Port of *England*: Some People from the Coaſt ſeeing this Ship thus ſail towards Land, where there was no Port, ran to give them notice thereof; But calling out aloud, and no one anſwering, they knew not what to think, judging they might be Pirates, who had not a mind to be known:

Strange Accident.

In

In the end, seeing the Ship like to be cast away, they resolved to Board her, and entering, they found nothing but this Cat, at which they were mightily astonished, and took the Ship into Port; It was laden with Corn, and after having heard that the People were lost near the *Isle of Wight*, they left it in the hands of the Justice, until it might be restored to the right Owners.

This great Storm, the cause of all these Accidents, was such, that it caused a great distraction and loss of People, along the Coast of *England*, as we heard since. When we came to *Portsmouth* we found out the Truth of this, and how the Sea had overwhelmed certain places a good way within *Portsmouth*, which is a pleasant Sea Port Town.

<small>Portsmouth.</small>

After having been some days at *Portsmouth*, to refresh our selves, and to wait for a Wind to carry us to *Havre-de-Grace*, where our Ship was to go, to leave there some Merchandize of *Barbary*: When the Wind was favourable to us, we set sail the 16th of *March*, and the next day in the evening we arrived at the Haven, for which I
praised

of John Mocquet.   193

for having delivered me
ly Perils and Dangers;
 Land to *Roan*, I there
y Materials, which were
ie Hoy; and having re-
ded them in a Boat upon
 went ſtraight to *Paris*,
ved the 25th of *March*:
I went to *Fontainebleau*,
ng an account of my Voy-
eſent him with the Plants
vhich I had brought, with
ajeſty was mighty well
juiring of me ſeveral
ch I anſwered him in the
I could: And deſiring
her of me, what it was
jdan did, I anſwered him,
ncamped in the Deſarts
ly: and amongſt other
him account of 3 Caval-
g to *Muley-Boufairs*, his
h whom he had War, the
come into his *Almahalle*,
nſelves to him, he deman-
if they came to him of
Free-Will, and having
n they did, and that they
Muley-Boufairs, becauſe
O   they

they had been falsly accused of a Robbery in the *Juderie* at *Morocco*: *Zidan* hearing this, asked them if they took him for a Receiver of Robbers, and thereupon commanded them to be Beheaded, shewing thereby a great Act of Justice for a Barbarian and Mahometan. Having finished this Discourse and several others to the late King, and presented him with the Plants and Rarities, and the White Honey of *Africa*, exceeding clear and excellent, of which his Majesty tasted, and caused me to lay it carefully up, I went back to *Paris* to think in good earnest of the Voyage that I had a mind to make to the *East-Indies*.

A Description of the following Cutts.

The First, *The manner of the Fights of the* Moors *and* Africans *of* Morocco, *and other* Arabians *of the Countrys of* Barbary.

The 2d, *The Customs of the* Arabians, *when they remove their Habitations, and carry with them their* Adouars, *or Tents, and take their Families to Sow and Cultivate the Land in any other part of the Country.*

Lib. IV. *of John Mocquet.*

THE
TRAVELS
AND
VOYAGES
OF
John Mocquet,
INTO

Ethiopia, Mozambique, Goa,
And other Places of AFRICA,
and the *East-Indies.*

BOOK IV.

Like as our defires are never fatisfied in this life, but continually coveting after new Things, until we are entered into a perfect enjoyment of thofe which we defire moft; fo, being returned from my laft Voyage of *Africa*, the defire of my former defign was

was renewed in me to go to the *East-Indies*, from which I had been diverted by the occasion that I have given account of in the beginning of my third Book; so that having taken a Resolution at this time, I took my leave of the King and Queen in the year 1607. and parted from *Paris* the 16th of *October*, with a design to pass into *Britagne*, and from thence into *Portugal*.

Embarking for Portugal.

I Embarked thence the 16th of *Nov.* in a Ship of *Poligaip*, belonging to one named *Joes Bigmin*, and we were about 18 or 20 men in all. This was in a morning, and in a very great Storm: We went on Board with no small trouble, the Waves covering us very frequently. As soon as we were there, we set sail, the Wind being for us: This Ship was bound for *Sevill*, but, as fortune would have it, being towards the Cape of *Pichoy*, we met with so furious a Tempest, the Wind being quite contrary to us to gain the Cape of *St. Vincent*, that we were forced to slacken in the River of *Lisbon*, where I was desirous to go; For it was the time the Fleet was preparing to go away. And arriving at *Sevill*, I had the

Lib. IV. of John Mocquet.

the trouble to return back to *Lisbon*; and perhaps, for all that, I might have lost the occasion of my Voyage.

We cast Anchor then at *Sta. Catarina*, a little above *Belin*, the 2d of December: I went on Shore, and lay at a place call'd *Belin*, where the Visitor of Health, hearing I was come without Licence, commanded me to Re-Embark, under the forfeiture of 50 Ducats. He made all this stir only for want of a little Present: After having ordered my Business, I failed not to go to *Lisbon*, where being come, I took a Lodging, and waited to Embark, and found there the Sieur *de-Herve*, who had been in the Service of the King of *Morocco*, and was very kind to these two Portugal Gentlemen, who were come out of Captivity; one being Son to the Vice-Roy of the *East-Indies*, *Henry de Saldaigne*; and the other, Brother to Don *Baptiste Fernand Sezar*, Provisor-General of the House of the *Indies*, and his Brother-in-Law, the Count *de Fera* went to the *Indies* for Vice roy. I desired my Friend, the Sieur *de-Herve* to speak to these Gentlemen, his Friends, who had so much

Belin.

Credit, that by their means I might pass to the *Indies.* *Pedro Sezar,* Brother to *Baptiste Fernand,* promised him to do all he could, so that he spoke to the Count *de Fera* ; and the said *Herve,* to oblige them the more, said, that I was his Brother ; For those Gentlemen were very respectful to him for having assisted them in the time of their Captivity with Money : They then desired me to speak to the Count *de la* *Fera* by the means of *Baptiste Fernand,* and told him that I was a very curious Man ; and he hearing that I had knowledge of Plants, was mighty glad, and told me that there was great quantity of good and rare Plants in the *Indies,* which he had proved at such time that he was Captain at Arms: After that, he asked me my Name, and having writ it in a Paper, he sent it by one of his Servants to the Proveditor of the House of *India,* who having read it, sent it to him again, saying, That a Stranger might not pass to the *Indies* without Licence from the King of *Spain.*

The Count *de la Fera,* seeing this, caused a Letter to be writ at that instant, in my presence, by *Baptiste Fernand,*

Count de la Fera.

Proveditor de la Case d'Inde.

nand, his Brother-in-Law, and sent it by the same Servant to Don *Christoval*, Vice-roy of *Portugal*, who commanded the Frenchman to be set down, that is to say, received. I was very glad of this Answer; and I with a Servant went to the House of *India* to carry this Licence to the Proveditor, Nephew to the Vice-roy, who kept it, and told him that brought it, that he could not set me down for this Permission; but that he would speak of it to the Count *de la Fera*. I was very sorry at this, and almost out of all hopes of going the Voyage: Hereupon I retired to my Lodging to consider of what I had to do, that I might not loose this opportunity. The next day, going to find out the Servant of the Count *de la Fera*, I desired him to go with me, as from the Vice-roy his Master, which he willingly did, but I could not obtain any thing at that time; but I lost not Courage for all that; and the day following I went again to the Servant, and desired him to go with me but once more; and so we went together to the House of *India* before this Proveditor, the Servant bring-

bringing him Word from the Count *de la Fera* his Master; The Proveditor seeing himself so much importuned from him whom he durst not displease, in regard he was one of the Grandees of *Portugal*, and Vice-roy of the *Indies*. He demanded of me my Name, and that of my Father, and of my Mother, and the place of my Birth; then he ordered me to be set down in the Book for a Natural French man. Thus at last I was received, of which I was exceeding glad, and gave the Servant many Thanks, promising to assist him all I could, as I did afterwards, he being sick: Two or 3 days after I went to receive my Pay, which was 7500 Rais, (there must be a thousand of them to make 25 Rials) and prepared my self to Embark in the Admiral, in which the Vice-roy was to sail.

The Author received for the Voyage.

When the time of Embarkment came, there was a great Confusion amongst us, were, being about 900. The Register called every one by their Name, to know if all were Embarked. My Host answered for me; and that he might not have any trouble upon my account, I was present at at the Lecture of all the Equipage: For it is a Register on shore which makes all this Inquest. These Ceremonies being over, we set sail; first, five great Ships or Carracks, which were, the Admiral called *Our Lady of Mount-Carmel* the *Olive*, the *Salvation*, *Our Lady of the Indies*, and the *Palm*; then 5 Gallies, *St. Jerom*, the *Good Jesus*, the *Holy Ghost*, *St. Bartholomew*, and *St. Anthony*; then after these a Carrack, and two Hulks.

We parted from the River of *Lisbon* the 29th of *March*, on *Easter-Eve*, and bore to the S.W. and to the S. We had great Winds in the sight of *Madera*, and passing close thereby, the Galley of *Good Jesus* lost us, and took her Course as far as *Mosambique*, where she was taken by the Hollanders.

Parting from Lisbon.

Amongst us was the greatest Disorder and Confusion imaginable, because of the Peoples Vomiting up and down, and making Dung upon one another: There was nothing to be heard but Lamentations and Groans of those who were straightned with Thirst, Hunger, and Sicknesses, and other Incommodities, and Cursing the time

Misery upon the Sea.

time of their Embarkment, their Fathers, and Mothers, and themselves who were the cause thereof; so that one would have thought they had been out of their Wits, and like Mad men, amongst the excessive heats under the Line, and the Abrolles, and Calms: This continued a long time and the hot Rains upon the Coast of *Guinea* was also very troublesome to us, which afterwards turned to Worms if that which was wet was not presently dried. It was a wonderful trouble to me, to see my Quilt wet, and Worms crawling all over. These Rains are so stinking, that they rot and spoil, not only the Body, but also all Cloths, Chests, Utensils, and other Things: And not having any more Cloth to shift my self withall, I was forced to dry upon me that which I wore, with my Quilt, by lying thereupon; but I was well fitted for that

Sickness of the Author. for the Fever, with a great pain in the Reins, took me in such a manner that I had a fit of Sickness, almost the whole Voyage; yet this was not all

Scurbut. for I had besides that, the *Lovenda* which the *Portugals* call *Berber* and

of John *Mocquet.*

llanders *Scurbus,* which
all my Gumbs, and ren-
of a black and putrified
Knees were so contracted
not bend my Limbs; my
highs were as black as
n-green'd, and was con
e continually Launcing to
black and putrified Blood.
o my Gums, which were
ue, and surmounting my
g every day out upon the
hip, holding by the Cor-
little Looking-Glass in my
where to cut: When I had
is dead Flesh, and drawn
lance of black Blood, I
Mouth and Teeth with
e next morning there was
nd my ill fortune was, that
Eat, having more mind to
n to chew, upon the ag-
e great pains which this
es. I found no better re-
he Syrop of Gilli-flowers,
d Wine: Great numbers
day thereof, and there was
e seen but Bodies a fling-
rd, and the most part Died
without

without help, some behind Chests having their Eyes, and the Soles of their Feet eaten up with Rats. Others were found Dead in their Beds, after having been let Blood, and moving their Arms, the Veins opened, and their Blood ran out: Oftentimes after having received their Allowance, which might be about a Pint of Water, and putting it near them to Drink, when a-dry, their Companions rob'd these poor Sick Wretches of this little Water, they being asleep, or turned to the other side. Sometimes being *Strange Thirst.* under Deck in a dark place, not seeing one another, they would fight amongst themselves, and strike one another, if they caught any about to Steal their Water; and thus, oftentimes were they deprived of Water, and for want of a little Draught they miserably died, without any one offering to help them to never so little, no not the Father the Son, nor the Brother the Brother, so much did every Man's particular Thirst compel him to Rob his Companions. I found my self oftentimes thus deceived of my allowance, but yet I comforted my self as well

as

Lib. IV. *of* John Mocquet. 207

as I could, seeing so many others in the same case: And this was the cause that I durst not Sleep too much, and commonly put my Water where it could not be easily taken without wakening of me.

After we had suffer'd thus much, and passed the Line, the Count *de la Fera*, Vice-roy, was took sick of a hot Fever, and continued so but 6 days before he died: He had a little before Commanded the *Estrinquere*, (which is he whose Office is to hoise the great Sail by a Wheel) to be made Prisoner, because he had *Amancebado*, that is to say, he kept a Concubine, which he had brought from *Portugal*, and she being with Child when she Embark'd, was brought to Bed in our Ship: The Woman was sent back to *Portugal* in the Hulk, in which was the Body of the Count *de la Fera*.

<small>*Count de la Fera falls Sick and Dies.*</small>

This Gentleman being dead, I Embalmed his Body, because of the hotness of the Climate; then having Embark'd it with about 50 sick Persons, who were to return again to *Portugal*, tho' not without great Intreaties to have the Licence of Captain *More*, Major.

Captain Major-Mor. Major. We called this Captain of the Vice-Admiral named *Don Cristoval de Norogne*, to Command in the Admiral, where the said Captain *Mor* being, did us a thousand sorts of Injuries and Cruelties, as well by Prisons, as by cheating us of our ordinary allowance of Victuals; for he reserved several Pipes of Wine, and a great deal of Flesh and Oil to sell at *Mozambique*. Don *Alfonce de Norogne*, Captain of our Ship, under the Vice-roy, when he was alive, was mightily displeased at this bad usage of Don *Cristoval*; but he died within few days, and his Body was cast into the Sea.

Having passed about 9 or 10 Degrees on the other side the Line, the Wind not being favourable to us, the Pilots held Council what they should do, whether to Tack about and return to *Portugal*, or to pass on, fearing they could not pass the Cape of *Good Hope*, in regard it was too late in the *Muessous.* year; because, that the *Mueson*'s, or Winds of the Season were almost passed already: After having well disputed upon this subject, they tack'd about to return to *Portugal*, and having sailed some

Lib. III. *of* John Mocquet.

some time, the Captain *Mor*, who had a mind to make himself by this Voyage, seeing himself at that time Chief Commander of the Fleet, threatned the Master and Pilot with ill Language, and commanded them to Tack again for the *Indies*: This was in the night, and thereupon Fires were made for a signal for the other Vessels to return; but we were not long together in Consort; for the rest knowing the Viceroy to be Dead, separated from us; and each held theirs apart, we continuing alone until we came to the Isles of *Angoche*, near the River of *Cumana*, where we found the *St. Anthony* and *St. Bartholomew* Galleys: We held then our Course, tho' our Men dying every day of the *Lovende*; At last we approached the Cape of *Good Hope*, seeing the signal of *Alcatraz* and *Mangues de Velours*; *Alcatraz* are Birds like Sparrows; *Mangues de Velours* are Birds like Cranes, having the bottom of their Bellies, and Backs white; and the end of the Wings, Tail, and Neck, black; and these Birds continually keep above 60 Leagues round about the Cape. These Signals did a little chear us up,

Cumana.

Cape de Bonne Esperance.
Alcatraz.
Mangues de Velours.

P and

and encouraged us to come nearer to this so dangerous and tempestuous place: For coming there, we had the most furious and greatest Storm that I ever saw; Our Carrack was about 2000 Tun, one of the Gallantest Ships in all *Portugal*, having been built above 30 years, and yet seemed to be but like a simple Boat, amongst these high and dreadful Waves. We needed little Fore-Mast to the Wind, and 30 or 40 Mariners at the Stern. In this Stormy Weather we could not keep our Ship with Wind, and were about a 100 Persons, 50 on each side, to Devise how to get again before the Wind, which we had lost. Our Deck was covered all over with Water, and it was impossible to get any farther than the Planks of the Ship, either behind or before. Amongst these Miseries and Calamities we expected nothing but Shipwrack, committing our selves to the Divine Mercy; and made a General Procession, Praying Devoutly to God, that he would preserve us from this imminent Danger; besides, we could no longer resist, because of the weakness and sickness of our Men: But

Furious Tempest.

Lib. IV. of John Mocquet.

But God of his Goodness heard our Prayers, appeasing by little and little this great Tempest, which we had so long endured ; so that having passed this dangerous place, we descried the Cape of *Aiguilles*, which made us judg that we had passed that of *Good-Hope*, and from thence we arrived at the Land of *Natall*, where it was very tempestuous, and almost as dark as night : We found there boisterous Winds, and we were forced to labour day and night to avoid the *Baixos ds los Judios*, or *da Judia*, that is, the Shelves of the Jews in the Channel of the Coast of *Sofala*, where there is a great many Ships lost, and where amongst others, happened that no less lamentable than memorable Shipwrack of the Ship called the *St. James*, in the year 1585. who going to *Goa* in the *East-Indies*, split upon these Rocks, and of 250 Persons, not above 90 escaped, by different manners, with as much or more misfortune and miseries on Land as they had enjoy'd on the Sea : There was some Fathers, Jesuits, and Dominicans cast away there, and others saved themselves. The strange and

Cape de Aiguilles.

Natall.

Baixos de los Judi-

P 2 la-

lamentable circumstances of the Accidents, have rendered this Shipwrack the most remarkable that ever happened in these Seas; which is the reason that these Rocks are so much feared, which are like great heaps of sharp Stones, and spikes of White Coral, and commonly covered with Water, so that they are not perceived until you are upon them, and the Ship splitting; but we by the help of God escaped them, so that having taken the height, and seeing our selves escaped, we made the best of our way towards this Harbour, where we found the two Gallies as I have said before, and knowing them again, we bore towards them, and cast Anchor 4 Leagues from the Isles, sending the Boat to Land to hear news from *Mosambique*, which is about 25 Leagues from thence. There came on board us a *Pangais*, who told us how *Mosambique* had been Besieged by the Hollanders, and that it was not above 15 days since they had raised the Siege, and had taken the Galley of *Good Jesus*, which they burnt; and having known by this Gallion that we were coming, they presently retired;

Hollanders at Mosambique.

for

for those of the Gallion knew nothing of the Death of the Count *de la Fera*, nor of the dispersing of the Fleet, they being separated from us hard by the Isle of *Madera*: We weighed Anchor from thence, not finding above 5 or 6 Fathoms Water. As the Wind began to clear it behoved us to cast our Anchors, and the next day to raise them again; this was the 15th of *Sept*. but the Currents of Water which run towards the Islands of *Angoche*, were like to have swallowed us up: We endured a world of Hardships in casting and weighing Anchor, which left me some Blisters upon my Hands; and as weak as I was, I laboured with all my might to be rid of these dangerous passages: In the end, we cast and weighed our Anchors so, that we arrived at *Mosambique* the 29th of *Sep*. and Anchored near the Isles of *St. George*, which is 3 or 4 Leagues distant.

Arrival at Mosambique.

The next morning we Anchored near ths Fortress. As soon as we arrived at *Mosambique*, we understood how our Vice-Admiral had passed the Cape of *Good-Hope* immediately after us, when the Storm was a little allayed; and how

Sea Monster how they had seen a Sea-Monster passing along by the Ship, which was of a strange form and wonderful greatness: He blowed and snored with a great noise, and kept his Body in a round like a Pillar, carrying a thing like a Shield before his Head, and a Saddle upon his Back: As he passed close by the Ship, he made so terrible a noise, that they thought themselves all lost; but he left them, and they saw him no more.

Being then arrived at *Mosambique*, we were mightily astonished to find there nothing to Eat, being then so fallen away by the fatigue of the Sea: We went on shore, having Anchored the *St. Bartholomew, St. Anthony, St. Jerome*, and our own, which was the Admiral: They were there full five Months, waiting for the *Muesson* of Winds to convey us to *Goa*. We endured there not a little; for as I have said, we could find nothing to live upon, there not being any Bread. The Sick were put in Cabins of Palm, some in the Fortress, and others in the City; but they Died by 10 and 15 a *Number of* day, and there remained 735 Buried, *the Dead.*

as

as the Chaplain of our Ship told me, who kept a List of them.

I went also on Shore, scarce able to go, and walked about the Streets looking for something to Eat; but I could find nothing save some little Fishes fryed, which these *Ethiopian* VVomen sell about the Streets, with some Cakes of Meal Baked upon the Coals, which they call *Mocates*. Mocates.

I bought some of this Fish fryed in the Oyl of *Gerselin*, (a little Seed like Carraways, which they make Oil of) which has a very ill Taste; Then retiring alone to make a Feast, and comforting my self the best I could, relying wholly upon God: I demanded a little Water of these VVomen, who gave me some, but it was so Salt that I could scarce drink any of it; for they had drawn it out of a nasty VVell, which was hard by the place where I was; But they fetch the good VVater out of the Continent, at a place called *Cabassie*: There is indeed a little Spring, but it was little better than nothing. Rape-Seed.

After that I went again on Board the Ship; Then the next day I returned again to Land, to look for some Cabin to lodge in, because the Hollanders had burnt all the Houses; and by chance I found a Soldier, who took me into his Lodging within the Fortress, where I carried all my Materials; But after having been there some days, as well to Purge my self, as to be cured of my Disease, comes some of the Servants of Captain *Mor* to look for me, and commanded me to follow them to speak with their Master: I followed them in abundance of pain, and they hastning me forward, which I did after the best manner I could through these Sands towards the Seaside: In the end, they laid me upon the Back of an *Ethiopian*, to carry me into his *Almadie*, which is a sort of a little Boat of the Country, made of a hollow Tree: They cast me within it as if I had been a Log of Wood; and one of the Serjeants Embarked with me: The Tide being come, he made the *Blacks* row, to bring me on board the Vice-Admiral St. *Jerome*. I was a long time in this *Almadie*, during the excessive heat of the Sun a Noon-Day, and I expected to Die with Heat and Thirst, and bought a

Almadie.

Lagne,

Lagne, or Nut of Palm of these *Ethiopians*, to drink of the Water of it, giving half to him who kept me Prisoner.

When I came on *Board*, he put me into the Hands of the *Merigne*, or Serjeant of the Ship, who demanded of him how he would have me fastened; to which he answered, by the Neck, the *Merigne* opened the Collars of Iron, and caused me to lie down all along, and shut my Neck betwixt two pieces of Wood: But seeing me Sick, he had some Compassion upon me and gave me a Pillow to put under my Head: *I* was in this miserable Condition from the 7th to the 28th of *October*, at which time *I* was set at liberty. *Imprisonment of the Author, and his Misery.*

I being then thus taken and shut np, about 4 in the evening comes the *Ovydor* or Judg of the Army, with the Regifter, and demanding of me my Name, and from whence I came, and who gave me Licence to pafs into the *Indies*; They knew it very well, but made as though they were ignorant thereof: For they hnew that I had Embarqued in the Service of the Count *de la Fera*; and besides, at such time when they themselves had been Sick *Nature of the Portugals.*

Sick, I had served and assisted them, for which they said then they were mightily obliged to me: But these Portugals being for the most part of the Race of the Jews, are by Nature Cruel and Ungrateful; When they had enquired concerning my Person, and writ it down, they demanded of me where my Chest and Utensils were, and to give them the Key: Their design was to Rob me of that little Money, and other concerns which I had.

They had taken a little before one *John Baptisto*, a Genouese, who had been Secretary to the late Viceroy, and had made much enquiry after him, telling him that he had some Papers and Memorials against the State of the *Indies*: The Captain *Mor* had deceived him; For he had caused him to come on Shore from the *Pangais*, where he was Embarked with Don *Louis Alves*, Brother to the Count *de la Fera*, desiring him to go with him to the Conquest of *Cumana*. This Don *Louis* carried 200 men to the assistance of *Monomoptata*, one of the Kings of the Lower *Ethiopia*, against another King his Neighbour, who made War upon him;

[margin: Voyage to Cumana.]

him; and the said *Monomoptata* had promised the Portugals to give them all they could Conquer. Now when this *John Baptisto* was come on Shore, upon the Faith of the Captain, who promised him that he should not have any harm done, he was immediately sent as a Prisoner to the Vice Admiral, and presently after I was taken as I have before given account, and found the said *John Baptisto* Prisoner, under Deck, not having then any Irons upon his Feet: He was mightily astonished to see me fastned so as I was, and endeavoured to render me what Consolation he could, that I might take it patiently: But this was not all my Misery to be thus fastened by the Neck; for Hunger, Thirst, and the Disease of my Gums tormented me much more; for they would not so much as give me a little Water to Drink; And by ill fortune I had taken no Money along with me, not knowing where they would lead me; and had not in all above two Rials, one of which I was Robb'd of, and with the other I prayed the *Merigne* to buy me some little Fishes, if any passed by our Ship,

John Baptisto taken.

Ship, when the Blacks come from Fishing abroad, who commonly pass by, asking in their Language if any one had occasion for *Somba*, that is to say, Fish, and *Macacoua*, or Fish dried in the Sun. I had still my Instrument-Case, and a Gold Ring upon my Finger, which I pawned for Victuals.

The evening being come, after the Inquest was made concerning the said *John Baptisto* and me, the Captain *Mor*, sent Soldiers to guard us, and ordered Irons to be fastened also upon *John Baptisto*'s Feet, then caused him to be put at the bottom of the Ship, and to shut the Hatches upon him, and the Keys to be brought to him; and continued thus five days, without having any thing given him to Eat: As for me, the *Merigne* in the evening took the Collars from about my Neck, and put Irons upon my Feet, and caused me to lie upon a Chest in his Cabbin.

Don Louis d'Alves. As for Don *Louis d'Alves*, Brother to the Count *de la Fera*, when he saw how Captain *Mor* had served his Secretary such an ill Trick, by thus falsifying his Faith, he was mightily troubled thereat; besides he had before fallen

fallen out with this Captain, and would have fought him, upon a difference about the Sea-Provision of the Count *de la Fera*, which was worth very near 10000 Ducats, in Victuals, as well Flesh, Biscuit, Wines, Oil, as other Refreshments for the Sea; and this Captain, who was before Vice-Admiral, and, since the Death of the Count, Admiral himself, had made use of some of them, and carried the rest to *Mosambique*, and there sold them. Don *Louis* seeing that he could obtain no Restitution of this wicked Man, he Embarked to go on his Voyage to *Cumana*, to the Conquest of the Gold, which this King, Enemy to *Monomopata* had; and Captain Mor thinking, that Don *Louis* upon his setting Sail would board the Ship where we were Prisoners, sent a great number of Soldiers and Cannoniers, with charge to fire at, and sink the *Pangais* of Don *Louis*, if he made the least shew to Board them. In the morning Don *Louis* having caused his *Pangais* to set sail, he put himself in a posture to Board our Ship; whereupon the Cannoniers turned their

Pieces,

Diffrence betwixt the Portugals.

Pieces, and the Soldiers with their Muskets cockt, to receive them; Some said, let us Fire before they come on board us; others said that they would not Fire becaufe thofe in the *Pangais* were their Countrymen, and their own Friends: In the end, Don *Louis*, (whether it was that he feared to be funk, or that he trufted not too much to the Faith of the Portugals his Compatriots) went directly on in his Courfe. Whereupon the Captain fent for the Mafter Cannonier, caufing him to be Imprifoned, and Irons clapt upon his Feet, bidding him prepare himfelf to be Hanged: But this Mafter Cannonier being a ftout bold Fellow, and not at all aftomifhed at thefe Threatnings, boldly told him that he confeffed himfelf he had more offended in Commanding, than he had done in Difobeying to Fire upon Don *Louis*.

This being thus over, the next day in the evening, the Captain fent one of his Men to take off my Irons, who left me Prifoner below Deck, with 6 Soldiers to guard me, who followed me every where for fear that I fhould leap into the Sea to fave my felf.

When

When I saw my self a little more at liberty, I assisted the Secretary *John Baptisto*, with a little Biscuit cut into little Bits, being black, rotten, and mouldy, and much ado to get that: I raised up, as well as I could, the cover of the place where I was enclosed, and thus gave him some little Bits, which was no small help to him.

But as God never forsakes his Servants in their Afflictions, the said *John Baptisto* told me in Latin, that he had found means to open the Pad-Locks of his Irons, and to take them of; and had also met with a Pipe of Wine, but could not get any of it without a hollow piece of Tinn, which he would use, putting a Stick through it with some Tow or Flax at the end, like a Sponge, and thus to draw out the Wine: I discovered this Business to the *Merigne*, who kept us Prisoners, and who was very well satisfied to have his part thereof, and not to say a word, getting me a Burrage of Leather, which I gave to the said *Baptisto* at night, when the Soldiers were busie at their sports above us, and before the Lamp was lighted: This
Wine

Wine was no small help to us, and I believe that without it we could scarcely have subsisted any longer; for I sopped in private a little Biscuit in this VVine, which heartned me mightily.

About 5 days after, when Don *Louis d'Alves* was gone, *John Baptisto* was taken out from under the Hatches, and was left under the Deck with me, but not without Irons fastned on his Feet, when, as for me, I had no longer either Collars or Irons: Now one day as I was walking backwards and forwards upon the Deck, I by good fortune found under a Cannon, a Stone Bottle full of *Syrop* of Gilli-flowers; this I communicated to the *Meregne*, who took and kept it up for us both: I made use of this Syrop very often, as well to drink as to sop a little Biscuit therein, and in a little time I perceived my Gumbs to grow better, and my Legs began to stretch, which was no small comfort to me; in short, I was quite cured of my Disease, also making use of some Remedies which I took out of a Chest full of Medecines which I found one day below Deck quite open.

Having

Lib. III. *of* John Mocquet.

Having continued about 22 days in this fashion; the Captain came one night very late on Board, and then I took occasion to Discourse him, to know what he had a mind to do with me, and why he let me thus languish; He made me answer, that I should come on Shore with him, to speak with Captain *Mor*. The 28th of the same month we went to see Captain *Mor*, who demanded of me, wherefore I came, and having answered, that the Captain had brought me to speak with him, he bid me wait till the next day, and commanded the Captain to take me to his Lodging.

The next day being come, he carried me to Captain *Mor* : Then Captain *Mor* enquired of me if I had liberty to pass into the *Indies*, and where my Licence was; I told him I had left it with the Proveditor of the House of *India*; Then he asked me if I knew any one at *Mosambique*, I told him no: Then he said do not go out of this Island without my Licence first had; and gave me a Line or two to the Register, and I had my Chest again, but my Money was gone.

After

After all these Troubles, walking one day about the Island, I went to visit a Portugal Gentleman of my acquaintance, who lodged in a *Horte*, or Garden of *Francisco Mendy*, Judge of the Orphans: These two offered me a place to make a Cabin of Palm; the which I gladly accepted; and went to Lodge there; tho' the Lizards and Ants came quite under my Beds-head. This *Francisco Mendy* kept Slaves, and sent me every day a great many Presents: He had a great mind that I should stay and live there, promising to give me one of his Nieces to Wife, Daughter to the Captain of *Cumana*, from whence the Gold comes; But I had no to mind tarry there, but rather pursue my Voyage to the *East Indies*.

Pau d'Anac Wood good for the Disease of Antac.

After having suffer'd considerably in this place, being ready to Embark, I went to the Firm-Land of *Cabassiere*, to look for a Barrel of Water, and a Root called by the Portuguese *Pau d'Anac*, that creeps along the Ground, and resembles much the Birth-Wort very long, bearing little long Pears, green and tender: The Root of it hath a wonderful Virtue in curing a Disease called

called *Ant.ic*, gotten by having to do with the *Ethiopian* Women, and there is no other Remedy whereby to be exempted from Death but this: The Root is taken, ground, with clear Water, of the weight of a Crown, which makes the Patient sweat so, that in a short time it Cures him. 'Tis a little bitter, and yet the Taste and Smell is agreeable enough. I bargained with some of these Blacks to fill me a Sack therewith, who led me into the Woods to look for it.

Going along with them I found a thousand sorts of Plants and Fruits to me unknown: At last we entered into a little Field, where we found some Blacks keeping of Corn for fear of the Elephants, who have Ropes which reach the length of the Corn, with Stones hanging thereon; As soon as the Elephants approach, they shake these Stones against one another, which makes such a noise, that it frights the Elephants away: In the night they make Fires, which these Animals fear mightily. They make a little Lodge at the top of a Butt, and there watch by turns.

Manner to Hunt the Elephants.

Q 2   Having

The Travels and Voyages Lib. IV.

Having seen this, we retired to the Habitation where they had prepared my Dinner: There I made the Seamen Drink so much that they had like to have overturned our Boat. This Liquor was called *Sura*, a sort of Wine made of Palms; and I was mightily troubled to see these *Ethiopians* so puzzeled that they could scarce put up the Sails; and in the mean time the Boat was full of Water: One of the Wives of these Blacks tumbled into the Sea, but I recovered her, otherwise she had been Drowned. These Men understood not one another they were so Drunk; but as good fortune would have it, the *Mocadon*, or Guider of the *Almadie*, was not so Drunk as the rest. 'Twas looked upon as a Miracle how we passed from *Great Cabassiere* to the little one, where there was a thousand Nets, Trees, and Branches, fixed all along the Coast to catch Fish withall.

Having then more happily than prudently passed as far as the *Little Cabassiere*, we went on Shore to provide fresh Water; but there was none but in a great Well where there was but little neither: The Mariners were there

there making Provision of Water, so that I could not have any till night.

The night being come, and not knowing where to Lodge, these *Ethiopians* led me to a place above a League and a half from thence, but the People would not receive us, so that we were forced to return to the Port by reason of bad Weather: At last, being arrived at the Port, I laid me down in the *Almadie*, covering my self with my Cloak, where I endured the Rain all the night.

The next morning we hoised Sail, and sailed directly upon the Banks, from whence we had much ado to escape: In the end, being come off therefrom, with a great deal of trouble, and the Wind carrying us by force towards the Main-Sea, which did us that favour as to bring us near to the Chapel of the Bullwork, where being come, I made a Vow, never to trust my self with such Mariners again, who made me run the greatest hazard I ever had in the whole Voyage: I ordered my Water to be brought into my Cabin, and prepared my self for the Embarkment to *Goa*.

White Prince of the Blacks. Whilst I was in this place, there came the Son of an *Ethiopian* King, from a great distance in the Continent, to see some of his Kindred: His Father and Mother were black, and he was white and fair - He brought with him one of his Brothers, who was black, and some Slaves: They came both into my Cabin, telling me, that having heard say there was white Men at *Mosambique*, they came purposely to see them.

The Portugals made him a very good Reception, to the end they might have Free-Traffick in his Fathers Country: 'Twas said his Mother had two other White Children; but that his Father killed them, saying, they must needs be by some other Man; and that as he came into the World with this colour, his Father had determined to kill him also; but one of his Friends persuaded him to the contrary by telling him that it was by Divine Permission, and so was saved. His Mother had possibly had these Men in her Imagination which were said to be at *Mosambique*, or else had happened to her by some other Course of Imagination. He was not in the least Tann'd or or Burnt with the Sun, and was about 20 years of Age, and his Brother about 18. They visited me 2 or 3 times in my Cabin, and I gave them to Eat and Drink of what I could have in the Country, at which they seemed to be very well Content.

I remember that being at *Lisbon*, I heard a Story of such a like thing which happened at *Genoua* not long before, of which they made a Song in form of a Romance, which I heard Sung in *Portugal*. There was a rich *Genoua*, who was Married to a very honest and virtuous Woman, of one of the best Houses in *Genoua*, who having conceived some displeasure upon the account of one of her Black Slaves which had been gotten with Child by another Negro Slave, she imprinted that so deeply in her Imagination, that being with Child her self, she was brought to Bed of a black Child; but the angry Father believing that she had dishonoured her self with some Negro, was resolved to kill her; but she fled away to her Friends. Whereupon he gave charge to one of his Servants to go and leave the Child some-

History of a black Genoway.

where

where, or to kill it: But the Servant moved with Compassion, (besides the Mother had recommended it to him) saved the Child, and caused it to be brought up, making the Husband believe he had made it away: A little while after, this *Genoua*, sore vexed with Spite and Anger, forsook *Genoua*, and retired into *Barbary*, resolving to turn Turk, and live in *Algier*. In the mean time the poor Disconsolate Mother took care to bring up this Child to years of Discretion, and gave him Order to go seek his Father through tne World; for none knew what was become of him. This young Black being upon the Sea, was taken by Corsairs, and carried to *Argier* to be sold, where he was bought by his own Father; but being troubled to see himself become a miserable Slave, his Father asked him whence he was, who learned of him the whole History of his Birth, at which being astonished, he acknowledged him for his Son, and resolved to quit the Country, and return with him to *Genoua*, and to be reconciled to his Wife: Wherefore having secretly provided for his departure

ture, resolved to embark all his choicest things, and what he esteemed the most, they departed one night out of *Algier* in a Boat; but as ill fortune would have it, they were taken by *Corsairs*, by whom they were both cruelly Massacred: Such end had the Adventure of this poor Black.

But to return again to our Embarkment at *Mosambique*; The Weather of *Muesson* being come, (which is a Wind that comes at a certain Season of the year, for there are but two sorts of Winds which raign in these Parts of *India*, East, and West; Don *Estevan de Tayde*, Governor of *Mosambique*, caused his *Pangais* to be made ready, burthen 30 Tuns, more or less, and to be laden with *Bretangis* and *Conterie*: *Bretangis* are a certain kind of Callico, dyed blue, and of a dark Violet; *Conterie*, are Beads of Glass or Amber, as well good as counterfeit, which is the Merchandize usual amongst these *Ethiopians*, who in exchange give Gold, Ambergreece, Eliphants Teeth, and other Things which these Countries of *Couama* produce, and the Cape of *Courante*, where these *Pangais* go. Now

Muessons.

Don Estevan de Tayde.

The Travels and Voyages Lib. IV.

Now, *Don Criftoval de Porogne*, alias Captain *Mor*, feeing thefe *Pangais* ready to depart, went with his Soldiers in Boats to take them, and bring them to Anchor along by the Gallions of the Fleet, which was near by: The which *Don Eftevan* perceiving from the Fortrefs, was mightily offended at; but not having Soldiers fufficient to go Succour, and Recover his *Pangais*, he commanded his Canoniers to Fire upon the *Pangais*, to fink them, not careing for the Lofs of his Merchandife; fo he might but fink Captain *More* alfo, at leaft to do him fome mifchief: The Canoneer took his Aim, and was going to fire one of the great Canons: But as good fortune would have it, both for one and the other, nothing but the Priming took Fire, and hereupon the principal of the City of *Mafambique*, ran in all haft upon the Ramparts to appeafe Don *Eftevan*, who was refolved to fink them all, and promifed him to procure the *Pangais* out of the Hands of Captain *Mor*.

The Reafon that moved this Captain to do thus, was nothing but Mallice and Revenge, to make the *Pangais* lofe lose the opportunity of the Voyage, to the no small damage of *Don Estevan*, to whom it had been above an hundred thousand Crowns Loss; for that year, for as much as he could not have sent the *Pangais* at any other time to bring back the Profits which he uplifts every year from those Countries of *Covama*.

Besides, he had endured a long siege of the *Hollanders* in this place: At last the accord was made betwixt him and Captain *More*, and he sent his *Pangais* to their accustomed Traffick; but yet they still retained betwixt themselves a secret hatred, and ill-will; Since which time R*uy de Mello* came to relieve Don *Estevan* of his Government; his three years being Expired.

This Country of *Covama* is the Finest of all *Africa*, from whence the best Gold is brought, and in the greatest quantity; insomuch, that the Captain of *Mosambique* during the three years that he Commands there, may carry away from *Mosambique*, *Sofala*, and *Covama*, above three hundred thousand Crowns, without reckoning that which he Pays to the Soldiers, and

some

Gold of Africa.

some Tibute which he renders to the King: While I was there I saw the Soldiers Pay, which was Gold in Powder, as it is found, giving every one so many *Carats*: This Gold is so yellow and pure, that our Pistol-Gold, and Crowns, seems to be but Copper thereto.

Traffick of Africa.

There dares none Traffick towards all this Coast of *Mosambique* without Licence of the Captain, who sends several Vessels to the Cape of *Courrants*, and to *Covama*, who return laden with the finest *Ivory*, for there the Eliphants are in abundance, and very great: They bring back also Amber-greace, and Gold, in liew of some small Ware which they give in Exchange to the Blacks or *Cafres*, who gather the Gold in the Field at the Foot of certain Mountains, at such time as the Floods of Water come, which running from on high, forces down store of Gold in Powder; and then each *Ethiopian* hath his little Brook, with a little Net, made in the Fashion of a Pock for to catch Rabets withal, but wove more slender, with which they stop all this Gold-Sand running from the Mountains;

tains; They sometimes find great pieces of it, and very fine, as I have seen some of them at the Senior *Francisco Meindi*, Judg of the Orphans at *Mosambique*, and one of the Richest belonging to the Captain: This Piece weighed about half a Pound, and was Refined: But he kept that as a rarity, for such Pieces are not often to be found.

Now the time of our Embarkment drawing nearer, and nearer, which was in the Month of *March*; I was not a little Joyful to quit this Desart Country, where I was ready to Dye for Hunger the most part of the time. As for the other Ships of our Fleet; I must not forget to tell that they were all cast away in their Voyage to the *Indies*. *Loss of the Ships.*

And First, the *Carraque*, called, *Nostra-Seniora d' Aiuda* was lost upon the Coast of *Ethiopia*, where the most part of the Men Died of Violent Diseases which are incident to that Country, and amongst others, a certain disease, which breaks out at the Fundament like an Ulcer, and is presently full of Worms, which Gnaw as far as the Belly, *Strange Disease.*

Belly, and so they die in great misery and torment: There hath been no better remedy found for this Disease, than the Juyce of *Lymon*, in washing therewith the Fundament; for that obstructs the Worms breeding there: I believe this Disease comes only by Drinking the bad Water which is there in great abundance.

Galion of the Holy Ghost. As for the Galion of the Holy Ghost, they seeing the Water coming in upon them, with such great Violence, were forced to Sail back to *Bresil*, where being come, they sent into *Portugal* to know what they had best to do, whether to return to *Portugal*, or to persue their Voyage; they were commanded to proceed: Having Chaulked their Galion, they set sail for the *Indies*, and *Cape of Good-Hope.* being at the height of Cape *de Bonne Esperance*, they met with contrary Winds, and Tacking about from one side to the other, continually beating about the Sea, they could no longer hold out, and the Vessel struck a Leak in the Fore-Castle, which the Master seeing, he, together with the Captain and Pilot, cast out the Boat in haste, with a Barrel of Water and some Biscuit therein, slipping down themselves

by

by a Rope; The Captain not being *Pitious Accident of a Ship.* able to hold so well as the rest, fell into the Sea, and they within were ready to cut of his Hands when he caught hold of the Boat; but one among the rest, crying out, 'twas the Captain, saved him: Several were kept off with Swords, and had their Hands cut as they laid hold on the Boat; There was but 16 Persons out of 300 saved. The Boat endeavoured to gain the Cape of *Courrants,* and sailed above 400 Leagues before they arrived at the place designed but in the end they came to *Mosambique,* and from thence to *Goa,* where I was told this accident.

    The Galion of *Good Jesus* was taken by the Hollanders near *Mosambique,* and burnt, setting the Men at liberty. *Mogincal.*
    The Carrack called the *Palm* was *Woman-Fish.* lost at *Mogincal,* where the Blacks Fish for *Pisce Mulier,* which is to say Women Fish: This Fish resembles a Woman, having the Privy Parts after the same manner, and carrieth her young under her Fins, which are on each side, serving for Arms, and goes often on Land, and is there disburthened of her young: The Blacks who Fish, are to swear not to have to do with these
                                                     She-

She-Fishes: Their Teeth are of great Virtue, (as I have experienced) against Hemorhoids, Bloody Flux, and hot Fevers, in rubbing them against a Marble, and agitating it with Water, and so to be Drunk. These Blacks are extream fond of these Fishes, and refresh themselves by having Communication with them. These *Pisces Mulieres* have a hideous Face, like the Snout of a Hog, and all the Body like a Fish.

These People also Eat human Flesh, for which they are called *Macone*: 'Tis said they drank the Blood of the Hollanders when the Portugals made a Salley out of *Mosambique*; And a Soldier of that place told me, that he saw a Black cut the Throat of a Hollander that remained upon the place, and swallowed down the Blood hot. They are very hardy and couragious in War, fearing neither Sword or Dart; yet there are some Cowards. The subjects of *Monomotapa*, when they kill any of their Enemies, cut off their Privy-Members, and having dried them, give them their Wives to wear about their Neck, of which they are not a little Proud: For they who have the most are the most esteemed, in regard that

Macone.

Barbarity of the Blacks.

Strange Customs of the Blacks.

Evi-

Lib. IV.   *of John Mocquet.*   235

Evidences the Husband to be the more hardy and valiant; They carry them before the King to declare where and when they purchased the same.

As for the Carrack called *Oleveira*, she was lost near the Isles *Quemades*, not far from *Goa*, being so close pursued by the Hollanders, that they were constrained to put out the Boat and save themselves by going a shore, setting Fire to their Ship.

Oleveira Carrack.

The Carrack named the *Salvation*, was carried towards the Coast of *Arabia* to the Confines of the *Abassins*, and was there also Shipwrackt. I believe this happened through the Villany of the Master and Pilot, who having a mind to Inrich themselves with the Money of private Persons, and the *Cavedal*, which is that of the King's for the lading of Peper, run purposely a-ground upon the Coast: Then was it time for every one to save himself, taking with him his Money and Arms; not thinking to lade themselves with Victuals. The Master and Pilot agreed before to put the Money into the Boat, with some Victuals and Arms, and some of their Confidents, went to cross the

q   Coast

Coast, passing the *Red-Sea* as far as the Persian Gulf, to recover *Ormus*: When this was known at *Goa*, they dispatch'd Gallies after them, and were taken towards *Ormus*, and brought Prisoners to *Goa*, whilst I was there.

Strange Adventure of the Portingals in Ethiopia. The rest (who were about 400 white Men and 300 Negro Slaves) set themselves in order to march along the Coast, and recover a certain Port of the *Red-Sea*, to Embark for the *Indies*: But as they marched with Colours displayed, and crying *Sautiago*, thinking to make the *Ethiopians* afraid of them, but it fell out to the contrary: Insomuch that being fatigued with Hunger, Thirst and weariness, and troubled with the Enemy behind, every one was forced to shift for himself, and the hindermost were killed by the *Ethiopians*: The rest who saved themselves fell into the hands of a most barbarous King, who seeing so many Blacks of their own Nation Captives amongst these Portugals, Hypocritically told them, that if they would render their Arms, they should receive no hurt; They believing that, and seeing themselves encompassed about on every

delivered up their Arms,
this *Abaſſin* King cauſed
taken, and led one after
a great place before his
afterwards having ſtrip-
rk-naked, ordered them
in a Ring, and cauſed an
roclaim their Death, ſay-
as his Pleaſure to have all
hopt off before his People.
opened by chance that in
p that was thus loſt, there
n Ambaſſador who had
Europe from the great
ia, to demand ſuccour of
Princes againſt the Turk.
fador having been well
id amongſt others by the
n, with noble and rich
returned in this Ship by
e *Indies*. I ſaw him at
about the City in great
ad his Turbant covered
s Stones. Now this Am-
ho ſaved himſelf among
Wretches, fell upon his
the King, deſiring, that
eaſe to give theſe Chri-
ives, ſeeing he had taken

q 2   from

The Travels and Voyages Lib.IV.
from them all they had, and suffer them to Embark in some Port of his Country; telling him amongst other things, that if he knew but the Power of *Spain*, he would not offer them the least Injury, and that their Prince was able in a little time to Ruin him. The King was a little pacified at these Words, and told the Ambassador that for his Sake he would give them their Lives, on condition they would presently depart his Dominions, or else he would put them to Death.

The Portugals seeing this, were not a little glad to have their Lives saved, got away Naked as they were, and Embarked in a Ship of an *Arabian*, Trafficking upon the Coast of *India*, who gave them Victuals and Passage upon hopes to be recompenced at *Goa*; and being arrived, the Master came *Good Office* to demand his Hire and Charges, but *ill requited.* was Laughed at. He came to the Viceroy *Andre Furtade de Mendoce*, but could not get any thing.

One of these Seamen that were saved being my Friend, told me, That the Master Cannonier mightily lamented the loss of a Stone of a strange Virtue

Lib. IV. *of* John Mocquet.

and excellent Odour, for having it a- *Odoriferent Stone.*
bout him, he seemed to have a Scent
of Musk and Ambergreece: The Virtue was such, that being Soaked in
Water, it was an excellent Remedy
against any Disease, and had experienced it upon several of their Men, who
as soon as they drank of the Water
wherein it was soaked, found themselves presently eased, and were cured
according to the quantity which they
took. The aptain would have given
him a 1000 Duckets for it, but he
would not take under 3 or 4000. He
came by it one day as they made a
Halt, taking his Harquebuss, and going about the Woods to shoot something to Eat, he found an Animal of
the bigness of a Deer, but a little higher, *Animal carrying an excellent Stone.*
who had two Horns below the Eyes,
and had the fortune to shoot him in the
Head: This Beast gave a leap to run
upon him, but he fell down dead. He
and his Companions cut him up to
Roast him upon the Coals; and as he
was going to Eat some of the Pluck, he
found this Stone in a little bag, which
at first he made no account of; but
having washed it he found it of so curious

rious and polished bright colour, and of so sweet a smell, that he kept it up carefully. The Coast of *Ethiopia* is full of excellent and odoriferous Herbs, and perhaps this Animal might feed thereupon, and that may be the cause of the Virtue of the Stone.

Thus was the greatest part of the Fleet lost: For of 14 Vessels there arrived but 4 at the *Indies*, with a Hulk which served us for a Patach, yet not without having the Masts broke in pieces. There was a Carracon of the Fleet which sailed back for *Portugal*.

Tragick History of Emanuel de Sosa Sepulveda.

But before we depart from this Coast of *Africa*, I will relate the strange Fortune which formerly happened to one *Emanuel de Sosa*, called *Sepulveda*, a *Portugal* Gentleman, and how he was lost upon this Coast of *Ethiopia*: This Gentleman, who was rich, being in the *Indies*, fell in Love with the Daughter of one *Garsias Sola*, Captain of *Bombain*, (a Fortress of the Portugals) esteemed one of the most Beautiful Ladies of the East, and had many great Suters to Marry her; But he not being able to bring his Designs to pass, because of her Father, who would

by

by no means give his Consent, tho' the Daughter was very willing he resolved to rid himself of the Father, and for this cause parted one day from *Goa*, with some of his Sworn Companions, with whom he Embark'd, and coming late in the evening to *Bombain*, they watched their opportunity, so that they found this Captain walking along by the Sea, and there killed him. This was so secretly done that *Sosa* had no great trouble to attain to his Desires, Marrying this fair Orphan named *Leonor*, whom he brought to *Goa*; where having for some time lived in pleasure with her, and having two Children by her, he had a desire to go with his Family to *Portugal*, to obtain from the King some Preferment greater than that which he had in the *Indies*: And for this cause, having bought a good Ship, and being Embarked at *Cochim*, with his Wife and Children, a great many Slaves, and others of his Train, he sailed away; But coming towards the Cape of *Currants*, and their Vessel running a-ground, they were forced to save themselves in the Boat: They thought to have arrived at the *Little Cafala*,

Cafala, where the Portugals have a Fort; for the great one is towards *Mosambique*; but they found themselves in a Country betwixt the Cape of *Currants* and that of *Good-Hope*, where they were troubled with the Blacks of the Country along the Seaside. These Blacks not fearing the Harquebusses, killed a great number of them, the rest, amongst whom were *Sosa*, his Wife and Children, saved themselves by recovering the Country, and came at last into the Power of a King of these Blacks, who treated them very kindly; But when they departed from thence, as they Travelled towards *Mosambique*, they fell into the Hands of the Enemies of this King, who did them all the Injuries imaginable, in killing the most part, and stripping the rest Stark-Naked: It was no small Grief to *Sosa* to see himself, his Wife and Children in this miserable Estate, wandering about the Desarts and Burning Sands of *Ethiopia*, without having wherewithall to Eat. Then began the just Judgment of God to fall on *Sosa* for the Murder of his Father-in-Law. He went up and down

down about the Woods seeking for Raisins to nourish himself, his Wife, and Children: But the greatest motive of Compassion was this poor innocent Lady, who seeing her self Naked, covered her self with Sand, that she might not be seen in this Condition, and made the greatest Lamentations imaginable, oftentimes telling her Husband, that their great Sins were the cause of so many Evils: But having continued some days in this Misery, after suffering the Death of her Children, overwhelmed with Grief, Hunger, and all sorts of Incommodities, was found dying by the wretched *Sosa*, returning from his Quest; yet he received her last Sighs, with Complaints and Lamentations of his loss; and knowing himself to be the cause of all these Misfortunes, went away like a Mad Man about the Woods, and was never after heard of. All the rest of his Company died after the same manner, except one Portugal, who with great difficulty escaped, and arrived at *Mosambique*, where he related this sad Story, of which the Portugals have made a Romance. They who have

Writ

The Travels and Voyages Lib. IV.

Writ of the *East-Indies* have made ample mention of this Tragical Accident of *Sofa* and his Wife, but they have omitted the Murder of his Father-in-Law, which was the occasion of drawing the Judgment of God upon him.

Language of the Blacks.

But before we leave these Blacks it will not be improper to speak something of their Language, because it's different from all the other People of *Africa*. That of *Mosambique* is called *Ethiopians*, and can number no farther than Ten, and begin thus; *Monti* 1, *Piri* 2, *Taton* 3, *Quinna* 4, *Chanon* 5, *Tandaton* 6, *Fongate* 7, *Nana* 8, *Quinda* 9, *Cohomy* 10: They call the Head *Mesora*, the Ear *Maro*, the Nose *Buonom*, the Mouth *Muromoiu*, the Face *Cohope*, the Arms *Menio*, the Feet *Mirengi*, the Hair *Cici*, the Teeth *Mannon*, and so of other Things.

Departure from Mosambique from Goa.

But to return to the 4 Ships which remained from the Shipwrack, *viz.* Our Lady of Mount *Carmel*, *St. Jerome*, *St. Anthony*, and *St. Bartholomew*, with which we parted from *Mosambique*, and set sail for *Goa* the 20th of *March* 1609. And having then put out to the Main Sea, the 23th of *March* we saw the Isle of *Comba*. This

This Isle is very high, and is to be seen above 25 Leagues distance: After that, we passed the Line towards the *Indies*, the 5th of *April*, and the 12th, being at 4 Degrees on the other side the Line, we found an *Arabian* Ship which came from *Dia*, and was going to *Mecca*; Our Vice-Admiral made towards her, saluting her with 2 or 3 shot of Cannon to make her strike sail; the which they would not do, until they saw the Bullets fly, then they lower'd their Sails, and came to us. The Captain came with 6 or 7 Arabians of good Fashion, carrying with him a Pass-port from the then Vice-roy of the *Indies*: The Captain seeing this Pass-port, durst not do them any harm, but having retained them 2 or 3 days, had great Presents from them, and sent to visit their Ship to see if there was any prohibited Goods therein, as Cinnamon, Cloves, and other things. There was about 700 Persons in the Ship, the most part Passengers, who were going in Pilgrimage to the Sepulcher of their Prophet *Mahomet*. This Ship was said to be worth above Two Millions, for there was nothing but Merchan-

Combo-Isle.

Arabian-Ship.

chandize of Silk, and other curious and precious Things.

After this Encounter we passed the Mouth of the *Red-Sea*, near to the Isle of *Socreta*, on the 7th of *May*, and there we had great Calms, which in regard of the want we were in for fresh Water, and other Necessaries, much troubled us. When we arrived at the Bar of *Goa*, we had but little Victuals left, and had we tarried but a little while longer we had all Died of Hunger: By the way we found a Ship which came from *Chaoul*, and was commanded by an *Arabian*: We commanded him with Cannon Shot to lower his Sails; for he would not obey at first; and being come on Board us, Captain *Mor* made him Prisoner at the Poop, where he was for some time; but having made some Presents to the Captain, he was let go, because he Traffick'd with the Portugals: We kept two of these Mariners to serve us for the knowledge of the Coast, if by chance we should meet with contrary Winds. One of these Mariners shewed me a Bird no bigger than a Linnet, and told me, it never stirred from the Sea, and

never

Socoreta Isle.

never went on Land but when the Female laid her Eggs, she mounts up out of sight, and so lays her Eggs one at a time as she mounts up; after this Egg comes down tossing in the Air, which is very hot in that Country, before it falls into the Sea, 'tis Hatch'd; after which, the Sea nourisheth it; which I found to be very wonderful and rare in Nature.

Wonderful Bird.

The 26th of *May* 1609. we arrived at *Goa the Old*, as they call it, and the 27th went on Land, being *Ascension-Eve*, to Dine at *Pangin*, before we should come to *Goa*.

Arrival at Goa in the Indies.

As soon as the Fleet arrived there, the Kings Packet was published, which was to be opened no where but at *Goa*, containing that in case the Vice-roy chanced to Die by the way, Senior *Andre Furtado de Mandoze* should be Elected; and if he was not there at that time, they should send for the Governor of the Isle of *Seilan*.

Andre Furtano Elected Vice-roy.

Andre Furtado having thus been received for Vice-roy, I went to *Reys-Magos*, (which is the Church of the *Cordelieres*, where the Vice-roys commonly reside whilst Preparations are
made

Reys-Magos, or the Church of the three Kings.

made for his Reception, to speak with him, and desire him to help me in my necessity: He made me answer, that I should come to him when he was setled in his Government: But all this signified nothing, for I could never speak with him until such time as he sent for me to go with him to *Portugal*, being relieved of his Charge by R*uy de T*a*lbe*, who came the next year to *Goa*: He sent for me then by his Cup-Bearer, to come and speak with him at the Pass of M*adre de Dios*, half a League from *Goa*; the which I did, and told me, if I would go along with him to *Portugal*, he would content me; to which I willingly agreed.

Madre de Dios, or the Mother of God.

I went to live in his House till we Embarkt, which was in *January* following: It was in *November* when he sent for me to this Pass, where there was a Captain who kept the Passage so that none could go into the Main-Land without being marked in the Hand, except those of the Country, and the *Portugals*, who must have the Licence of the *Coregidor*. I desired then this Captain from *Andre Furtado*, to give me an *Almadie*, with Mariners, and

and a Naique for Guide, which he willingly did, and recommended me mightily to this Naique, telling him that I went to look for Herbs for *Andre Furtado*, which was true, and accordingly brought some which served him for Fomentation of the Opelation of the Spleen. Passing then to the Main-Land, we went by these Places in the Habitations of the Gentlemen *Bramenis*; and having demanded some Water to drink at the House of one of these People, he gave me some, but stayed to see if I drank without touching the sides of the Cup, the which I knew not, and Drank without any Ceremony, which the Son of this Gentleman seeing, cried out as loud as he could to his Father, who was in a little place behind the House, who presently came running in great Anger, so that I was constrained to march of, and make clean the Cup by my Naique to appease hem.

After that I passed by a Pagod or Temple, very well built, and entering therein I found one of the Natives stark-naked, adorning their Idol with Flowers, which had a Head like a

Calf,

Calf, when presently an old Woman amongst them cried out to me, Why I came in there with my Shooes; my Naique excused me in telling her that I knew not the Custom.

Paygods.   As for the Pay-gods, they have several sorts of them; Some for War, others for Peace, and for Love, where the Maids coming to be Married, are brought to be Defloured; and their Idol hath the Privy Parts like a Man. The Damsels, who serve these Pay-gods like the Vestal-Virgins, continue there from 10 to 20 years of Age, and Dance all night long, carrying lighted Lamps in their Hands, and go to Sleep round about their Idols. I saw there very beautiful Girls and Women They Marry their Daughters at 8 or 9 years of Age; when they are once past 12 or 13, they are not regarded, because they believe them to continue no longer Maids, considering the heat of the Country: At the end of 20 years, these Religious Women that have thus served the Pay-gods, are kept in a certain place the rest of their Lives.

Indian Women Religious.

After I had gathered some Herbs which I had occasion for, we went to a little Habitation of Gentiles, where I demanded by my *Truch-man*, if they had any Victuals to give us for our Money, for there is no Inns or Taverns there; but there were some little Shops where they sold Fruit, and other things fit to Eat: These Gentiles having Compassion on me, there was a Woman, who put me under a Gallery of her House, where there was a Napkin full of Leaves and Plantane, accommodated with Thorns; then she threw me some Rice thereupon, with a certain Sauce which they call *Caril*, I Eat all this, and when I was about to Drink out of a little Vessel of Copper that they had given me full of Water, they began to cry out upon me, because I touched it in Drinking, for they never touch the Cup in Drinking, only heaving it up with the Server whereon it stands, and so Drink.

The Floor and Pavement of their Houses are composed with Cow-Dung, which they make look exceeding bright, and think that it keeps away the Ants, which are there in abundance; and they can keep nothing free from being destroy'd by these little

Ants troublesome.

tle Animals, to prevent which the have also Cupboards bore upon Piles set in Vessels full of Water, where th' Ants drown themselves by thinking to mount up. Near to this Habitation, found a great Tree, laden with *Ta-* *marins*, of which I gathered a few They had yet nothing but a sower Taste, I carried away the Husk, which are almost like French-Beans, but larger and greater.

Tamarins.

Now as I returned by a very Desart Place, I saw some of these Gentiles running in great haste; and having caused my Truch-man to ask what ailed them, they answered, that their Father was gone to Drown himself, a little after I saw them return, bringing back their Father, and Comforting him after the best manner they could: He was troubled for some Misfortune that had happened to him. It is a common thing with these People to Drown or Poison themselves, or to Die after some such way, when any Accident happens to them.

Indians *subject to* *Dispair.*

As for the Women, 'tis the Custom, that when the Body of their Dead Husbands are Burnt, they cast themselves

Lib. III. *of* John Mocquet. 242

selves into the Funeral Pile, and Burn themselves, after being first adorned with their richest Accoutrements and Jewels, Dancing at the Sound of Instruments, and thus Die with a wonderful Constancy, speaking in the Fire to the very last: Those who do not this are held Infamous so long as they live, not daring to shew themselves before others, nor to appear before their Friends and Kindred. Such as have a weaker Courage Poison themselves, seeing their Husband Dead, and are Burnt together with him. *Women who burn themselves.*

'Tis remarkable that the Body of the Woman hath such an Oyley Property, that one Body will serve like Oil or Greese to consume the Bodies of 5 or 6 men. The Moors and Mahometans who inhabit the Main-Land of *Goa* towards *Pichelin*, do not allow this sort of Cruelty in the Women; but when they see they cannot obtain this favour, they Poison themselves.

This Custom of Burning themselves hath continued, as they say, ever since a certain Gentile King, who reigned amongst them; who seeing how all the Men of his Kingdom died, and know-

R 2 ing

ing that it was their Wives which Poisoned them, to have other Husbands; and that those who had Children should continue alive to take care of them, but without Power ever to Marry again, instituted this: They observe this very strictly, and do nothing but Groan, Weep and Lament, during the rest of their Life; and at certain hours of the day and night, howl and lament after so strange a manner, that 'tis a great pity to hear them.

As for my part I was sometimes Deafened with the clamours and noise of some or other who had lost Husband or Children: I have heard a *Bramin* say, (who had turned Christian) that they who have lost a Child, mourn and lament 20 years entire: *He* told me also, that a certain Woman of those who us'd to serve the Pay-gods, that after being retired into a *House* where they pass their time with Men, she *Resolution* entertained one who heated himself so *of a Lover.* with her, that he Died upon the spot, at which she was so afflicted, that when they Burnt his Body, she Burnt her self with him, seeing he had Died for Love of her, tho' she was no other than a good Friend. As

As I returned from my little Voyage, I paffed by a Valley where there was a very neat and pleafant Fountain, which came out from a Rock flat and hollow, and the Water which came out run through little holes in the Rock: 'Twas impoffible to empty it, though there was but very little Water therein: For in taking out that which was there, more runs out, like a ftrong and active Spring: After this, I went to Embark at a Paygod, which is in a certain place along by the River, it being fo deep that 'tis impoffible to find the bottom. They have made there large and fpacious Steps along by the fide; and there the Gentiles come every year, 2 or 300 Leagues diftant, to wafh themfelves at certain times, and fometimes there are affembled there above a 100000 Men, Women and Children, cafting abundance of Fruit in this River, who believe that at the end of the year it comes again upon the Water. Thus Satan deceives them, for there are always fome or other who tarry there for fecurity, who fometimes drown themfelves out of a Fond Devotion.

Foolifh Opinions of the Indians.

Another Voyage of the Author.

Pichelin.

As I Embarked by these Steps, I returned to the *Madre di Dios*, from whence I set out about *Dec.* Then I made another little Voyage to the Main-Land of *Pichelin*, to procure some Drugs and other Rarities of the Country, and took again my Truch man, with the *Almadie*, and the Mariners which the Captain of the Passage had given me, who having expresly commanded them to Obey me, and to conduct me where I had a mind to go.

We departed in a very fine evening, and travelled all night, the Moon shining, insomuch that we arrived at *Pichelin*, a very pleasant City, where is a great number of Gentile Merchants, and belongs to *Dealcan*, it being some 4 Leagues from *Goa*: We went to the Lodging of one *Manate*, a Gentile, who received us kindly upon the Acquaintance he had with our Truch-man, and put me to lie under a little Pent-House, where an Indian Woman brought her Daughter to lie with me, as this *Manate* had counselled her; but this Girl not above 13 years of Age, seeing I would not touch her, fell to Weeping and Groaning, thinking to force

force me to have to do with her, and her Mother did all she could to appease her; I understood not the ground of all this Mystery.

The next morning, I saw a Jogue-Gentile, who was all perfumed with incense, and stark Naked, squat upon his Tail before a Fire of Cow Dung, and with Ashes thereof all bepowered his Body, having long Hair like a Woman, which he held on the top of his Shoulders: This was the most hideous and monstrous Spectacle that ever was seen: For he remained still looking on the Fire, without so much as turning his Head. *Strange fashion of the Jogues.*

These sort of People are sometimes 4 or 5 days without any meat, and use extraordinary Abstinence: All these Gentiles, and especially the Bramins, never Eat any living thing, or that has had life, and will not taste of Red-Herbs, saying, that they have Blood in them; They Eat Rice and Milk, and call the Cow their Mother-Nurse. About the Desarts they have Hospitals where they Feed the Pilgrims that pass that way: When some rich Men Die they leave something to the Hospitals. *Hospitals amongst the Indians.*

The Travels and Voyages Lib.IV.

To this purpose, I will relate what happened to one of my Friends, coming from the Kingdom of *Pegu* to *Cochin*: This was a Fleming, who was Married at *Lyons*, and had two Brothers Married at *Goa*, to the *Metices* of *Cochin*: These 3 were taken in the Ship *Good Jesus* by the Hollanders, who put them on Shore; And as they came along by the Sea-side, they had but one pair of Shoes amongst them three, the which they wore by turns: He who wore the Shoes went upon Land, and the two others, bare-footed, went in the Water along by the Shore, not enduring the Soles of their Feet upon the Ground, it was so hot and burning at that time: They were ready to Die with Hunger and Thirst, not finding any thing to subsist upon in these Desarts: And being very weak, and in great Distress, they espied two Gentiles, who ran towards them, crying out to them to stay a little; but they not knowing what they meant, feared at first that it was to Rob them, but having nothing to lose, they resolved to tarry, and these Gentiles being come to them, courteously offered them Meat and

Cochin.

Courtesie of the Indians

and Drink, for which they thanked them, saying, they had no Money to pay for it: They spake by Signs, not being able to make them understand otherways: But these Gentiles pointed towards Heaven, as if they would have said, 'twas God who commanded them to do thus; so that these 3 easily consented thereto, and afterwards pursued their Voyage: This shews how these Gentiles are content when they find occasion to do good to poor Travellers, they being all very pious People, who endure all sorts of Ignominy and Injuries, such Lovers are they of Peace and Tranquillity. This Goodness and natural Humanity of these poor Idolaters, abused in so many other things, is an excellent Lesson for Christians instructed in the True Religion, which they make so little account of, since the Natural Light of these blind Infidels, shames the Super-natural Gifts of those who profess Christianity.

After I had gathered together, and bought all the Drugs and other Things which might be of any use to me, I began to think of my return with my Truchman and Mariners; and going along

along the Coast, which was very green, pleasant, and abounding in all sorts of Plants; When I saw any Herb which pleased me, I commanded them to fetch it.

Indians kill not Animals.

The Portugals put a thousand Affronts upon these poor People, and sometimes they make shew as if they would kill some Bird, or other Animal, which these Gentiles have pity on, and presently buy them to set them at liberty: Yet since they have found out that the Portugals do this on purpose to have their Money, knowing their bad Intention, they buy not these Animals as they were wont to do.

Rude Comportment of the Portugals towards the Indians.

When a Portugal has a mind to have some new Cloths, he makes no more ado but goes to the Shop of an Indian, with a Tailor, and there chooses his Stuff; then orders it to be cut out in his presence, and when it comes to be paid, he bids the poor Gentile follow him to his Lodging to take his Money, where being come, he pretends that his Companion, who has the Key of his Chest, is not there; and so the other whatever he can say or do, can have nothing of him but this excuse: And

2 or 3 days after, the Portugal tells him he owes him nothing: They use the same Tricks to all other Merchants, and Tradesmen: They have done as much to me, when I have paid any thing for them; for some time after they made as if they knew me not: Yet it ought not to be thought strange if they do thus in the *Indies*, since they play the same Pranks in *Lisbon* it self; where one of my Hosts told me, that one day having Dressed up a Hat for a *Castilian*, and asking him for his Mony, shewed him a Pistol cockt, telling him, if he had a mind to be paid, he must follow him into *Flanders*, where he was going, and this was all he could get.

As soon as they arrive at the *Indies*, they make themselves Gallants, calling themselves *Fidalgues*, or Gentlemen, tho they be but Peasants and Tradesmen: They themselves relate, That a certain one among them named *Fernando*, who had kept Hogs in *Portugal*, coming to the *Indies*, and adding 3 Letters to his Name, caused himself to be called *Don Fernando*, and was in a little time so well known and esteemed amongst the Women *Metices*, that one having chosen him

Nature and Quality of the Portugals in the Indies.

him for her Servant, she caused him to Ride about with a Chain of Gold about his Neck, and a great many Slaves after him; But one day it happened that his Master's Son, whom he had served in his own Country for a Swine-heard, having met him in this Rich Equipage, riding about the Streets of *Goa*, saluted him, saying in his own Language, *Deos Guarde de Fernando Como Esta*; which is to say, *God save ye Fernando, how goes it*: But the other making shew as if he knew him not, ask'd, who he was; to which the other made answer, Was not he the same who formerly kept Hogs for my Father; This Gallant hearing this, drawing him aside, told him, he was, and was here called *Don*, and was looked upon as a great Gentleman, praying him to hold his peace, and gave him Money; yet this hindered not his being known by several, who made their own profit thereof.

Portugal Pride.

But since I am fallen upon this Discourse, I will add, that when these Portugal Soldiers first arrive at the *Indies*, wearing their Country Cloths, those who have been there a long time be-

before, when they see them walk about the Streets, call them *Reipol*, laden with Lice, with a thousand other Jeers and Affronts: When I was there, these Newcomers durst not stir out of their Lodgings until they were dress'd like the other Indians; And then they know them no longer, using Majestick Gravity, and observing the *Sossiego*, after the Spanish manner, always having their Boy, who carries their *Parasol*, or Cloak; without which they dare not come out of their Lodging, except they have a mind to be esteem'd *Picaro's*, or poor miserable Wretches; as in truth they are to those who know them: As long as they are there, instead of vile and base, as they be, they esteem themselves all *Fidalques* and Noblemen, changing their more obscure Names to more Illustrious: I knew one who Enrolled himself for the War, and he changed his Name 3 or 4 times, as 'twas found out by the Secretaries and Registers of *Goa*.

When they hear of any one that knows them, they are so wicked as to send to ask whether he knew such a one or not, and who he was, of what
Cast

Cast or Race, and if noble and honourable, so that if the other answers, that he is some *Picaron*, or miserable Fellow, this Friend reports it to the other, and then for meer Spite, complots with his Associates against him who has told this Truth, and meeting him in the City at their advantage, give him so many Blows that they kill him, or leave him for Dead: This is the cause that one must take care how he tells the Truth of such who are enquired after: But on the contrary, if they tell all the glorious Things in the world of him, of his Nobility, Valour, Power, and other Qualities, tho' never so false; Then he of whom all this is meant, coming to meet the other, immediately salutes him, Embraces his Thigh, and prays him always to say the same of him, and that he is wholly at his Service, ready to reward him with his Life and Fortune.

Revenge of the Portugals. When they have a mind to *d'Accouchillar*, or Slash any one with their Swords, they send Notes to their Friends to desire their assistance against one who has offended them: If he to whom this Note is sent does not come, and

and excuses himself, because such an one is his Friend, they cry him about for a faint-hearted Coward; and 'tis he on whom they will wrack their Revenge, if he has not a care of himself. These are the Actions at this day.

One day standing at my Lodging Door in the Street of the *Crucifix*, I saw two Companies of Soldiers, the one coming from the *Misericordia*, and the other seeming from the *Cordeliers*; and drawing nigh one to the other, laid hands upon their Swords with great fury, but the Rascals did one another no harm, being the numbers were equal: But when 10 or 12 meets with one or two, then you shall see them do wonderful Exploits.

There was one amongst the rest, who to shew himself a Champion, challeng'd another to fight him hand to hand, who appear'd but plainly with his ordinary Arms; But the other wicked and false wretch, carrying with him a Harquebuss, presented it to give Fire, at which the first cryed out that he should kill him like a man of Valour, and not like a Coward; yet he would not hearken to this, but told him, that

The Travels and Voyages Lib. IV.

if he had a mind to have his Life given him, there was one thing he muſt do, and the other demanded, what it was; this Wretch who had his piece cockt, told him that he muſt deny *Jeſus Chriſt*, which the other having baſely done, he firing, ſaid to him, get thee the right way to Hell, and ſo parted.

Horrible Trick.

    'Tis impoſſible to tell the Wickedneſs, Inſolencies, and Irreverences they commit in the Churches during Divine Service; which I have often seen, whilſt they were ſaying Maſs at *Goa*, hearing them ſpeak out aloud, and crying ſo to one another, that none could hear any thing of the Service, making all that noiſe in the Indian Language, and bawling as if they were in a Fair, or in the Fields; and ſome will ſend their Slaves to fetch their *Eſcritorio* to take ſome Letters out to ſhew: Then when they ſee the Holy Sacrament raiſing, they give themſelves 3 or 5 blows upon the Breaſt, and preſently fall again to Bawling, Laughing, and Mocking as before: There is nothing amongſt them but Uſury, Covetouſneſs, Theft, and ſtrange Oaths, and ſuch that the moſt

Irreverence in the Churches.

Eſcritorio.

Lib. III. *of* John Mocquet. 249
moſt ſubtile might be cozened and deceived.

I have remarked that they have a ſort of Honour amongſt them, when they meet about the Streets, the leſſer number gives way to the greater, and if they are but two, they muſt begin to Salute 3, when they meet 'em, and ſo of the others: And indeed I was once ſo deceiv'd; for, being in the company of 2 or 3 of them, as we met with two others, not knowing their faſhion, I began to Salute them firſt, for they were of my acquaintance; but the others check'd me for it, ſaying, I knew not the Cuſtom, and for the future muſt take care how I did the like. *Manner of Saluting.*

They go in the night, with their *Carpauſſes*, which are Dreſſes for the Head, after the manner of a Coat, plucking up and down the Vizard when they pleaſe; and about Supper-time go away to ſuch Houſes where they know there is ſomething to take, knocking at the Door if 'tis ſhut, and enter if they find it open, their Faces hid, asking for the Maſter of the Houſe, they demand of him to lend them 2 or 300 Cheraphins, otherways they will Kill him, and ſo carry away the beſt Things in the Houſe. *Robberies as Goa.*

A Portugal Gentleman related to me how he had been thus Robb'd by that sort of People, as he was going to Supper; For his Slave having opened the Door upon their telling him they had a word or two to say to his Master, entering in by force, and leaving one at the Door, took at the first bout all the Plate which was upon the Table, demanding of him 200 Cheraphins if he had a mind to have them again, which he gave them, and so they went away. If the Justice goes to take them, they have great Bags of Cannon-Powder, with Matches tied about them, threatning to throw them amongst those who offer to approach the Door.

Jealousie of the Portugals. The Portugals are grown so extream jealous of their Wives that you must not so much as look them in the Face; and if they see them but speak to any one, they presently Strangle or Poison them; and when they have Strangled them, they call their Neighbours to their Succour, saying, that a Swooning Fit has taken their Wife upon the Chair; But they never come again to themselves: Sometimes they send for a Barber to Blood them, saying, that they are not well; When the Barber is gone

John Mocquet.

ey undo the Fillet, and let
n out until the poor mise-
re dies; and then also they
eighbours, to see as they
sad Disaster has happened
e in Sleeping.
e are who take their Wives
o Bath in some Brook or
ere make them Drink their
nd a little while after, send
to look for their Mistress,
find Drown'd, which the
owing before, seems to be
onished and grieved at.
ifferent ways, they make
ives, on the least suspicion,
ds relate the Story amongst
There are some who have
vay 3 or 4 Wives.
omen also, when they think
ds entertain any other, rid
f them by Poison, or other-
ake much use of the Seeds Datura.
hich has a strange Virtue; *Poison.*
, or *Dutroa*, a sort of Stra-
great and high Plant, bear- Cisampe-
owers, like the *Cisampelos*, los.
Now he who takes too
tity thereof, Dies in a little
g and weeping like a Fool.

Thus

The Travels and Voyages Lib. IV.

Thus the Women who have particular Friends, gave of this Herb to their Husbands, mixing therewith other Drugs, which is such that the poor Husband falls into a Fury, and Raving, snatches up a Pike or Hallberd to guard the Door, without saying a word to such as come either in or out: Then the *Seniora* or *Lady*, sends for her Gallant, and passes the time in presence of the Husband until the Operation of the Drug (which continues about 24 hours) is over: He who has taken it, not remembring what he has seen or done, so mightily are his Thoughts and Mind agitated and troubled with this Herb.

Strange Actions.

As for the Slaves, 'tis pity to see the cruel Chastisements they give them: For they run them through with double Irons, then give them with a Cudgel, 500 blows at a time, and make them lie along the ground on their Belly, and then comes two, who by turns strike the poor Body as a Log of Wood, the Master Portugal or *Metice* being present, counts the Blows with his *Rosaire*: And if by chance they who thus strike are not strong enough to his mind, or have an inclination to spare their Companion, he causes them to be put

Cruel Chastisement to the Slaves.

put in the place of the Patient, and to be foundly banged without any Mercy.

As I was in my Lodging at *Goa*, I heard nothing but Blows all the night long, and some weak Voice, which Breathed a little, for they stop their Mouth with a Linnen Cloth, to hinder them from crying out. After they have been well beaten, they cause their Bodies to be sliced with a Razor, then rub it with Salt and Vinegar for fear it should Fester.

They have another sort of punishment which they call *Pingar Viue*, which is to drop Lard put into a red hot *Pelle*, upon the Body of the poor Patient, stark naked and lying upon his Belly. The Parents of these miserable Wretches are sorry they brought them into the World, to feel such Torments, which pierces them to the very Entrails. *Cruelty of the Portugals.*

I have sometimes seen part of these Barbarous Cruelties which afflicted me so much, that I have still a horrour when I think thereof. There was one day a poor Indian Girl, who came running to my Lodging, crying out for help, and praying me to be a means to obtain Mercy; but I could not save her, to my great Sorrow; For she was taken

taken and laid all along on the Ground and Baſtinadoed without pity.

There was a *Metice* Woman who had by theſe horrible Chaſtiſements killed 5 or 6 Slaves, which ſhe cauſed to be Buried in her Garden; And one day as ſhe ordered another to be thus puniſhed, he who gave her the Blows going to leave off, the miſerable Creature in the mean time Died; and when he told his Miſtriſs that ſhe was Dead; no, no, ſhe anſwered, ſhe counterfeits, *Daly Daly es, Rapoſe Veille*, that is to ſay, Lay on, lay on, 'tis an old Fox.

Daly daly es rapoſe Veille, i.e. Give it her, give it her, 'tis an old Fox.

Another had a Slave who was not vigilant enough, and ready to riſe when ſhe called her, her Miſtreſs cauſed an Horſe-Shoe to be nailed upon her Back, inſomuch that the poor Creature died ſome time after, the place thus abus'd being invaded by a Gangreen.

Unheard of Cruelties.

Another, for not being nimble enough, had her Eye-Lids ſowed to her Eyebrows, which had like to have coſt her her life, her Face being ſwell'd ſo.

One day I heard another young Indian or Chineſe Woman, who was Chaſtiſed after the ſame manner, the blows ſounding very loud, but ſhe did nothing but groan, ſo low that one could

could scarce hear her very cry, saying, *Ja Ja Me Signor*: I then demanded of my Host's Brother, what it was, who told me, 'twas a Slave a Chastising, and that she would have three times as much if she complained; and that this was nothing to what others endured; and that there was another of them who was hanged in a Chamber by the Hands, for 2 or 3 days together, and that for a very small matter, as for letting fall some Milk as he thought; for they would have made him believe he drank it: And having asked him if they ever let him down to give him any thing to Eat, he told me, no, but sometimes, as a great favour, would let him a little lower, just to give him a little Rice sopt in Water, and presently hoise him up again: But that this would not be all, for after that he would be well Bang'd, and that they only tarried for his absence, that they might begin again this cruel Chastisement.

Ja ja mi Senior.

Portugals without Compassion.

He told me also, how his Brother, who was Master of the Lodging, having one day bought a Japan Slave, a beautiful Girl, and how in Dineing with his Wife, he happened to say in Jesting, that this Slave had exceeding White Teeth,

Teeth, his Wife said nothing at present, but having watched her opportunity when her Husband was abroad, she caused this poor Slave to be taken and bound, and pluck'd all her Teeth out without Compassion; And another's Privy-Parts, whom she conceited her Husband entertained, she ordered a red-hot Iron to be run up, of which the miserable Creature Died.

Cruel against Nature.

Such is the cruel and Barbarous treatment, which the *Portugals* and others use to their slaves of *Goa*, whose condition is worse than that of Beasts: I will add also that my Host, tho an *Indian* had Learnt these Rigorous ways of Chastising, and indeed having a *Coulombin-slave*, which is a certain Country in the *Indies*, and had a mind one day to have him meet him at his house; this Slave knowing that 'twas to chastise him, ran and cast himself into a Well near to the *Misericordia*, and there all bruised his body, Insomuch that his Master having caused him to be drawn out, was forced to cure him himself, for he was a Surgeon. But sometime after his Master being resolved to correct him, this poor Slave fled out of the Lodging: But being forced to return,

turn, there being Guards at all the Ports and other places, so that he was not able to save himself; any way this miserable wretch seeing there was no way to escape the hands of his cruel Master in dispair, came in the Night, and hanged himself upon the Grates of the Window of his Masters Lower-Hall; who in the Morning found him there Hanged, not being quite Dead, and taking the pains to cut him down, caused him to be brought again to Life, by the best treatment he could, for he would not Loose him, because he got him good Money, and the same Slave was still with his Master when I Lodged at his House; and I often saw him cruelly Chastised, and could not prevail to get him excused, because the Master shut the Kitchen-Door upon him, where he did his Execution, at which I was not a little sorry.

Strange dispair of a slave.

One day, as his Wife and he was thus Chastising a poor Slave of *Bengal* a young Girl, their Cook, whose Legs and Arms they brake with great blows of a stick, I endeavoured to help her; But they both earnestly intreated me to forbear, otherwise they and I should
fall

Pity not permitted at Goa.

fell out; So that I was forced to let them alone: For 'tis not the custom there to succour such, except one has a mind to fight and be killed by them afterwards, so mischievous and perverse is this Nation; Insomuch that a *Portugal-Gentleman* being in bed with his Wife, in the Night Dreamed that she committed Adultery with one of his Friends, after he was awaked, he was so Transported with Rage and Jealousy, that he killed her at that instant with his Poynard as she slept, and then fled away to the main Land of *Goa*, and from thence to the Court of *Dialcan*; in whose service he put himself, in the City of *Isapor*. For this King seeing him a Cavalier of good fashion, received him into his service, giving him means to entertain himself, and to be Lodged near his own person, and also hoping to make him deny the Law of Jesus Christ; and embrace that of Mahomet, he gave him one of his Sisters in Marriage, but for all that the *Portugal* would never Apostatize whatsoever *Dialcan* or his Sister could do, which this Prince seeing, was resolved to put him to Death; But she having notice of it advertised her Husband thereof,

Strange History of the Jealousy of a Portugal.

thereof, advising him to save himself with all possible speed, and he asking her if she would follow him, she made Answer that she willingly would with all her heart; so that one Night having provided a great Number of precious stones and other Riches, with two good horses, they set out upon the high way, and made such haste that they soon arrived at *Pichelin*, and from thence passed to *Goa* where this *Cavalier* so ordered the business by Friends and Money; that he had his Pardon for the Murder he committed upon his first Wife, excusing himself to the Justice that she had dishonoured her self.

In the mean time, *Dialcan* seeing the next Morning that neither this *Portugal*, nor his Sister came to visit him as they were wont to do, soon doubted of the business, and having understood that they were fled, sent a great Number of Horsemen after, to catch them, but all in vain, for they were already out of his reach: This mightily vexed the Prince, and caused him to be a greater Enemy to the *Portugals*, than ever he formerly was: For they have no greater Adversary than he, who hath several times besieged them at *Goa*, but

Dialcan an Enemy to the Portu-

at

The Travels and Voyages Lib.IV.

at present they have made truce together, and I saw an Ambassador from him at *Goa*, when *Andre-Furtado* commanded there, who Marched about the City in great Pomp and Magnificence, after the *Moorish Indian* manner.

Ambassadors at Goa.

I saw also other Ambassadors from *Pegu*, and *Calicut*, and it was a very fine sight to see them March, in order with their Guards about the streets, who carried Bows and Arrows in their *Palanquins*, going with this Ceremony to find out the *Vice-Roy* in behalf of the Kings their Masters, to confirm the Peace in their Ports and Coasts, as far as their power permitted 'em to do. But *Andre-Furtado*, being Exasperated against the King of *Pegu*, would not so much as read his Letters, but tore them, telling the Ambassadour that he would come and visit him within a few days; and that he remembered how he had given Port, and entertainment to the *Hollanders* their Enemies, against what had been concluded upon by the Peace and accord made betwixt them: And that he had also an intention to visit the King of *Achin* in *Sumatra*, for he had also received the *Hollanders* into his Ports to Traffick, tho he

Designs of Andre-Furtado.

he at the same time knew that they were their Sworn Enemies: The Ambassadour of *Pegu*, was not a little ashamed at this reception, to see himself thus rejected of the *Vice-Roy*, and returned very sad and discontented to his Master: These designs of *Andre-Furtado* were never effected, for not long after came an other *Vice-Roy*, who was more intent in filling his Coffers than the War, during his 3 years, which is commonly worth to them above six hundred thousand Crowns; especially those who cruelly Tyranize over the poor People.

As for *Andre-Furtado*, he had done great exploits in the Wars of the *Indies* during his Life, and had acquired such Renown that all the Kings, as well Gentiles, as Mahometans, trembled for fear when they heard that he was declared *Vice-Roy*: He had taken and chained a King Named *Cognale*, very strong and puissant, whom he led to *Goa*, where he had his head choped of, bringing thereby no small terrour and fear upon all the People of the *Indies*.

He had also given Testimony of his valour against the King of *Achin*, whom he bravely besieged him in the City of

Laudable qualities of Andre-Furtado.

The Travels and Voyages Lib. IV.

Siege of Achin. of *Achin* in *Sumatra*, and I have oftentimes heard him relate this exploit, when I returned from the *Indies* with him, telling me amongst other things how in this siege, there came such multitudes of *Sumatrans* upon him, that not being able to resist with so few Men, as he had, he was forced to raise the siege; but after such a manner that he first embarked all his Canon, and then the most part of his Men, by little and little, not making any shew of retiring, but leaving some of them all the while to skirmish; himself encouraging them to stand briskly to it, and to retire themselves gradually and orderly towards the Sea: Insomuch that he ordered the business thus, that he carried of and embarked all his Men, as well Dead, as wounded and sound, and was himself the last Man that embarked; thus dexterously deceiving the Enemies, who questioned not but to have had them all that same day in their Power.

Siege of Malaca. He told me also of the memorable siege of *Malaca*, which he had defended, being then Captain against the whole *Holland-fleet*, and about 14 thousand Gentiles, there being ten or twelve
Kings

Lib.IV. *of* John Mocquet.

Kings of those Countries, at that time assembled there with them, and how the *Hollanders* had Landed a great Number of huge pieces of Cannon for Battery, wherewith they fired without intermission: In short, he was besieged both by Sea and Land, without any hopes of Succour, not having 50 white Men with him in this fortress, where he was forced to watch Day and Night, which had caused him to have a dangerous Distemper, of Melancholly an Oppilation of the Yellow Jaundies for some space, and yet every where giving such good orders, he had remained Vanquisher of all his Enemies, until such time as to Succour him, came the *Vice-Roy, Dóm Martin-Alfonce*, who hearing thereof, at the siege of *Achin*, where he was, immediately hastened thither with all his Fleet; of which the *Hollanders* being soon advertised, presently reimbarked their Canon, and the *Indian* Kings were retired each one into his own Country: But in the mean time the Army of the *Hollanders* being come to encounter that of *Portugal*, and thundering their Canons at one another, setting fire to each others Ships, and

Naval fight twixt the Portugals and Hollanders.

burning some, and sinking others. But in the end after a long fight and great loss on either side, the *Vice-Roy* saving himself from the conflict, had fled to *Malaca*, where he died of sickness and grief: Thus much this Valiant Captain *Andre-Furtado* related to me a little before his Death at our return; being then at the hight of St. *Helens*, for I took care of him in his Sickness, and being retired into his Chamber, discoursed with his Gentlemen and Soldiers of all his Wars, Adventures and Conquests in the *Indies*; and I certainly believe that had such a Man continued *Vice-Roy*, a little longer there, he would have amplified the Christian Faith amongst these Infidels.

It was told me amongst other things, that in this Naval Fight of *Malaca*, there was a Portugal, Captain of a Galion, named *Louis de Sosa*, who escaped from the Fight, and flying away with the first, left his Ship, and sav'd himself in the Boat on Land: Then he made such haste that he arrived in the night time at *Goa*, without making himself known; and entering his House, his Wife being in Bed, whether he suspected she played false, or for some other cause, he he ran his Sword quite through her Body, she casting her self at his Feet, desiring him to have a care what he did, but this softned not his cruel Courage, for all that he left not off his purpose, shewing himself more cruel to his Wife than the Hollanders his Enemies; after having left her Dead upon the place, he fled to the Main-Land, and tarried till all was quiet, and then returned to *Goa.*

Since, as I returned from *Reys Magos*, with one of his Servants, who had put the Irons about my Neck at *Mosambique*, being then *Merigne*, or Serjeant of the Ship, but afterwards at *Goa*, had put himself into the Service of this *Louis de Sosa*, arriving both together very late at *Goa*, I went to Sup at the House of the said *Sosa*, who made me very welcome, upon the acquaintance he had with this Servant; and desired me also to visit a Nephew of his, who had a Wound with a Pike in the Groin, when he went to see the Women; 'Twas then I learnt the History of this *Louis de Sosa*, of my Host who told me several other things, too tedious to relate.

But since I am upon the Discourse of the cruel and strange Deportments of the Portuguese at *Goa*, and of the rest of

S the

the *Indies*, I will relate some Histories that happened in or before my time.

Tragical History of a Portugal Soldier.   A Portugal Soldier falling in Love with a young Woman at *Cochin*, Daughter to a Portugal Married there; he so bestirred himself that he accosted a Maid-Slave of the House, telling her, he was of a very good Family, and mightily Enamoured with her Mistress, and entreated her to acquaint her of his good VVill, and if it was possible, so to order the business that he might speak with her: The Slave gained by VVords, but more especially by Presents, which is the best means in those Countries to have what you please with the VVomen, gave her Mistress to understand, that a Gallant young Portugal Gentleman was mightily Enamoured of her, and ready to Die for Love: The young VVoman allured with this discourse, was mighty curious to know who he was, and how he came to see her; for in that Country the Maids and VVomen of Quality are seldom seen, for they go about the City in *Palanquins*: At last, she so ordered the Business, that her Mistress promised to speak with him at a certain hour in the night, which being come, the young Portugal having discoursed

coursed with her of his amorous Passion, she was no less enflamed than he, being of an Age fitting to pass her time, and in a Country so hot, that where any Man can only have the means to speak with a Woman or Maid, he is sure to obtain of them what he desires, if the least occasion present it self: In short, they both resolved to fly away together in some clear night, with the Woman Slave, which they after perform'd, and the young Woman taking her Rings, Jewels, and store of Silver, they Embarked for *Goa*, where being come, and having taken a Lodging somewhat private, they there for some time led a very pleasant Life: But the Soldier, who was mightily addicted to Gaming, soon found an end of what his Mistress brought with her, and beginning to be a weary of her, he conspired the Death of two young Women, seeing they had no longer wherewithal to keep him in his Rioting; and having sent the Slave into the City, he Strangled the Mistress, and hid her; and the Slave returning, he did the same to her, and Buried them in a private place in the Lodging. These Murders continued a long time without being known, until the same Wretch was taken for another Crime, and Condemned to be Hanged, as he was upon the Ladder, he confessed this lamentable and cruel Tragedy, which mightily astonished all the People, and heaped an eternal Regret upon the Disconsolat Father, who had made search in every place for his dearly Beloved Daughter

Another Tragical Act.

I saw another at *Goa*, who often came to the Lodging where I was, who suspecting that his Wife had played a false trick with a Mate of a Ship, so watched his opportunity, basely disguising himself, that he caught the other near the Church of *Misericordia*, and Stab'd him with a Knife in the Groin, when he was not at all thinking of him; tho' he had notice enough of the other's intention; and for this cause wore a Coat of Mail, with two Pistols, but that stood him in no stead: For the Indian was more nimble in Stabing, than he to avoid it; and from thence went straight home to his House, to do as much to his Wife also, who was soon advertised of the Death of her Friend, and seeing no way to save her self, her Husband being already come to the Door, out of Despair, she cast her self out of the Window, where he receiving her upon the point

of

of his Sword, left her ſtark-dead on the place, then he retired into the Main-Land, until they had need of Soldiers at *Goa*; for there are Edicts and Proclamations of Pardon made for all thoſe who are accuſed of any Crime whatſoever, ſo that they may return ſecurely to their Houſes: Such is the Juſtice of thoſe Countries, where they kill one another for every ſmall trifle.

If they have a Quarrel with any one of low Condition, and but little Credit, they take not the trouble to be Revenged upon them themſelves, but ſend their Slaves to Slaſh or Cudgel with a Bamboo, thoſe who have not ſaluted them very low, or unawares have not taken of his Hat before them: They are Covetous of ſuch Vanities, with which they feed themſelves very much.

To this I will add that of the Daughter of the King of *Siam*, who having a White Elephant, a thing very rare in the *Indies*, the King of *Pegu* his Neighbour, made cruel War upon him to have him, and had him in the end, overcoming this King of *Siam*, whoſe Daughter was taken in the War, and carried Captive to *Goa*, where I have often ſeen her, ſhe being then not very young, *Adventure of the Daughter of the King of Siam.*

young, and came to see my Hostess, who was a Chinese, for they were great Friends, and commonly Eat with us, comforting her self at the recital of her Miseries, and how she had been sold to a great Portugal Lord by one of those of *Pegu*, who had first taken away from her all her Jewels and precious Stones, she not being then above 8 or 9 years of Age; altho' great search had been every where made for her, but that the Soldier not having a mind to discover her, for fear of being constrained to restore all these Riches, had come to sell her to the Portugals, her Father's great Enemies, who also uses them no better when he can catch them: For some of them he causes to be put stark-naked in Frying-Pans of Copper, upon the Fire, and thus to be roasted by little and little: Others he causes to be put betwixt two great Fires and set down, and thus to Die in Torments; others, he exposes in the Park of his Elephants to be crushed and knocked down by by them, and a thousand sorts of barbarous Cruelties, which he exercises upon these poor Portugals.

Cruelties of the King of Siam.

This King of *Siam* once having a mind to make War upon another King his

his Enemy, was resolved to send for some of the greatest Lords of his Kingdom to be Commanders of his Army; But some making shew as if they were Sick, by the Counsel of their Wives, who could not endure them out of their sight, of which the King being advertised, sent for these Women, and having caused their Privy-Parts to be cut off, and to be fastned upon their Husbands Foreheads, he caused them thus to walk about all the City, and then to have their Heads choped of.

Strange Cruelties.

This same King hearing, that his Concubines exercised amongst them the Sin against Nature, with Counterfeit Members, he commanded them to come before him, and having caused every one to have a Viril-Member to be painted upon their Thigh, forced them thus to go about the Streets, and than commanded them all to be burnt: Thus you may see what cruel Punishments these Gentile Kings exercise without Pity upon those whom they have a mind to be Revenged on.

It was a Chinese, named *Joan-Pay*, Secretary to Don *Andre Furtado*, who related to me all these Histories, to which I will add what was told me in those

The Travels and Voyages Lib. IV.

Countries of the Kingdom of *Pegu*, next to that of *Siam*, where had happened some years since the most strange and prodigious thing in the world: Some Sorcerers and Witches so ordered the matter with the King of *Pegu*, that he took such a hatred against his Subjects, that he was resolved utterly to root out and extirpate them; to bring this to pass, he expresly commanded that none on pain of Death should either Plough or Sow the Land for the space of 2 or 3 years. The Ground having thus continued Incultivated for some years, without Reaping any thing, there fell out such scarcity and necessity amongst these poor People of *Pegu*, that having consumed all their Victuals, and all other things fit to be eaten, they were forced after the manner of the *Anthropophages*, to Eat one another. And what was most prodigious and terrible, and never before heard of, to keep publick Shambles of the Flesh of those they could catch about the Fields, the strongest Killing and Massacring their Companions to have a share of them; insomuch that they went to hunt after Men as some Savage Beasts, and made Parties and Assemblies for this end. During

Horrible Famine.

ring this horrible Famine, the People of the Kingdoms round about being advertised of this extream necessity, equipped a quantity of Vessels laden with Rice, and other Victuals, which they brought to *Pegu*, and sold it there for what they pleased: Amongst the rest, there was a Merchant of *Goa*, who arriving there with a Boat laden with Rice, as he went from House to House to put off his Merchandize, taking for payment, Money, Slaves, or other things they could give him: He happened upon a House where they had not wherewithall to Buy so much as a Measure of Rice, and yet ready to Die with Rage and Hunger, but they shewed this Merchant an exceeding Beautiful Woman, whom her Brethren and Sisters had a mind to sell for a Slave for certain Measures of Rice; the Merchant offered 2 Measures, or Bushels, and they would have 3, Remonstrating, that if they killed this Girl, the Flesh would last them and nourish them much longer than his Rice; At last, when they could not agree, the Merchant went his way, but no sooner was he gone, than they killed this young Woman, and cut her to pieces: But the Merchant being not a little

Sad History of a Peguan Damsel.

tle enamoured with this Maid, and besides having Compassion of her, mightily desired to save her life, soon returned again to give them for her what they demanded: But he was mightily astonished and sorry when they shewed him the young Woman in pieces, telling him that not thinking he would return, they did it to satisfie Hunger: Such was the end of this *Peguan* Damsel, and many others had the same Fate. This Merchant related this Tragedy to one of my Friends, who passed from *Portugal* to the *East-Indies* in the Galion of *Good-Jesus*.

Now to return to those of *Siam*, the cause why the King of *Siam* so barbarously uses the Portugals, is, that they use the same Treatment towards his Captive Subjects. I have seen one of them at *Goa*, above 90 years of Age a Joyner by Trade, and Slave to a Portugal Gentleman, to whom this poor Man was forced to render every day to the value of two *Tangues*, whether he wrought or no; and went thus to seek work about the City, with his Tools: My Host having one day called him to make something for him, he told me all the Cruelties which was used against him:

Cruelties of the Portugals.

him: For when he failed to pay his two *Tangues*, his Master tied him like a Beast to a Stair-Case, and gave him so many Blows with a Stick, that he left him bruised and maimed; and told me that he had been a Slave for above 40 years, and had gained his Master good Money; and yet he gave him to live upon but a measure of Rice raw every day, without any other thing, as they do to all the other Indians, and sometimes two *Baseruques*, (which are some two *Deniers*) to have some *Caril* to put amongst the Rice.

Miseries of the Slaves.

Thus you may see, how these Slaves live, without either Bread or any other Meat but Rice boiled in Water; insomuch that several die with Hunger and Work: They lie upon the Ground, on little *Esteres*, or Matts, made of Bullrushes, or the Bark of Trees.

The Portugals acquire much Reputation of making good Christians; for having caused them to be Baptized, they thus make them Die miserably: Also the *Japans* knowing their Letchery and insatiable Avarice, seem to have had some reason for their rising against them: For these, who are a subtile and wary People, seeing that the design of the Portugals

gals, after having made them Christians, was to dispossess them of their Lands and Goods by all Inventions; therefore they did not care for their Amity, much less did they desire 'em to Govern, and this perhaps was one of the causes that they have Martyred so many Jesuits who were utterly innocent of all this: For these *Japans* are mightily Jealous of their Wives, and the Portugals had no other aim but to gain them, especially those of the greatest, with whom afterwards they do what they please; which was the reason that moved these People to so much Cruelty.

Dominati-on of the Portugals what?

Japans jealous.

I have found out in the *Indies*, that the Whoredoms, Ambition, Avarice, and Greediness of the Portugals, has been one of the chiefest causes why the *Indians* become not Christians so easily: This is the Reason why the People of the Portugal Churches, who are in those parts, mightily desire some French, Dutch, or Scots to be with them, because these People lead a life less impure and scandalous; which is the thing that most chiefly maintains and upholds Religion in that part of the World. I have there known a Father Jesuit of the Country of *Artois*, who lived in *Sal-sete*;

Religion how and by what maintained

fete, which is a little *Isle* not far from the main Land, depending upon *Goa*; he was there as Curate in a great Parrish, and understood very well the *Indian* Tongue: But afterward the Jesuites took him from thence to send him to *Chaoul*; and I then saw the poor People of his Parish, who mightily lamented that they had lost him, some saying that they had rather have had their Arms cut off, than have seen him taken away from them; For they feared to have some *Portugal*, who would Tyranize over them.

Thus ye may see what honest Men can do amongst the very Infidels, who know how to discern the good from the bad.

As for the Father Jesuits, they pass as far as *China* to make there some fruit, and fit their beards and hair after the *Chinese* manner, and have their Cloaths made after the same fashion, and Learn the Language to Accommodate themselves the more easily thereto; but they dare not Preach the Gospel there but in private, for fear of being put to Death: I have been told at *Goa* that they have Converted great Numbers of them, yea, the very *Mandarins* themselves, *Jesuits in China.*

The Travels and Voyages Lib. IV.

selves, and Governors of Provinces: They have a Church, and Colledge at *Macao*, an *Isle* and City of *China*, and there they Learn the *Chinese* Language:

This is about 45 Leagues from *Canton* one of the greatest Cities in all *China*, where they go through a gaeat River, much bigger than the *Sene* at *Roas*, and is joyned with the Sea.

Canton a great City.

At the Port of *Canton* are continually above three or four thousand very large Boats; and there a great Number of Birds of the River retire themselves which they leave in the Morning to go into the fields to seek their Living, some on one side, and some on the other; then when the Night comes, the *Chinese* sound a little horn, which is heard at a great distance, and then these *Ducks* return every one to his Boat, where they have their Nests, and hatch their young ones.

Fowls.

Ducks of China.

A Man who shall have a Boat garnished with these Ducks is rich; For they sell 'em raw in the Market, and some they also Rost to sell.

A *Portugal* told me at *Goa*, that going from *Macao* to *Canton*, he had been Cozened by a *Chinese* after this manner; for having bought one of these
Rosted

Rosted Ducks at a Cooks shop, seeing it look well, and appearing to be very fat, he carried it with him on board his Vessel, to eat it, but when he had put his knife within it to cut it up, he found nothing but the skin which was upon some paper, ingeniously fitted up with little sticks, which made up the Body of the Duck; the *Chinese* having very dexterously plucked away the flesh, and then so well Accommodated this skin, that it seemed to be a true Duck; of which the *Portugal* was so ashamed that he durst not say a word thereof, to any one for fear of being Laughed at, both by the *Chinese*, and his Companions; and so eat the skin alone of the Duck without making any further ado. *Guile and deceits of Chinese.*

These People of *China* are very subtill, and great cheats, patient in Labour, they wake all the Night long: And when two or three are upon one piece of work, some go to sleep whilst the others work, they come to relieve one another by turns. If they see any Merchant that has Money to lay out, they do all they can to have his traffick; fetching all sorts of Merchandise, if those do not please they go for others, untill they *Chinises cunnig Merchants and desirous of Money.*

they have catched his Money.

There the custom is for all People of the same Office or Trade, to live together in the same street, as all the Painters in one street, all the Shoe-Makers in another; and so also the rest of the Tradesmen, the persons of honour are in one street, the less Noble in another, and never mix together, thinking that a great shame and disgrace: They also bring up their Children in their own calling and no other, and observe this very strictly: When they have a mind to marry their Children, they cause them to come all to a certain place designed for that purpose, which is a great Hall, and there put all the Males on one side, and the Maids on the other directly over against one another: The young women have their faces covered with a Vail, and the Boys go to choose which pleases them best, and keep to those whom they have taken by the hand; this is the manner of their Marriages: The *Portugals* are mighty desirous to have these *Chineses* for Slaves, because they are not only faithful and industrious, but also very active in business.

Marriages in China.

When the *Portugals* come to *Canton* there

there are *Chinefes* on purpose, who make it their Trade to go into the Country towards the Habitations, and Villages: And when they see there some pretty little Boy or Girl, they entice them away with little toys, promising them more; then when they see them at a little distance, they carry them away by force, and hide them in certain places waiting till Night comes, and then come to the Sea side, where they know there are Traffickers, to whom they sell them for 12 and 15 Tays a piece, which is about 25 Crowns.

My Hostess at *Goa* told me that she had been thus deceived by a *Chinese*, at 8 years of Age: A young *Chinese* Slave gave me an account returning from the *Indies*, how he had been also thus trappan'd by a little Cake, which had been given him, made of a sort of paste fried, of which they make very much use.

Chineses, how stole away.

In *China* are a great Number of Hogs like wild Boars, of whom they make Gammons to sell to those who belong to the Sea, and especially to the *Portugals* who come there; and have also the same cunning tricks with the Rosted Ducks, to pluck away the flesh, leaving nothing but the skin, which they

they fill with black Earth, with the bones therein, then rub it so well with the fat that it seems to be the flesh it self: They sell this by weight, and 'tis no easy matter to discern the right from the wrong: Nay, if you put your knife in it, if it be but as they cut it in slices: you may perceive the deceit.

Trick put upon a Portugal. In the *Isle* of *Macao*, where the *Chineses* and *Portugals* inhabit together, there was a *Portugal* Merchant very rich, who being in Love with a *Chineses* woman that was Married, used all the Solicitation and Courtship he could to oblige her to condescend to his will, but not being able to bring his designs to pass, he continued to importune her, insomuch that she declared it all to her Husband, who prudently told her that she should permit him to come at an hour appointed, and that he would make shew of going abroad, and then presently return and would knock at the Door: Having thus agreed betwixt them, it was put in Execution and the *Portugal* had assignation of the Lady, who failed not to come at the time appointed, not a little Joyful of this good fortune at last. But no sooner was our Gentleman entered the House the Door shut, than the Husband knocks at the Door, at which the

Good

Good Wife seeming to be mightily astonished, prayed the *Portugal* to hide himself in an open Tub or *Pourcelainfat*, and having caused him to enter therein, and Locked it fast, opened the Door to her Husband, who without making shew of any thing, let him there soak till the next Morning, when he ordered this Tub to be carried to the Market, or *Lailan* as they call it, saying that there was some of the finest sort of *Pourcelain* therein to sell, and that there was so many Courges, or Dozen, and carried a sample thereof in his hand: When he had agreed with some one for the price, they opened the fat: And then appeared the poor *Portugal* ashamed, and almost starved, and every one mightily astonished to see him there in that condition, and the *Chinese* himself pretending great wonder thereat, and the *Portugal* had his belly full of Jearing and hissing at, without any other harm.

When the *Chineses* can catch any *Portugal*, they use them very scurrilously as it happened to a *Portugal* Captain, who going from *Macoa* to *Canton*, the Mandarin Governor of the province sent for him, telling him that he had been advertised that the *Portugals* had carried away a great many *Chinese* Captives, and for

Treatment of the Chineses towards the Portugals.

that

that cause he must be content to be put to Death, and have his Ship Confiscated: The other thought this very strange, and began to entreat the *Mandarin* as well as he could with fair words and promises to let him go; but the *Mandarin* not having a mind to quit him at so easy a rate, commanded him to be stripped stark naked; and to lie along upon the ground as the *Portugals* do to their Slaves, and others, then caused him to have three blows with a Cane slit in two, and then was let go.

Now when there arrives any Ships in the Ports of *China*, to put off their Merchandise, the *Chineses* coming for the custom, take the length and the breadth of the Ship, then after that they know within a very small matter what the Ship carries, they pay accordingly without regarding what the Merchandize is.

As for the *Chineses* at their meat, they eat like Gluttons, and with an ill grace, as I have often taken notice of, in eating and drinking with them. They have this custom, never to touch the meat they eat, but have two little spatules of hard wood very neatly made like forks, which they hold betwixt their fingers, they eat the flesh of Dogs, which is a great dish amongst them, they are also mightily used to Rice, and little Bread. As for their Houses, they are very sumptuous, and adorned with all sorts of pretty Devices: They also are very Voluptuous, as well Men as Women.

But to return to *Goa*, I think it not much amiss to relate what a Portugal Gentleman told me of their Adventures, which was that once going to War towards the South Sea, with the Naval Army of Galiots, (which every year go out against the *Malabars*) about the middle of *September*, when their Winter is past, and at the same time another Army goes out to the North Sea, which is towards the Red Sea.

The Captains of the Army held Council together to go into a Habitation of the Gentiles, along by the Coast near to *Cochin*, to take away by force a Golden Pagod, very great, with other little ones, who were in a certain Temple there: But forasmuch as these Gentiles were Confederates with the Portugals, they would not do this enterprise in the day-time, but went one night to go ashore in this little City, not far from the Sea, where the Pagod was, and setting foot on Land, they set Fire in every place to fright these poor People, and so went straight to the Pagod, but the Fire passed so quickly, that before they had Power to take the Idol it forced them

them to retire a little faster than they came, and had no more time than only to snatch the Pendants and Rings from the Ears and Fingers of these poor Religious Women, who were shut up, Dancing all the night in their Pagod, according to their Custom: They were near 500, and seeing the Enemy entering, they all assembled themselves together, fastening their Legs and Arms one within another, that 'twas impossible for the Portugals to draw so much as one of them out: But seeing the Fire at their Heels, they only snatched away the Jewels from their Ears, their Fingers they cruelly cut off to have the Rings, and they made such a lamentable noise, that 'twas a great pity to hear them: The Portugals flying away from the Fire, left all these Religious young Women to be Burnt, none being able to succour them; and thus cruelly do the Portugals treat their best Friends and Confederates: He who related to me this pitious History, was named Don *Louis Lobe*; who was of this enterprise, and told me, that this uproar moved him from his very Heart to Pity.

As for what concerns the City of *Goa*, and the Country round about, I pretend not here to make an exact and ample Discription; yet I desire the Reader to take

take notice, that that little which I speak is no more than what my Memory was able to furnish me withall; for being upon the places, I was so carefully watched, as are all Strangers, and especially the French, that I could put nothing in Writing; And this was the principal cause of my Imprisonment at *Mosambique*, being accused of having made a Ruttier of the Sea, which thing the Portugals fear the most, not being willing, that the French, English, or Hollanders, should know any thing of those Countries.

 I will say of *Goa* in a few words, that it is a City excellent well scituated in an Island, environed with the River, some part level, and other mountainous, and may be about as big as *Tours*, but Peopled with all Nations of *India* : It is very well built, in its Churches, Hospitals, Colleges, publick Palaces, and particular Houses of the Portugals and Natives, which are of a reddish Bastard Marble, and Free-Stone: The other Houses of the Indians are like Cabins built with Earth, and some Stone: They have a great number of Gardens, with *Tanques*, or great Ponds to Bath in, and many Fruit-Trees : The Country is good and fertile, bearing Rice twice a year : The Gentiles have liberty of their Religion, but are not suffered to have any

S 4   Pagod

Pagod or Temple within the City, but only in the main-land, and out of the Isle.

When these Gentiles and Idolaters come to Die, if they leave little Children, the Jesuits are careful to take and bring them up, and instruct them in the Faith; and therefore for their Pains, they seize upon their Lands, Inheritances, and Goods: My Host, a Christian Indian, told me, that he had been served after this manner, without being a jot the better instructed.

As for the Men of War, they are about 1500 or 2000, according as the Fleets arrive. I saw a General-Muster of all the Inhabitants bearing Arms, as well the Portugals as Natives and Indians, and were found to be about 4000: They did that, being that time in fear of the Hollanders, who scowered the Sea with a great number of Vessels. I neither knew nor met with any Frenchman there, but a good Father Jesuit, named *Estienne de la Croix*, Native of *Roan*, of whom I received no small kindness: I also saw 3 others, who had escaped from the *Maldives*, amongst whom was one named *Francois Pirard*, a Briton, who has Wri the History of his Voyages: I was told that 3 Months before I arrived at *Goa*, there went away from thence, a French Gentleman named *de Feynes*, who caused him himself to be called the Count of *Monsert*: He was mighty skillful in the Art of Blowing up places; which was the cause of his Misfortune; for coming from *Persia* to *Ormus*, as he was discoursing there, that he knew the way of Blowing up a Fortress, was it never so strong, he was presently laid hold of as a Prisoner, and carried to *Goa*, where he was kept in Prison for fear he would observe the Fortresses; and the first Fleet that returned to *Portugal*, he was sent therein, and kept Prisoner at *Lisbon*, until Monsieur *du Mayne* went into *Spain*, who obtain'd his Deliverance.

As for what concerns the Fertility of the Land of *Goa*, and what it produces, I remit you to what has been written by the Portugals; only I say, that the Fruit most necessary for the life of Man, is that of the Palm. This Tree is Spongy, having little Strings or Veins environed with a Pellicule, and draws its substance from the Sandy-Earth, from which it also draws great abundance of moisture, which is necessary for the greatness of the Fruit it bears, and the quantity of *Esura* or Wine which this Fruit renders. Of the Nut of this Palm-Tree, so celebrated in the *Indies*, they draw abundance of Meat and Drink. There are plenty of these Coco's, or Maldives;

Maldives; but amongst others, they remark one sort thereof which comes from the bottom of the Sea, the Fruit is bigger than the common Palm; 'tis also very dear amongst the Portugals, who suppose it to have a great Virtue for the Disease of the Lungs, and for the *Astmatiques*, or Shortness of Breath, and against Poison. The Nut thereof is very great, long and black, in form of a Gondale; The Tree that bears this Fruit is not to be seen, growing at the bottom of the Sea: but when the Sea is agitated, the Fruit is born from the bottom to the top, and is found upon the Shore.

I come now to my return, when the Senior *Andre Furtado de Mondoso* returning to *Portugal*, sent for me to go with him. We parted then from the Bar of *Goa* the 2d of *Jan.* 1610. Being Embark'd in a Ship called *Nostra Segniora di Beigna di Francia*, which was very heavily laden and cumbered, insomuch that 'twas no small confusion to be there; *Andre Furtado* was very sick when he Embark'd. At last we set sail with a great deal of trouble, because the Ship had Cinnamon almost as far as the middle of the Mast, every day taking care to put by so much out of the way.

The 16th of *January* we saw the Desarts

farts of *Arabia*, and sailed with a very good Wind as far as the Land of *Crimbe*, or Country of the *Abaffins*, and passed along by the Coast the 9th of *Feb*. But the 11th we feared to be lost by a contrary Wind, the Ship beating upon the Sea, and drawing in much Water. The Senior *Andre Furtado* sick as he was, seeing this extremity, got upon the Deck to order the Ship to be lightned and pumped, and about 300 Black Slaves, with some Mariners, were 3 days and nights, and had much ado to empty it.

The 15th of *Feb.* we saw the Isle of *St. Lawrence*, mightily covered with Fog, and bearing about to pass the Cape of *Good-Hope*, with a favourable Gale of Wind, we passed it the 16th of *March*.

Being at the height of the Isle of *St. Helens*, we were in great doubt whether we should go on Shore to take there some fresh Water, and the Passengers and Mariners disputed ftifly against the Master and Pilot, but they put it all to the Sieur *Andre Furtado*, who was then mortally Sick, and who said that he had no Orders from the King of *Spain* to go to the said Isle, except it was in case of great necessity, and that he feared to find there some Enemies, who might give them trouble, it being the place where they

com-

commonly came: Thereupon he commanded a review to be taken of the fresh Water that remained, to know if it would hold out for every one to have half a Pint a day for 4 Months, for we reckoned we had so long to sail: This enquiry exactly made, 'twas found within a very small matter of this measure; so that we made the best of our way, the Wind being favourable. We could not persuade Senior *Andre Furtado*, tho he was sick, to repose himself in this little Isle of St. *Helen*; so that in the end this poor Gentleman, being weakened and overcome with sickness, died the first of *April*: His Body was Embalmed that it might be carried to *Portugal*, for in the Ships there is never want of *Camfre*, *Benjoin*, and Aromatical Things for that purpose: There was a Portugal Barber, who knew only how to Shave and let Blood; and having a mind to make Balm, in causing the *Benjoin* to be melted, and to fill the Body therewith: I releived him from this trouble and apparent Error, and made him acknowledge his Fault; and so having Embalmed the Body, and put it in a Coffin, It was laid up in the Guard-Robe of the Chamber, with a lighted Lamp by it, and we carried it without any smell or inconveniency as far as *Lisbon*.

We

We passed close by the *Isles* of the *Acores* and along by them, were great debates betwixt those of the Ship, some were resolved to go on shore by force, which the Captain, the Master and Pilot would by no means yeild too: This came all from the passenger Souldiers, who came to dispatch their business in *Portugal* for Recompence of their Services in the *Indies*: For then the King gives them some Captain-ships of Fortresses in the *Indies*: But the Captain caused some of the most Mutinous to come before him; (for they were ready to lay hold upon their Arms, and made no small stir and ado, thinking themselves still in the *Indies*) but he soon made them to know their duty; and persuing our course with a very good wind, we arrived at *Cuscais* the 2d of *July*, and the next day I went on shore, leaving all my things on Board, which were there above a Month without being able to get them out; there being Guards which stole them all away. At the Months end the Kings Duty being paid, the small things were brought on Shore, and there was several who found their Chests fast shut, but nothing within them: I was one of those also; but it was small loss to me, not having brought back any thing of value from
those

commonly came: Thereupon he commanded a review to be taken of the fresh Water that remained, to know if it would hold out for every one to have half a Pint a day for 4 Months, for we reckoned we had so long to sail: This enquiry exactly made, 'twas found within a very small matter of this measure; so that we made the best of our way, the Wind being favourable. We could not persuade Senior *Andre Furtado*, tho he was sick, to repose himself in this little Isle of St. *Helen*; so that in the end this poor Gentleman, being weakened and overcome with sickness, died the first of *April*: His Body was Embalmed that it might be carried to *Portugal*, for in the Ships there is never want of *Camfre*, *Benjoin*, and Aromatical Things for that purpose: There was a Portugal Barber, who knew only how to Shave and let Blood; and having a mind to make Balm, in causing the *Benjoin* to be melted, and to fill the Body therewith: I releived him from this trouble and apparent Error, and made him acknowledge his Fault; and so having Embalmed the Body, and put it in a Coffin, It was laid up in the Guard-Robe of the Chamber, with a lighted Lamp by it, and we carried it without any smell or inconveniency as far as *Lisbon*.

We

We passed close by the *Isles* of the *Acores* and along by them, were great debates betwixt those of the Ship, some were resolved to go on shore by force, which the Captain, the Master and Pilot would by no means yeild too: This came all from the passenger Souldiers, who came to dispatch their business in *Portugal* for Recompence of their Services in the *Indies*: For then the King gives them some Captain-ships of Fortresses in the *Indies*: But the Captain caused some of the most Mutinous to come before him; (for they were ready to lay hold upon their Arms, and made no small stir and ado, thinking themselves still in the *Indies*) but he soon made them to know their duty; and persuing our course with a very good wind, we arrived at *Cuscais* the 2d of *July*, and the next day I went on shore, leaving all my things on Board, which were there above a Month without being able to get them out; there being Guards which stole them all away. At the Months end the Kings Duty being paid, the small things were brought on Shore, and there was several who found their Chests fast shut, but nothing within them: I was one of those also; but it was small loss to me, not having brought back any thing of value from those

those Countries, where I had nothing but bad fortune; and was very well content that I was safely returned tho I was not a little indisposed in my person, because of these salt and spiced waters, which I had then been forc'd to drink till they so heated my Stomack, that my mouth cast out burning Vapours, and I could scarce quench my thirst.

At length being restored to my health by cooling remedies, and seeing my self strong enough to reassume the way to my dear native Country, where I had a great desire to see my self again after so many fatigues and dangers, I embarked the 17th of *August* in a Ship belonging to one *Picare Simon* of *Rochelle*. and in our Company was another Ship called also the *Dauphin* of *Rochelle*: But being in the Sea, we were so beaten with Storms, that the *Dauphin*, mightily desired us to keep by them; but one Night in a very great Storm, her Sails split and tore to pieces, they were forced to bend their main Top Sail in stead of their main Sail, insomuch that in the Morning we saw her at above 3 Leagues of us, and had put abroad their Ensign to cause us to come up to her; which we did as soon as might be, and coming near her, we saw them crying out for *Misericorde*, or mercy, for they were

were sinking: We boarded them at the *Poop*, and they saved themselves, who could in our Ship; it was a great pity to see them in this extremity: I saved one of them along by the side, who fell from the Stern of our Ship: Thus was the Ship lost and all the Merchandise that was in her; and afterward we arrived at *Rochelle* the 3d of *Sept.* from thence I came to *Paris* the 23 of the same Month, when our young King *Lewis* XIII. (whom God preserve and prosper) was gone to be Crowned at *Rheims*.

I had heard no News of the unhappy accident happened in the Person of King *Henry* the Great, my good Master, untill we were in sight of *Lisbon*; for then, according to the custom, there came a *Caravel* from the Port to see and know who we were, who told us that sad History, which I could scarcely believe, but coming to Land it was too much confirmed, to my Eternal regret and sorrow.

FINIS.

THE TRAVELS AND VOYAGES OF John Mocquet,

INTO

Syria, and the *Holy Land*.

BOOK V.

Aving return'd to *Paris* from so many long and troublesome Voyages after the Death of King *Henry the Great*, whom I can never sufficiently lament, and all other good French Men, I had a desire to make a Religious Voyage into the *Holy Land*, there to go pay (like a good Christian) so many Vows I had made to God for the innumerable Perils and Dangers, from which it hath pleased him, mercifully to preserve me so often.

Embarkment at Marseilles.

In this Resolution I parted from *Paris* the 19th. of *July*, 1611. and took Coach to *Marseilles*, where I arrived the 14th. Day of *August*, and tarried there for some Days to wait for passage, which at last I found in a Ship of *Toulon*, called the *St. Francis*, belonging to *Ode Bergue*, and *Vander Strate*, Merchants of *Toulon*, and *Marseilles* : There embarking, the 8th. of *September*, we set sail, and the

Sardania. 12th. saw the Isle of *Sardania*, which we left on the North-East; and the 15th. we saw the Coast of *Barbary*,

Guerite Isle. passing near the Isle of *Guerite*, which is a little Island not far from the main Land, where the Robbers and Pyrates lurk, as well *Turks* as *Christians*; we had this Isle towards the South-West.

Malta.
Sicilia.

The 17th. we passed along by *Malta*, then by *Sicilia*, where we found a Ship in the fashion of a Galiot, who came directly towards us to know if they durst engage us; but when they had perceived our Strength, they tacked about, taking their course towards *Barbary*, seeking other Prey more easie to surprize.

The 21ft. we paffed along by *Can-* Candia.
dia, where there is a little Ifland cal- Agofe *Ifle.*
led *Agofe,* which advances into the
Sea with a Point towards the South :
Then the 27th. we went to the Ifle of
Cyprus, towards the City of *Bafe,* Cyprus.
not far from the Coaft, and went to
pafs the Cape *de Gate,* defigning to
go to *Famagufta:* But having a fharp
Gale, and good for our Voyage, we
continued our courfe, bearing to-
wards *Tripoly* in *Syria,* where we ar- *Arrival at*
riv'd the laft Day of *September;* the Tripoly.
next Morning, the 1ft. of *October,* I
went on fhore to lodge in the City,
in a Campo near the *Juderie,* or *Jews-* Camps.
Place: Thefe Campo's are great Houfes, with large Courts and Fountains,
where Strangers retire themfelves for
fhelter, like Inns. Thefe belong to
fome great Perfon, who letts them
out; and he who is the Porter thereof, whom they call *Boabe,* receives
the Money of the Paffengers, and
gives it to the Mafter, of whom he
holds it upon Rent.

 Having tarried fome time at *Tripoly,* *Voyage to*
I had a mind to fee Mount *Lebanon;* *Mount Le-*
and for this effect took a Turk, with *banon.*

an Ass to carry our Victuals: We left the City the 11th. of *November*, and went over very high Mountains, and troublesome to pass, and in the end arrived at the Lodging of a *Chaldean* Archbishop, called Father *George*, who received us after the best manner he could. His House is right above Mount *Lebanon*; his Church is under his Habitation, and a Water-mill underneath his Church. I saw a good Father, a *Chaldean* Priest, and Kinsman to this Archbishop, who came from grinding his Corn, as he shewed us by his Visage all white with Meal; and seeing him in this case, we knew him not to be of the Church, until the next Morning, which was *Sunday*, when I saw him go with the Host in his Hand from thence to a Village, there to sing Mass. The Father *George* lived there with his Mother, Sisters, and Nieces, making one and the same Family altogether. He shewed me a Chapel above his House, upon a little Rock, right under Mount *Lebanon*, and told me there was there a Hole, out of which every Year, upon the 1st. Day of *May* only, gushes an abundance of Water

Water, at such time as they sing Mass in the Chapel. The Mountain is covered all over with Cyprus-Trees. The Place is very agreeable; but the Winter is there very troublesome, because of the excessive Cold, and great Snows, which mightily afflicts these good Fathers, so that they are constrained for that cause to pass the Winter near *Tripoly*, and return there again in the Spring.

 The next Morning after we had heard Mass, we set forward towards the Place where the Cedars are, about *Cedars.* Three Leagues from thence; where being come, we had such a cold blast of Wind, that my Turk blew his Fingers: I order'd him to get upon a Cedar-Tree to break me off some Branches, but he tarried there not long; for the Cold soon made him to descend, that he could not get me so much as I desir'd. But I feared he would tumble down, being half frozen; and besides, he had not eaten his Breakfast, because of their *Roma-* *Romadan,* *dan,* in the which they fast till Even- *or Fast.* ing, not daring to eat any thing upon pain of Death, except it be in private, and those who observe not strictly their Law ; and when I saw him tremble in good earnest, I presently made him come down, fearing to lose him.

Canibi.

From thence we reassumed our way to return to *Canibi*, which is a Place belonging to the *Chaldean* Patriarch, and had very bad Weather of Rain ; so that we arrived there late in the Evening, after having passed many little Habitations, situate for the most part upon the side of inaccessible Rocks, and are almost all *Chaldean*, and *Greek* Christians, with some few Moors amongst them. We were there very well received, and drank excellent Wine, which grows in these Mountains.

Inundations.

The next Day having heard Mass, we returned to *Tripoli*, where I passed a very troublesome Winter, because of the great Inundations of Water which came from the Mountains, and so swelled a little River which runs through the middle of the City, that it bore down part of the Houses, with great loss of Merchandise, and Water-mills, which it carried

ried quite away, with the Stone-bridge. This was the cause that Bread was there very scarce and dear, that we had much adoe to get a little black Biscuit, half spoiled, which was sold me by weight, and at what rate they pleased, and that by halves; and the People already began to cry out for Famine. The House of the Consul of *France* fell upon him, and killed him: Several other Houses fell also by this disaster of Inundation, which came in a Night without so much as dreaming of.

    The City of *Tripoly* is situated in a Valley below Mount *Lebanon*, and has still an old Castle with square Towers, built formerly by the French, the then Lords of the *Holy-Land*: There is at present a Garrison of *Turks*. The City may be as big as *Pontoise*, and there is but a small River that passes that way, which is very subject to break out of its Banks when the Snows of the Mountain melt, and then does a thousand Mischiefs, as I have seen when I happened to be there: All the rest of the time one may pass almost dry upon the Stones. The City is

A Description of Tripoly.

very

very well built; the Houses low, except those of the Great Ones; and there inhabits a great Number of *Grecian* Christians, *Jews*, some *French*, and *Italians*. Those of *Marseilles* trade mightily there.

There is also a Bassa, or Governour, who, in the Summer, goes with his Nobility to lie in Tents in the Meadows betwixt the Port and the City, and there exercise themselves at the Launce, and Sword. This City is about Nine Days Journey from *Aleppo*.

Parting for Jerusalem. The Spring being come, I began to think of going to *Jerusalem*; and for this purpose, parting the 9th. of *April*, 1612. with a *Mouquary*, or *Turkish* Carrier, we took our way towards *Damascus*, and the first Night lay in a little Meadow by a River-side, where we endured no small cold, because of the Winds which come from these Mountains laden with Snow. The next Day we raised our little Caravan, which consisted of *Turks* and *Jews*, and a *Greek* Christian and his Sister: This young *Grecian* Girl was not above Twelve Years of Age, and was very vertuous and brisk, being mounted upon

upon her little Afs, which was led by her Brother. We paſſed many Mountains, and arrived at a Habitation of *Arabians*, where we had but very bad Lodging, lying along the Walls of the Houſes which are in very dirty Places: I made my Pillow of a Stone.

The next Day we went to Dine at *Armel*, a little City of the *Arabians*, and then retired into a Houſe of Pleaſure very ſtately and magnificent, but there was none in it; it ſerves only for a retiring Place, and Lodging for the *Caravans*, they giving ſo much to the Porter who is the Keeper thereof: This Houſe is furniſh'd *a la Moreſque*, and ſtrong enough to hold out an Aſſault. A certain *Turk* who returned from the Baſſa of *Tripoly* cauſed it to be built after this manner: The Baſſa commanded him to be taken and brought into his preſence, telling him, That being his Subject he was greater than he, in regard of the ſumptuous and ſtrong Houſe which he had cauſed to be built, that he might rebel againſt him; and thereupon commanded his Head to be chopp'd off in recom-

Armel.

*After the Mooriſh manner.

recompence of several good and notable Services he had done him.

Parting from this Place, we went along by a Rivolet to lodge upon a little Hill within the enclosure of certain Walls very low, where there was a small Cottage of the *Arabians:* We lay along the Wall, and passed the Night with great fear of the thievish *Arabs.* We parted from thence betimes in the Morning, and came to *Bailbec,* a very ancient City, where formerly lived Christians, the Ruines of a Church remaining there yet. I went into the City with my *Mouquary,* which was the *Turk,* that furnished me with a Horse to ride upon, and there we sought for a little Wine, but privately, it being forbid to sell any: We found some White, very good, at the House of a *Grecian,* who earnestly desired us to hide it. They failed not to come to search our Cloaths, and other things, but they could not find it, for we had locked it fast up. We lay without the City along the Walls which are made of great Stones, not of Masons Work, but roughly set one upon another, each one above

Lib. V. *of* John Mocquet.

12 or 15 Foot long. The Baſſa of this Place went out about Noon with all his Cavalry and Infantry, going to ſome Place, not far from thence, upon a Quarrel which he had againſt the Baſſa of *Damaſcus*. He marched in excellent good order, eſpecially for *Turks* and *Arabians* to obſerve.

We diſlodged from this Place two or three Hours before Day, paſſing by Rocks, of which the moſt part were broke and thrown down, and the Veins and Pipes bigger than ones Arm are ſtill to be ſeen, through which flowed the Water before they were broke down: There is amongſt others one of theſe Rocks ſlit in two, about 3 or 4 Leagues from *Damaſcus*; and the River of *Jordan*, which comes from Mount *Lebanus*, paſſes with great ſwiftneſs very near it, there is a Bridge over which we paſſed: Along by this River are places cut like Caves within the Rock, where lived formerly certain Hermits; and truly the Place is very proper for a ſolitary Life, being exceeding deſert, and of difficult acceſs. We went to lie in a certain Habitation, and the next Day we arrived at

Aquaducts.

Jordan.

at *Damascus*, which was on *Palm-Sunday* Eve, the 14th. of *April*. I went to take a Lodging in the House of one *Ibrahim*, a Rabbi of the *Jews*, to whom I had been recommended by a Cousin of his, which I had known at *Tripoly*. He received us after the best manner he could; but we supped but badly, because it was the Day of their Sabbath, in which they dare scarce touch any thing. The next Day I so ordered the Business with this *Jew*, my Host, that he gave me one of his Servants to conduct me, and help me to buy an Ass. They were at that time making Preparations for their Passover, and I saw them buy Sheep in a Market for that purpose, and this Servant chose the fattest for his Master; so that I had much adoe to hale him to the place where I knew there was an Ass to be sold, which had been brought from *Tripoly* with us: I bargained for it for 19 Pataques and a half one, for the *Jew*: I exchanged my Money, taking for *Spanish* Money, Pieces of Albouquelque, to give to the Cafars, and gained 55 for 50; for the Cafars go for as much

as

Damascus.

Passover of the Jews.

Pataques.

Cafars.

Lib. V. *of* John Mocquet.

as those of *Spain*. Albouquelques are pieces of *German* Money, having the mark of a Lyon; the *Turks* take it for a Dog, and therefore call them Albouquelques or Dog-pieces. I desired also my *Jew* to find me out a *Turk*, which he did, and promised him a Patache a Day, but he was to find himself with Victuals.

Albouquelques.

As for this City of *Damascus*, it is very fine and pleasant, having most delicate Gardens, and is seated in a Valley, as it were in the middle of a Meadow; and there is a Lake and a River which pass cross it, with many excellent Fountains: Amongst others is to be seen that of St. *Paul* near to a Mosque.

This City is divided into two, by a great Church-yard of some 400 Paces, after the Moorish manner: The whole City may be as big as *Orleance*. It is of great Trade; and amongst others, there is a great Street, where there is nothing but Merchandice of Drugs and Spices. This City is encompassed with Walls, but not round about, and has a very strong Castle, and great number of Gardens in the adjacent

Damascus described.

cent Parts. There is a Baſſa, or Governour, and a multitude of *Greek* Chriſtians there, but no *French.* It is about Three Days Journey from the Sea, and Five from *Jeruſalem :* Formerly it was the greateſt Commerce of the *Indies, Perſia, Chaldea, Armenia,* and other Places.

Cafars, or *Toll.*

We left *Damaſcus* the 16th. of *April,* and went to *Saſſa,* where was a Cafar, or Toll : But my *Turk,* to ſave me from paying any thing, and thinking to have the half of that which belonged to the Cafar, put upon my Turbant, which was of the *Greek* Colour, another of white after the *Turkiſh* manner, and paſſed thus without being taken notice of by the Cafars, or elſe they were aſleep in their Houſes; for we ſaw none coming toward us as we paſſed over the Bridge which is there : So that we eſcaped, and went from thence through a very bad way full of great Stones, where I endured no ſmall pain, ſcarce being able to draw my ſelf out from amongſt them, becauſe of the Water and Mire which are together; and this bad way continued almoſt the whole Day. But as

we

we were a good way in these Boggs and Quagmires, we saw coming towards us a *Turkish* Cavalier, with a Harquebuse at his Saddle-bow, and passing near to me, he demanded, *An ta Frangi?* if I was a Christian; and having answered him, Yes, he returned in a Fury towards my *Turk*, who was before me, and held his Sword at his Throat to kill him, had not a poor *Arabian*, who was at work hard by, run to his succour, praying this Cavalier to be pacified; and from thence he came to give me a Blow with his Sword, but I gat my self out of his way, and he spurring his Horse upon me, cryed *Rou*, which is to say, Return; but my *Turk* so ordered the Matter, that he was content to take a Piece of Money, and the *Arabian* also mightily desired him. After that, my *Turk* took away my white Turbant, shewing him that I had one of the right Colour underneath, and that this which he had given me was to keep me from the Sun. This, with the Money, contented him, and preserved us from the Danger of being soundly beaten, and also of returning

Adventure of a Turk.

back

back to *Saffa*, where the Cafars and *Sub-Baſſa's would not have pardoned us. I then threw away his white Cap, contenting my ſelf with my own, not having a mind ever to rely any more upon what he told me. We were in continual fear left theſe Cafars ſhould come after us, upon the Information of this Cavalier, but they did not; yet my Turk was under ſuch a mortal Apprehenſion that they would, that he turned about ever and anon, and pricked on the Aſs as much as he could. We went to lie at *Conetra* in a Campo, where we payed a Cafar.

* *Soubachins.*

Conetra.

The Chelubin, which is to ſay the Lord of the Place, who underſtood a little of the *Gemique* Tongue, (which is corrupted *Italian*,) ſpake for me to the Cafars, that they might uſe me kindly, and take no more of me than he ordered them. He came with other Cavaliers of his Company to diſcourſe with me where I was with my Aſs in a Court; and having perceived my Kit or Gittern amongſt my things, he deſired me mightily to play upon it, which I willingly did, and preſented

sented him with a curious great Pomgranate, which had been given me by one of the Bassa's of *Damascus*'s Gentlemen. He was very well content therewith, and thought himself well payed for the Kindness he had done me with the Cafars. These Cafars are the Farmers and Toll-gatherers of the *Turk*, and are always Three together; one for the Grand Signior, another for the Soldiers of the Country, and the third for the Soubachin, or Governor of the Place. I lay there in a Stable of Mules and Camels, upon a little Grass which I had bought, having no better Lodging that Night than my Ass.

Cafars, or Toll-gatherers.

We parted from thence about three Hours before Day, and found the Company which was going after the *Chec-Marabou*, who parted from *Damascus* two Days before us, whom we overtook along by the Sea *Tiberiades*. This *Chec-Marabou* goes out every Year from *Damascus*, to go in Devotion to *Salomon*'s Temple in *Jerusalem*, and those who go with him, (which are they of the Country,) pay nothing; they are sometimes 5

Chec-Marabou.

or

or 6000. I was very glad to find this Company, for fear that my *Turk* should play me some Roguish Trick, though the *Jew*, *Ibrahim*, had made him put his Hand upon mine, promising, upon the Law of *Mahomet*, to guard and protect me as himself, and to bring me back again to *Damascus*, or at least a Letter from me to this *Jew*: But yet I trusted not so much to that, as to make me neglect being upon my guard, knowing well the Humour of this cursed and unfaithful Race of People, who will kill a Man for a small matter, and especially the *Christians*, whom they greatly hate, and serve them only for their own Profit, of which they are as greedy as Hell can make 'em.

Turks Covetous and Wicked.

We passed then a great Number of Woods, and at length came to *Jacob*'s-*Bridge*, where there was a Cafar, through which passes a very swift River, which is that of *Jordan*, and which runs from thence into the Sea *Tiberiades*, not far distant from thence. These Cafars were *Arabs*; and my *Turk* thinking not to pay so much, to save something for himself, endeavour'd to per-
swade

Jordan.

swade them that I was a *Jew*, and that I was going to *Zaphet* where their Synagogue is; but these *Arabs*, who were very cunning and subtle, saw by my Looks that I was not like a *Jew*; and an old Man, all scorch'd and burnt with the Sun, asked me, *Hady Frangi*? which is as much as to say, if I was a *Christian*? My *Turk*, and another of our Company, earnestly entreated them not to take much of me, and that I was a poor miserable Wretch, and made me pass before with the others, they tarrying there to pay; but for all that, they payed much more, (or at least made me believe so) than I had done: But it behoved me to pass that way whether I would or not. When you have passed the Bridge, you see in this River a little Island, where there is an ancient Building, which they say to be *Jacob*'s House.

<small>Zaphet.</small>

<small>Jacob's House.</small>

From thence we passed through Deserts, where was a great Number of Tents of the *Arabs* on each side, and began to mend our pace for the great Fear we were in, without resting or refreshing our selves at all; and I was very angry with my *Turk*, who would not

not give me time to eat a bit of Bread, being very weak, having set out a little after Midnight, and made so much way; and besides, our evil Fortune was not to find the least drop of Water to drink. When we had passed all these Habitations of *Arabs*, we went to pitch along by a Rock, where it was exceeding hot, and there seeking for Water we found some, though very little, which was Rainwater kept there a long time. We had a mind to taste of it; but it was so bitter and stinking, that it was impossible to swallow the least drop thereof, tho' I formerly had drank that which had been very bad, and fancied that the Lizards, Serpents, and other venomous Creatures, which are there in abundance, had come to drink, and to plunge themselves therein. Our *Turks*, though they are exceeding dry, and are rustical and rough in their manner of living, could not drink the least drop thereof. By good Fortune I had still a Pomegranate or two left, of which I gave to every one a little bit to refresh their Mouths, not daring to eat any thereof before them,

them, without giving them some, tho'
I had very great need of it my self:
But it behoved me so to do, if I had
a mind to live quietly; my endeavour
being to humour them as long as I
was with them.

Thus passed we this troublesome
Way as far as the Cistern of *Joseph*, Cistern of
where we drank some of the Water, Joseph.
which is very good and fresh, and filled also our Teronques therewith.
This Cistern is a little Place raised up,
where there is a Building, in which
live certain *Arabs*: It is covered with
a Cupolo, sustained with Four Pillars
of White Marble; but at present
there is but Three entire, the other being broken.

Having drank enough, we went
on our way; but these *Arabs* striving
to force us to give them something
for this Water, my *Turk* ran to hinder
them from taking my Bread which I
had brought from *Damascus*, where I
was furnished with Provision for several Days; but at last it behoved us to
give them something: And thus escaped we from their Hands, passing a- Valley of
long by the *Valley of the Five Loaves*, the Five Loaves.
where

where our Lord wrought that famous Miracle: From thence we came to the Sea of *Tiberias*, the 18th. of *April*, and found the *Chec-Marabou*, who was going to *Jerusalem* to the Temple of *Salomon*, accompanied with 4 or 5000 Persons of all sorts. The Place where we were, was then called *Lameny*; there we pitched our Baggage hard by a Bush, and in the mean time I went to bathe in this Sea, to ease and refresh my self a little: I found the Water thereof very sweet and still, and excellent good to drink, having a very soft Sand at the bottom. The River of *Jordan* passes with a very swift course just through the middle, without mixing it self therewith, and from thence runs into the dead Sea near *Jerusalem*, from whence it is plainly to be seen from Mount *Olivet*; for it is in a Valley, having the Land of *Arabia* very high, and Desart on the other side, as I saw from Mount *Olivet*.

This Place of *Lameny* hath Cafars, but I met with none of them: I there saw all these *Marabouts Santons*, who dance before the *Chec*'s Tent; and it is a fine sight to see them perform their Ceremonies

Sea of Tiberias.

Lameny.

Ceremonies and Follies, ranging themselves all into a Ring, as in a Dance, then clapping their Hands, and crying *Nila Nilala*; then bowing, and heaving themselves up with a great force: There was a *Santon* that led them by Signs of his Hands, Gestures, and Motions, like a Master of Musick, and who was in the middle of the Dance, following with his Face towards them. It would be impossible to represent all the great Follies and silly Tricks which they shew in these Dances; for there are some of them, who going out of the Dance, cast themselves all along upon the Ground; then two of these *Santon-Marabouts* take him, one by the Head, and the other by the Feet, and stretch him out as far as they can; after that, this Man pretends himself dead, and makes as tho' he had great Convulsions and Tremblings, shaking himself mightily two or three times, then seems as if he gave up the Ghost; the *Marabouts* seeing that he neither stirs nor takes his Breath, look upon him as a dead Man; he who is at the Head, takes his Right Hand, and puts it up-

Strange Dances.

on his Face, then does as much to his Left, and after that, puts them upon his Belly; he who is at the Feet plucks him very hard, and the other holding him by the Head raises him upon his Feet; whereupon presently this dead Man reviving, runs to dancing with the others: They employ themselves thus 4 or 5 at a time, one after another, going to this fine Sport.

As I was beholding these Fooleries, there was a *Moorish* Woman hard by me, who seeing all this, entred into such a Fransie, that she fell to shaking and crying out like the rest, so that they had much adoe to quiet her, making as if she had been ravished into an Extasie.

The Evening being come, they all fall to their *Sala* or Prayers, and light a great Number of Lamps before the Tent of the *Chec-Marabou*, who is the Captain of the other *Santons* and *Marabous*, placing before his Tent all the Standards, where there is writ in *Arabick* Letters something of the Law of *Mahomet*: Afterwards in the Morning, when the Caravan comes to decamp, all these *Santons* take every one,

one

one of these Ensigns, and go singing before the *Chec*, who is encompass'd about with these Standards; then he mounts upon a fine Horse, with some other Cavaliers that accompany him, and march thus in great Ceremony before the Caravan.

As we thus parted from *Lameny*, my *Turk* took me out of the way of the *Chec*, telling me, That in the way where the *Chec* was to pass there was abundance of Water, which my Ass could not pass over: He thus deceived me on purpose, to make me pay the Cafars, with whom I believe he participated. We went over Mountains very high, and almost inaccessible, with no small trouble; and there was also some *Turkish* Men and Women with us, who had taken this way as the best.

At Night we arrived at *Eonjir*, Eonjar. which is a place some two Musquet-shot from Mount *Tabor*: We thought Mount Tabor. the *Chec* would have come there also, but he came not that Day; which those of the Campo seeing, they caused us to enter into the Court for fear of the *Arabs*; and there I accommodated

ted my felf in the middle, with my Afs clofe by me. There was fome *Greeks* who invited me to fup with them, giving me fome Rice and parch'd Beans. After Supper, as I was going to fleep hard by my Baggage in the Court, a Janifary, who came along with us that Day, with 3 or 4 *Turkifh* Women, fent for me, (he being under a Vault, with a great Number of *Arabs*,) and invited me to eat fome Almonds and Raifins with him; and befides that, fpoke for me to the Cafars, fo ordering the Bufinefs with them, that I fhould pay nothing, telling them that I came in Company of the *Chec*, where all was frank and free: But I was fince fhewed the contrary at *Nabelous*.

<small>Turkifh Courtefie.</small>

We parted from that Place before Day with Three or Four *Turkifh* Merchants (the Janifary ftaying there to attend the Coming of the *Chec*) and came to *Gigny*, paffing on Foot over Mount *Thabor*, which is very high, and elevated, covered with Trees like Oaks, bearing Acorns, with Leaves which prick like Holly-Oak. This Mountain is above a League high, and

and the Circuit of it is near Three, the top whereof is plain, and had formerly some sort of Building and Dwelling-place for Hermits, but all is ruined; the Country round about is nothing else but Woods.

Gigny is a little City; where being come, we went to put our selves into the Court of the Castle during the great Heat of the Sun; and being there, a great many *Arabian* Cafars came armed with Bows, Arrows, Darts, and Harquebuzes, who encompassed me about like ravenous Wolves, crying out *Alcafar ara Drehen*, Give us Money. I excused my self after the best manner I could, that I might not give them all which they demanded; but the Master Cafar, without saying a Word to me, at my first Refusal, gave me such a Blow upon the Shoulders, that he broke his Staff, and presently sent for another as big as his Arm, with which he treated me so cruelly, that I was forced to give them as much as they would have. My wicked *Turk* all this while was gotten far enough from me, and caused this Tragedy to be acted, having

Gigny.

Rude Treatment of the Author.

for

for that purpofe led me out of the way of the *Chec*, that he might the more eafily rob me: When he was returned, I gave him Money, telling him that he might go his ways where he would, and that I would have no more to do with fuch a wicked Man in my Company: But he told me that he was obliged to bring me fafe to *Jerufalem*, and to bring News from me back to *Damafcus*, if I returned not with him: Finally, I was forced to bear with this Tyrant, who was never content with what I gave him, and befides denied what I had given him at *Damafcus* for Advance, and that which I gave him alfo at *Gigny*, thinking to have it over again.

We departed thus from *Gigny* the 22d. of *April*, and came to *Caranouby*, a Place of the *Arabians*, in the Country; and there the *Arabs* came from all Parts to fee me, being on Horfeback, with Launces in the manner of Pikes, for that is their ordinary Arms: They endeavoured to rob us; but fome of them were purfued by thofe of the Caravan, who caft Darts, Stones, and Clubs at them, and the *Arabs* rode away

Caranouby.

Lib. V. *of* John Mocquet.

away like Lightning through the middle of the Fields. There was one of them taken, who was led before the *Chec*, who caused him to be soundly Bastinado'd for his Theft.

Now my *Turk* who sought nothing more than to ease me of my Money, stirred up two *Arabians* to demand *Alcafar* of me, or Tribute. I was not a little surprized at that, seeing my self in the open Fields, where there was not any appearance of a *Cafar*; however, I told them that I owed them nothing in that Place: But my *Turk*, who had brought them, urged me very hard to pay it, that he might have his Share thereof, yet I would not give them any thing; and seeing my self near the Tent of a *Turkish* Gentleman, I took the more Heart, knowing very well that he would not suffer me to be abused; so these *Arabs* were forced to go their ways as they came. But my Traytor, the *Turk*, bore me a Spite, and acted the same in a very base manner; for the next Day parting from *Caranouby*, and passing through the City of *Herodes*, where St. *John* was beheaded, and
where

where still a great Number of Marble-Pillars are standing, and Olive-Trees very old, we came to *Nabelous*, a great City, which is said to be *Samaria*. The *Chec* went to pitch his Tent in a great Enclosure, a quarter of a League below the City; and then my *Turk* putting me close by an Olive-Tree, with my Baggage, and my Ass, went straight away to give the Cafars notice: I was a good way from the Tents, and this Villain had separated me from the Company of Three *Turks* that were Brothers, very civil Men, where I was left alone amongst the poor *Arabs* who followed us to *Jerusalem*. As I was thus under the Olive-Tree, eating of that little which I had; for I could find nothing, save a little Paste fryed in Oil, two *Arabian* Cafars came to me, and without a Word speaking, one takes me by the Throat, dragging me along, and the other belaboured me with a Cudgel behind, making me go by force, pretending to lead me before the Soubachin at *Nabelous*. I could do nothing else in this Extremity, but call God to my Succour, and He forsook me not: For at that Instant, a

very

Nabelous.

Cafars Tyrannous towards the Christians.

very honest *Turkish* Gentleman seeing me thus basely used by these cruel Rascals, came out of his Tent, and took me by force out of their Hands, demanding of them what they would have for their Right? they asked Seven Sequins; which was a vast Summ out of the little Money I had remaining. At last this *Turk* so perswaded them in my Behalf, that they were contented with Six Pataques, which are worth about a Crown apiece, which he caus'd one of his Servants to carry for 'em. But afterwards one of these Cafars returned again, demanding of me half a Pataque more, and that by the same means I should go thank the *Chec*, the which it behoved me to do, by the Counsel of this *Turkish* Gentleman; and this Cafar gave me a little Paper, wherein was imprinted the Grand Signior's Mark. Behold the Treatment which I had at *Nabelous*, where the Christians are extreamly tyrannized over.

A little below this Place is a very fine Fountain, adorned with Marble and Stone; they say it is *Jacob*'s Well, or that of the *Samaritan* Woman. In the

the Evening my *Turk* came to me again, pretending ignorance of what had happened: But it behoved me to endure that also, and overlook it as my best way. The *Chec* continued two or three Days at *Nabelous* touching the Sick; for they present these sick People to him, and he stretches out their Arms and Legs: then for his Pains he has Money given him, which his Secretary receives, giving little Tickets like Countercharms, and Notes for it.

We had there great Rains, which we were forced to endure Day and and Night very patiently, without having any thing to shelter us: But seeing it continued without ceasing, I placed my self with these Three *Turkish* Brethren, not trusting my self any longer with my *Turk*, and followed them into the City, with my little Baggage, not knowing then where this my gallant *Mouquary* was.

An Ancient Vault. We took up our Quarters in an old Vault full of Spiders: This Vault is so ancient, that they say 'tis above Three Thousand Years since it was made. In this Place lodge the Camels

mels, and the Caravans, which go and come. I tarried thus in this dark Hall amongst the Mules and Asses, not having my self so much as a Wisp of Straw to lie upon, and being so crowded that I could not lie down, but was forced to remain close by my Ass, who was very impatient; for I cou'd get him nothing to eat.

Having there passed this bad Weather, the next Day my *Turk* came to seek me out, pretending himself to be mighty busie in looking for me; but he was a Drunkard, and minded nothing else but drinking of Shirbet, which was sold in the Tents, from which he never stirred all the Day long, nor the very Night, and would fain have perswaded me also to go there to drink of this Liquor, which they swallow down hot: It's of a very unsavoury Tast, and blackish Colour; the *Syrians* call it *Cody*. In *Tripoly* are a great many Vaults like Taverns, where they most commonly go to drink this Shirbet, which is made of Seed and Water boiled together.

Leaving this Place, we went to pitch our Tents two or three Leagues from *Jerusalem*, in a Place where formerly was a Chapel, which is half ruined, and there is a pleasant Fountain hard by upon the way.

Arrival at Jerusalem. The 27th. of *April*, 1612. we arrived at *Jerusalem*, and were there first: Not far from the City I met with the Soubachy, or Governour, who came out with a great Number of Cavaliers, and all in good order, going to meet the *Chec-Marabou*. This Soubachy ask'd me if I was a Christian; and having answered, Yes, he commanded my *Turk* to take me to the Gate of *Jafe*, and to leave me there at the Gate until he had fetched me a Trucher-Man, which was a *Greek*, belonging to the Cadi or Judge. My *Turk* failed not to do what the other had commanded him, and made me tarry at the Gate of *Jafe*, where I was a long time waiting for the Trucher-Men, and an Officer of the Cadi, to visit my Baggage. They being come, caused me to enter into the City, and led me where the Religious dwell, where they view'd my things,

things, leaving me with these good Men, whom I saluted. After Dinner, they gave me a *Greek* Trucher-Man to accompany me to *Bethlehem*, whither I went, passing by the Fishpond of *Bersabee*, and drank at a Fountain which is upon the Bridge: From thence we went to the Turpentine-Tree, where the Blessed Virgin reposed her self, going from *Bethlehem*; then to the Cistern, or Well, where the Star appeared to the Three Kings going to Worship our Lord; my Trucher-Man made me to drink of the Water which is very good: Not far from that Place we saw *Jacob*'s Tower, which is almost quite ruined; after that, the Place where the Prophet *Ely* slept, upon a Rock along by the Highway; they shewed me still the Mark of his Body in the Rock: From thence we went to see the Field of the Shepherds, and near to that, the Five Cisterns which *David* caused to be made; there are Three of them open, and the other Two stopped up; they are all round in a Ring, some Three or Four Foot one from the other, about a little Stone's-cast from

Bethlehem.

Description of several Holy Places.

the Highway: We there found some *Grecian* Women, and Maids, who were drawing Water, which my Trucher-Man caused me also to drink of, being very excellent. When we came to *Bethlehem*, we went into the Monastery, which is a Place very agreeable; and then the Father Guardian, a good and devout Religious Old Man, put on his Ornaments, and gave me a lighted Wax-Tapor, shewing me all the Holy Places, and amongst others, the Place where our Lord was born; then the Place where the Three Kings worshipped, and and that where St. *Jerome* was buried, and other Places: But should I give an Account of all, I wou'd never have done; I therefore remit my Reader to the more particular Descriptions which have been made of these Places.

After having visited this Holy Place, on *Saturday* Morning the 28th. of *April*, and heard Mass, which was said upon the Manger, and bought some Beads which the *Greeks* make there, I went to see the Grotto where the Virgin fled, when *Herod* slew the Innocents.

Monastery of Bethlehem.

Innocents. As I was coming out of this Place, I met some *Greek* Women, who came to desire me to give some Remedy to their sick Children, because they had heard that I was a Haquin, or Surgion. I instructed them, according to my small Capacity, and as that Place would permit. Round about the City of *Bethlehem* are Vineyards: It is now nothing but a lttle Village, full of old Ruines; and not far from thence is a Monastery, the Ruines of the City of *Bethuly*, where there is no Habitation.

Bethuly.

As for the Place of the Manger, it is at this Day nothing but an old strong Vault, sustained with little Pillars of Marble to keep it from falling: The Vault is gilt with counterfeit Gold; they descend by ten or a dozen Steps: In the Place of the Manger is a great Marble-Stone.

After that, I reassumed my way to *Jerusalem*; where being come, it behoved me to sell my Ass to maintain me, as well at the entrance of the Holy Sepulchre, where I was to give 14 Sequins, which are about Twenty Crowns;

Crowns; as also to give my *Turk*, who so insulted over me, that I could scarce find Money enough to content him: He brought one of the Citiers, or Serjeants of the Cadi, to have me before his Master. When I had payed him by the Hands of my Trucher-Man, yet he almost deny'd that I had given him any thing, and would have done it, had not this Trucher-Man been with me to witness that I had payed him; and he was then contented: yet he alledged, that he had bought me an Ass, not having Money enough to pay for him, as if it behoved me to pay it, as if I had been obliged thereto, and that I had not given him enough for the Courtesie, which he would shew to be as much as the Principal which I had agreed with him for a Month. In the end, seeing my self so pestered with this Man, who threatened to have me before the Cadi, or Judge of *Jerusalem*, I was forced to pluck a Ring from my Finger, and give it him in the presence of the Trucher-Man. But I saw him no more, since I gave him a Letter to the *Jew*, *Abraham Rabbi*, to shew him that

The Author quits his Turk.

Lib. V. *of* John Mocquet.

that he had put me safe and sound in *Jerusalem,* as he had promised.

The *Saturday* following, in the Evening, some Pilgrims that were there, and I, went to the Holy Sepulchre to do our Devotions; the Governour of the City having sent the Keys upon Request that was made to him, being there were lately Pilgrims arrived; and in entring the Church they cried to me *Hada,* which is to say, that I came the last; for the others had been there already to do their Devotions some Days before, and were minded to return there again upon this occasion: Being there, we went all in Procession; and the Father *Bucher,* a Cordelier, made a Sermon, shewing us every Place where our Saviour had suffered any Pain; as the Place where is the Pillar to which he was tyed and scourged: Then we went to the Holy Grave, where he lay and was buried; this is like a little Cupolo, having within, a great Number of lighted Lamps, and an Altar where they say Mass, which is upon the Sepulchre it self: From thence we went to Mount *Calvary,* and saw the Hole where

where the Cross was fasten'd, which is garnished on the inside with Silver; the Rock hard by, is slit to the bottom; there are some Signs of a Chapel below. After having heard there a short Sermon, we went to the Place where our Saviour was set, having the Crown of Thorns upon his Head; then where he was put Prisoner to wait for his Death and Passion, where he was anointed, which is a Stone of Marble as big as a Tomb, compassed with Bars of Iron; and in short, all the Holy Places of Devotion which are within the Enclosure of the Holy Sepulchre. After that, at Break-of-Day, I heard Mass in this Place of the Holy Sepulchre, Confessing my self, and Communicating as devoutly as I could, in a Place so Holy and Venerable, and that with so much Contentment and Satisfaction, that I don't believe I ever received the like; rendering infinite Thanks to my God, for having preserved me from so many Perils and Dangers, and for having brought me into this Holy Place, here to do the Duties of a good Christian and Catholick.

Having

Having thus finished my Devotions, I returned back to the Monastery, and after Dinner taking one of the Religious, with one named *Grand Fils*, a *Parisian*, who was also there: We went to the Street which is called *Dolorous*, through which our Lord passed, bearing his Cross; we there saw the Place from whence *Veronica* threw the Linnen from her Door upon our Lord's Face; then where *Pilate* said *Ecce Homo*; and the Places where St. *Paul* was put into Prison, where St. *Stephen* was Stoned, where the Virgin *Mary* was Buried; the Sepulchres of *Joseph*, and St. *Anne*; the Place or Mount of *Olives*, where our Saviour ascended into Heaven, leaving the Prints of his Feet in the Rock, but at present there is nothing left but the print of his Left Foot; the *Turks* having transported the Right into *Solomon*'s Temple, as I was there told: Then the Place where our Lord wept over *Jerusalem*; the Place where *Judas* hang'd himself, where *Lazarus* was raised from the Dead, where the Three *Maries* went to seek our Lord, to desire him to come to see their Brother;

Holy Places.

ther; and the Stone is still to be seen which our Lord sate upon: Then the Castle of *Eniaus*, where he made the Feast, where he healed the Blind, where St. *Peter* wept for his Fault: Then the Sepulchre of *Absolon*, which is cut in the Rock like a Tower, having upon it a Head of a wonderful bigness, and there is a Window on the side towards the Valley of *Jehosaphat*, through which they say the Children still cast Stones as they pass by, out of disdain that *Absolon* had made War upon his Father: Then the Place where our Lord fell into the Torrent of *Cedron*, the Marks of his Arms and Hands still remaining upon the Rock: Then where he was Interrogated under the Golden Gate; where he was put in Prison, in the House of *Ann*, upon Mount *Sion*; the Olive-Tree to which he was tyed, which is still green, and raised from the Ground round about; the *Greeks* hold this Place: Then the Stone of the Sepulchre, the Place where St. *James* was Beheaded, where *Abraham* would have sacrificed his Son *Isaac*, which the Æthiopians keep, and which is near to the

the Sepulchre. In short, all the other Holy Places which are in *Jerusalem*, and thereabouts, as they were shewed us by these Religious who conducted us.

Now for the City of *Jerusalem*, as it is at this Day mightily diminished, from what it formerly was, it may be about as big as *Blois*, and is situated upon a Heighth amongst Mountains, not having any thing of plane but toward the side *Jafa*: 'Tis encompassed about with good Walls, built not so much in compass as was the ancient City, which was very great, as the Circuit and Ruines do still shew: They have left Mount *Sion* out, to take in that of *Calvary*. All the City is full of Ruines, and ancient Vaults, and inhabited by People of all Nations and Religions, as *Jews*, *Greeks*, *Latins*, *Moors*, *Turks*. The Governour of the City is called the Soubachin, who depends upon the Bassa of *Damascus*. The Temple of *Solomon* is built very great and high, covered with Lead, and gilded; and all round about is built Places like Chapels: It is built with Freestone. This Place serves them

Jerusalem Described.

them for a Mosque, where the *Turks* will not suffer either the *Christians*, or *Jews*, to enter. The Country round about, as all the rest of the *Holy Land*, is incultivated and desart, full of old Buildings, and Ruines, and is very stony. In short, it throughly feels all over, and in every Place, the grievous Curse of Almighty God, for the Iniquities of the People whom he so loved, for whose sake he render'd this Country the most Agreeable and Fruitful in the whole World. This may serve for an Example to us *Christians* at this Day, who do so badly observe his Holy Law, to which, by his Grace, he has called us in the room of those whom he has cast off, for their Disobedience and Ingratitude. When I had satisfied my curious Devotion in all this, I came back to the Monastery, and the next Day I prepared for my Return, taking a Mule of the *Atelas*, and a Guide and Trucherman of the *Christians*, who was a *Greek*, to whom I gave Seven Sequins.

I then

I then left *Jerusalem* on a *Monday*, and passed through the Valley of *Terebinte*, where *David* overcame *Goliah*. In this Place we found a great Number of Cafars, but the *Atelas* spake for me to them, and so freed me from that Penalty.

Parting from Jerusalem.

From thence we passed by the House of *Jeremiah*, from which runs a pleasant Fountain, which Passengers drink of: Then we came to *Ramah*, a little City, where we lodged at the *French* Consul's House, and the next Morning went to *Jafa*, tarrying there all that Day, waiting for the next Morning; we lay under an old Vault along by the Sea-side. This was a great City, and a good Port, but now all in Ruines, and there is but Three Towers to be seen entire, and some little Houses: There is here nothing to be found either to eat or drink, and you must bring your Provision if you have a mind to eat. The Morning being come, the *Atelas* giving order for our embarking, and having given us a *Greek*, with a great Boat like a Patache, we parted from thence

Ramah.

Jafa.

the

the 1st. Day of *May*, and came to the City of *Cæsarea*, which is quite ruined, and went to cast Anchor near *Caiphas*, in a Place where was formerly a Monastery. We went on shore to look for some fresh Water, and were refreshed by bathing our selves: There was with us a *Turkish* Chiaux, and a Janisary.

Cæsarea.

The next Morning leaving this Place, we went and cast Anchor a little below Mount *Carmel*, where *Elias* made his Abode; then passing along by St. *John of Acre*, formerly *Ptolemedes*, a very pleasant City, upon the Sea-side, and where dwelt formerly the Knights of *Malta*; then we anchored before the City of *Tyre*, where some of us went on shore for Victuals, and to see the Place where, they say, *Sampson* threw down the Temple upon the *Philistines*: This Place is all desart and ruined, and there is a great Number of Marble Pillars, and amongst others, one of a wonderful length and breadth, very smooth, and almost Seven Fathoms about, and seems as if there were Three in one, 'tis broke at one end: They say it is that which

Mount Carmel.

Acre.

Tyre.

Sampson

Sampson cast down, but that is false; for the Scripture tells us, that this was at *Gaza*, another City far from *Tyre*; so that these Pillars must be of some other ancient Building. We took some Refreshments in the House of a *Greek*, who makes Brandy under an old Vault. At Evening we returned to our Petache, designing to set sail after Midnight. As for the rest, this City of *Tyre*, or *Sur*, is quite ruined, inhabited only by some *Moors*, and *Greek* Christians, which live there in Vaults under the Ground. There is to be seen a great Number of Marble Pillars which keep up the Walls, being placed and layed cross one upon another, to hinder the Sea from undermining the Walls. This City was once of a vast Extent, but at present is like a Desart.

 Parting from this Place before Day, we cast Anchor at *Sydon*, or *Sayette*, where we saw upon a little Hill the House of the *Canaanite*, hard by the Sea-side. We went on shore for some Refreshments, and dined in the Ware-House of the Christians, with the Consul of that Place, who told me that
some

Sydon.

Fortune of a Ship of Malta. some Days before came there a Ship of *Malta*, who had a Protection from M. *Joseph Facardin*, Governor of *Sydon*, and that this Vessel returning into the Sea to look for some Prize, had met with a *Turkish* Caramousin, whom she took, and boarded her with some Knights and Soldiers, who leaving their Admiral some Leagues from thence, came to *Sydon* to take in some Refreshments, and by chance the Brother of him who had lost the Ship was there at that time; who, when he saw his Brother's Ship, he cried out to the *Moors* of the City, How was it possible that they would suffer those Dogs, the Christian Robbers, (for so they call us,) to come thus within their very Port, after having taken their Goods. Whereupon those of the City immediately ran to Arms, and leaping into Boats, fell upon this Caramousin, and fought them on all sides: They within defended themselves valiantly, as long as their Powder lasted, but the most part of them being killed or wounded, the rest were forced to yield, and be carried into the City, where they had their Heads chopped off,

off, being 16 in all. A few Days afterwards the Admiral sent his Boat to *Sydon*, to enquire after his Men; but there was Seven or Eight of them arrested and made Prisoners while I was there. The Consul told me moreover, That M. *Joseph Facardin* had promised him to let them escape in the Night-time, without the Knowledge of the People who were exasperated against them.

This *Emir Joseph*, commonly called the *Ermine of Sydon*, or *Emir de Sayede*, is very courteous and kind to the Christians; and is said to be descended from those ancient Kings of *Jerusalem*, who were of the Blood of the Princes of *France*; and this is he who is said to be since come into *Tuscany* to the great Duke, with an Intention to become Christian, and to propose Means to the Christian Princes how to chase the *Turks* from those Parts.

Leaving *Sydon*, we went to lie at *Baruth*, which is a Place very pleasant and delectable, having two little Fortresses upon the Sea-side. They say that this *Baruth* is the Place where St. *George*

Baruth.

St. *George* flew the Dragon, and delivered the Maid, as the Pourtrayes shew which are made thereupon.

Tripoly. The next Day, the 6th. of *May*, we arrived at *Tripoly*, where I continued for some Days, employing my self in gathering certain curious Plants, bearing excellent and odoriferous Flowers, of which I gathered a great quantity upon Mount *Lebanus*, and about the City of *Tripoly*; all which I lay'd safe up to carry to the King, as at my Arrival at *Paris* they were planted in the Garden of the *Lovre* which is before His Majesty's Chamber, whom I shewed several excellent Flowers.

The Bassa of *Tripoly* is a Man very Proud and Cruel; and I was told there, That once he being amorous of a very beautiful young Woman of one of the best Houses in the City, and seeing that he could not bring his Desires to pass by any sort of Artifice, he resolved to use Violence; and watching his opportunity when she went to the Stoves with her Mother, as it was their Custom; where pre-

Barbarous Cruelty of a Bassa. sently going, he took this poor young Woman by force, and having had his Will

Will of her, he took his Gangear, or Knife, made in the form of a Croisant, and ript her open quite from the Privy-Parts up to the Neck. Behold how these Barbarians give Satisfaction to their desires, how horrible and wicked soever they be!

I was also told how that this Bassa, at the Arrival of a certain *French* Ship, called the *Dauphin*, belonging to the Sieur *de Moisset*, had a mind to go on board her, where having been treated with all the Complaisance imaginable, at his coming out from thence one of his Favourites reproached him for eating with the Christians; at which he was in such a Fury, that he cast his Gangear at him, with which he so wounded him, that had not the Surgeon immediately dressed him, he had died thereof upon the Place. They relate several other cruel Acts and Violences of this Man, which are very ordinary and common to all these Race of Infidels.

After having tarried some time at *Tripoly*, I parted from thence the 18th. of *May*, and embarked to return to *France*. We passed along by the Isle

Isle of *Cyprus* the 21st. and the 25th. we saw the Coast of *Turkey*, then the Mounts of *Phenico* and *Sately*, and not far from the Isle of *Rhodes*, which we left towards the North-West. After that, we passed by the Isle of *Candia*, where we espied Two *Turkish* Caramousins, driving full sail upon us; but when they saw themselves too weak for our Vessel, they tacked about again: We chased them with our Shot, but Night coming on, they escaped us; they being in great Fear, and using their utmost endeavour with Sails and Oars to get themselves out of our reach. From thence we passed along by the Isle of *Malta*, and the 12th. of *June* saw the Isle of *Sardania*, which we left to the North-East; and in the end, by the Grace of God, arrived at *Marsailles* the 19th. of *June*. I made not long stay there, but only to carry a Letter which I had for Monsieur the First President of *Varix*, at *Aix*, from whence I returned again to *Marsailles*, and from thence came streight to *Paris*, where I arrived the 24th. of *July*, 1612. *For which, God be Praised for evermore.*

END of the FIFTH BOOK.

THE

THE TRAVELS AND VOYAGES OF John Mocquet,
INTO SPAIN.

Being design'd to travel to other Places, and the Causes which made him desist therefrom.

BOOK VI.

BEING returned from *Syria*, and the *Holy-Land*, with quantity of curious Plants, and other rare things, which by my diligent Search in several Places I had procured to present to the King, and

Queen-

Queen-Regent, I failed not, so soon as I came to *Paris*, to go do my Reverence to Their Majesties, who were very glad to see my Rarities, and commanded that a fit Place should be given me in their Palace of the *Thuilleries*, there to frame a Cabinet of all sorts of Rarities, and other curious things which I had gathered together in all my Travels throughout the World. But after having so well begun what I had at that time in hand, I judged that to pursue it according to my Desire, it would be necessary for me to undertake some more Voyages, and I had no less design than to encompass the whole World, first by way of the Occident, and from thence by the Orient to return again into our Occident; an Enterprize, I must confess, so great, that the only Presumption of so much as ever having it in my Mind, I believe would have gained me Glory enough; and yet I hoped, that by the Grace of him who had always conducted me every where, I should have been able to have brought it to pass. But I was defeated of these my Purposes by the Occasions following.

Cabinet in the Thuilleries.

With

With this Intention then I left *Paris*, and followed Their Majesties to *Tours*, in the Voyage which they made there in the Year 1614. in *July*. From thence I embarked upon the River *Loir*, to go to *Nantes*, and to St. *Leiger*, to wait for occasion and conveniency to pass to *Portugal*, from whence I was to pursue my Designs. But having put out to Sea, the Wind turned so contrary, that we were forced to draw back to St. *Leiger*, tho' not without a deal of Trouble; and there hearing that the King was at *Nants*, I took the Occasion to go there to furnish my self with some Passports which I had forgotten; and which I judged needful for my Voyage.

This being done, I returned to St. *Leger*, but I found that the Vessel in my absence had set sail, having a right Wind; and which was worse, had also carried away all my Provisions which I provided for the Passage, with some other things, which I never could hear of since. This was a great Hindrance to me, and also an unlucky Presage for my grand Design. Yet it hindred

Voyage into Spain. me not from embarking as well as I could in another Ship of *Aulonne* which was going to *Andalusia*: The Ship was called the *Florisand*, and the Master *Franchois Michaud*. We first of all put in at *Aulonne*, then with a right Wind we set out Seven or Eight in Consort, for so many Ships we were in all, bearing towards *Spain*; and having continued some time upon the Sea, and given chase to some Cruisers, we arrived in the Cape of St. *Vincent*; and taking Cognizance of the Cape, we ran along by the shore near the Port *des Algerves*, where some of our Ships anchored to Traffick, and the rest bore to *San Lucar de Baramede*, where our Ship was bound, being laden with Cloth.

Being arrived in this Place, I began to think of some way how to transport my self to *Sevilia*, to get Knowledge as well in Physick, and the Art of Apothecaries, (of which the Practise is something different from ours,) as also to find means to pass to the *East-Indies*, and accomplish the Voyage *Design of the Great Voyage.* which I had proposed to my self; which was to go streight to *Mexico*, and

and from thence to embark for the Coast of the South-Sea, and so to follow the Coast of the *East-Indies*, along by *China*, *Camboja*, *Siam*, *Malaca*, *Peru*, *Bengall*, *Coromandel*, *Malabar*, *Goa*, *Diu*, *Ormus*, and from thence to return by Land through *Persia*, and *Babylon*, to *Aleppo*, and from thence by Sea repair to *France*, my own native Country; thus to accomplish so great a Voyage, and by the Example of those famous Heroes, *Magallan*, *Drake*, *Cavendish*, and *Oliver Van der Nort*, to encompass the whole Universe. But God had otherways disposed thereof, and for my own Good; his Pleasure being always Just, for his own Glory and our Salvation.

Parting then from *San Lucar*, following the *Mareme*, along by the great River *Guadalquivir*, I came to *Seville*, and immediately placed my self in the Shop of the most famous Apothecary of the whole City, in the Street called *di los Francos*: The Master was named *Alonso Rodrigo*, a *Portuguese*, with whom I continued for some time, both to learn the Language, of which
I had

Seville.

I had already some Knowledge, and to have also some Knowledge of Drugs, of which this Man made the greatest Traffick: For he had Two or Three great Magazines in his House, and as much or more in other Places of the City, where his Children put off the Drugs.

After having tarried some time with him, I left him, for the great Desire I had to find an Occasion to embark; but I was still detained by another, named *Juan Sancha*, who had also dwelt with this *Rodrigo*, and was Apothecary to the Army, and the Frontier Cities in *Africa*, for the King of *Spain*: He was to have a Shop at *Marmorre*, a Place which the *Spaniards* had newly taken in *Barbary*, and laboured mightily to perfect this Shop which he was to send to this Fortress. I tarried then to help him, and continued there from the 3d. of *November* to the 8th. of *January*, until his Shop was finished. From thence I went to walk in the Fields to take the fresh Air, because of the great Filth of this City of *Seville*; which causes there

a very

Lib. VI. *of* John Mocquet.   331

a very bad Air, which is purſued by a great Number of Diſeaſes.

As I was traverſing on Foot ſome Mountains, to obſerve the Nature of Trees, I met with an honeſt Cavalier, named *Pedro Sancha*, as I knew ſince, who courteouſly invited me to come and lodge at his Houſe in a little City called *Corea*, or *Coria*, not far from thence, which I could not well refuſe. He entertained me very kindly, and I ſtayed there till the next Day; then I reaſſumed my way to the Mountains, where I was for ſome Days taking notice of the Plants, and found ſtore of Roſemary, and a great quantity of Maſtick-Trees, with which the Country is mighty abounding; amongſt others, I gathered ſome Thiſtles called *Chameleonis-Ally*, ſome Flowers of Narciſſus, and ſome Mandrake-Apples, which they call *Sebollas de Villana*: After that, when I ſaw that I had but bad Entertainment in theſe Deſarts, where moſt commonly I found nothing but Water, and ſome Raiſins to eat, and ſometimes a little Bread, in the Shepherd's Cabins, I returned towards *Corea*, and viſited my honeſt
                                    Hoſt,

Hoft, the Sieur *Pedro Sanche*, who was very glad to see me, and made very much of me. He afterwards came to see me at *Seville*, to have the Interpretation of some Receipts which had been given him for his Wife who was with Child.

From thence I returned to *Seville*, where the Sieur *Juan Sanche*, the Apothecary, would have perswaded me to tarry with him; but I had my Voyage of the *Indies* so in my Head, that I had no mind to tarry there, but took my way streight to St. *Lucar*, and sailed along the River, with a great many other Persons for Company in a Boat.

We arrived in the Night-time at St. *Lucar*, and I went to lodge with my former Host, who was called *Baſtanuil B·ſcain*. I continued there for some Days to wait for an Occasion to embark: But my bad Fortune would have it so, that the Vessels which were then in the Port, durst not venture out, because they had Advice, that from *Argier*, and other Places of *Barbary*, were put out to Sea near Fifty Vessels, who guarded the Coasts,

and

and were separated 10, 15, and 20 Ships, towards each Height and Cape, where they thought they were to pass; so that they took all they could meet with.

Seeing my self thus retained, and without much Commodities to live by, having already spent the most part of what I had, I was constrained, in expectation of better Conveniency, to place my self with an Apothecary of St. *Lucar*, who made me promise to serve him for some time. But as Fortune never left Persecuting of me, so this poor Man returning one Night from Supper in the City, was arrested Prisoner by the Command of the Duke of *Medina Sidonia*; and after that, the Justice came to his House and seized upon all his Papers, where the Alguaziles, or Sergeants made a strange Ravage. They accused him for having made some Libel against the Duke. I spent this Night with no small Trouble and Uneasiness.

The next Day I went again into the Fields to go towards the Port *St. Mary*, where I made so much haste, after having passed many Places by
Water,

Water, and bad way, that I arrived there at Night in Company of a Religious *Jacobin*, who shewed me a great deal of Courtesie, and caused me to lodge with him in the House of a Muleteer. The Day following, I took the way of *Xerez de la Frontera*, and had no small Trouble before I could come there, for the great Abundance of Waters which I found by the way. At last, having escaped them as well as I could, and being very weak in regard of the great Hunger I endured, by good Fortune I met with two Men in sight of *Xerez*, who courteously invited me to eat with them; and being sate down to eat, they fell to discoursing of several Things, and amongst others, came upon my Subject, speaking of Hunger, and that it is the most easie to be supported, when one stirs not from a Place without doing any thing, or when one is at Work, and thinks of doing some other thing: At last one of them concluded, that he was sensible of more Hunger when he was doing nothing, than when he was at work, and found that there was some

reason

reason for it, in regard that Action diverts the Thoughts: And I remembred that I heard reported, how that the several sorts of Plays, as Cards, Dice, Tables, and others, were at first invented to amuse Men during a great Scarcity of Victuals, and by this means to divert them from thinking upon their Hunger. And therefore 'tis said, That *Drake*, that famous *English* Captain, returning home from his great Voyage about the World, (which he had encompassed,) one Day, as he found himself in great necessity of Victuals, and saw his Men ready to starve with Hunger, he caused them to play to divert themselves; and when they were thirsty, he advised them to sleep to refresh themselves. This Scarcity was so great, as I have heard some *English* say, That they were forced to eat some Blacks which they had brought along with them, and having found near *England* a Vessel loaded with Victuals, they eat so much thereof, that the most part of them died by over charging themselves.

But

Xerez.

But to return to *Xerez*: Being arrived there, tho' not without abundance of trouble, passing through the City, I by chance found my self near the Shop of an Apothecary, where there was some Surgions discoursing together. When they saw me, they cast out some Words of Mocking, because of my Garb, *à la Francois*: But I returning towards them, told them a few Words of Chirurgery in *Latin*; which they being ignorant of, they knew not what to answer, except by naming to me, to surprize me, a certain Composition called *Hieralogodii*; but I asked them, if they knew not whether it was *Hieraspachii*? which is one and the same thing; at which they were put to a *Nonplus*. And thus I left them there, and kept on my way, and by good Fortune met in this City with a *French* Man, a *Britan*, who lived with a Cavalier, and took me along with him, where he made as much of me as he could. There I found a *Persian* Slave, who hearing me speak of his Country, and the *East-Indies*, was so overjoy'd, that he called me his Kinsman, and made me me as good Chear as he could in this House, where he had much Credit.

This City of *Zerez* is fituated on high in a very pleafant Country, as all the reft of the Province of *Andaloufia*, and is not far from the little River *Ovadalet*, famous for the great Battel fought there, where *Roderick* the laſt King of *Spain* loft his Life, with all his Nobility, at which time the *Moors* render'd themfelves Maſters of all *Spain*. The Soil is very fertile in Corn, Wines, Oil, and all forts of Fruit, and produces alfo thofe excellent Horfes call'd Gennets.

When I was there, I was told how that the Judge of that Place, whom the King of *Spain* had eftablifhed there, not having a mind to do a piece of Injuſtice, as the Gentlemen and Hidalgo's of the City defired him, they had invited him to a Supper, with an Intention to put an Affront upon him; but he doubting of their Ill-will, would not go to them: At which they being vexed, made his Image, and burnt it in a Fire before his own Door in a Bravado; and in the mean time,

time, he not daring to ſtir out of his Houſe, which was as it were beſieged by them. Upon which, his Wife went ſtrait to Court, to make her Complaint to the King, and to demand Juſtice of him, which was granted her: For the King of *Spain* commanded theſe inſolent Hidalgo's, or Gentlemen, to come before him, and ordered their Proceſs to be drawn immediately, and condemned them every one to have their Heads chopp'd off. But when they ſaid for Excuſe, that they were drunk when they put this Affront upon the Judge, they were pardon'd, and had his Grace, except Two Brothers, who never would confeſs themſelves to be drunk when they play'd this Prank, and were ſo glorious, that they choſe rather to have their Heads cut off, than to confeſs the ſame, as the reſt had done. And hereupon came the Proverb, That *Los Hidalgos di Xerez Son Borrachos*, The Gentlemen of *Xerez* are Drunkards.

After

After having tarried some Days at *Xerez*, I returned to the Port St. *Mary*, expecting to find an occasion for my Embarkment: But being there, I could not by my utmost Endeavour, procure Licenſe to paſs to the *Indies*, in regard of the rigorous Injunction not to ſuffer any Strangers to go to the *Indies*, but eſpecially the *French*; yet if I had had Money to give, perhaps I might have had this Permiſſion; but I had not ſo much as a Maravedis, nor Hopes to meet with any there, beſides that I found my ſelf ſomewhat indiſpos'd. All this, with the bad Entertainment which I receiv'd amongſt theſe People ſo Uncharitable and Diſcourteous, gave me cauſe to deſire my Return, and thought to embark my ſelf in ſome *Aulonnois* Ships, to return with them to *France*; and indeed I gathered together ſome rare Plants, which I put into a Veſſel, with ſome other things, of which I never ſince could hear any notice, but that they had caſt all into the Sea. In the mean time I wondred why this Ship did not ſet ſail, but ſhe was hindred by the Decrease of the Moon; for the Sea does so follow the course of this changing Planet, that it is taken notice, that the Ebbing and Flowing is in the heighth, when the Moon is in Conjunction.

This Ship of *Aulonne* which I waited for, was called the *Gift of God*, and belonged to one *Peter Bled*: In the mean time the Vessel departed without taking me in, and I remain'd there in no small trouble and misery; and had no other Recourse, but to put my self into a Boat which I found going to *Calix*, not far from thence; and nevertheless we had no small Trouble in our Passage, because of the contrary Winds. We at last went on shoar in a desart Place, about a League from *Calix*, to which Place I went on foot along by the shore: I there found Acquaintance, but I could not stay there long, because the City was filled with Soldiers belonging to the Army of *Dom Lous de Fajardo*, Admiral of the *Spanish* Fleet, who was just returned from *Mamorre*, which he had taken from the *Moors*, and had

had there found a great Number of Pyrates, of whom some he had hanged, and put the rest to the Oar; the rest were partly sunk, and some burnt themselves in despair, rather than they would yield.

 This City of *Calix*, or *Cadis*, was the *Gades* so famous in ancient times, where 'tis said that *Hercules*, after having overcome the *Gerions*, planted his memorable Pillars, as being the end and utmost Bounds of Navigation at that time; but since, in these last Ages, the *Portugals* and *Spaniards* have happily found the *Plus Ultra*, which has given them Passage at their Pleasure through all the Orient and Occident. These *Gaditanian* Pillars were upon the Two Mountains *Abyla* and *Calpe*, placed upon the Extremities of the *Straights*, one in *Africa*, and the other in *Europe* side, now *Ceuta* and *Algezira*; or else the true Pillars compos'd of Tin, Gold, and Silver mixed together, which were by *Hercules* put into the Temple of the *Parques*, and afterwards in the Temple dedicated to him in the City of

Calix.
Gadis.

Ceuta.
Algezira.

Parques.

Gades.

Gades. This Straight has since been called *Gibraltar*, or *Gabel-Tarif*, which signifies Mount of *Tarif*, in Memory of that Renowned Captain who commanded in Chief in the *Sarazen* War, which began the Conquest of *Spain*.

The City of *Gades* in ancient times was not very Populous, and is at this Day a little City, celebrated for the Salt-pits, and Almadraves, or the Fishing for the Tonny. This was formerly an Isle distant above 700 Paces from the main Land; but at present there is only a little Causey which separates it therefrom.

Seeing then that I could not conveniently tarry at *Calix*, I went into the Fields towards an old ruined Tower, which they call the *Tower of Hercules*, not far distant from the *Straights*. I found there some rare Plants, which I loaded my self withal, and saw this Tower, into which I entred, though not without a great deal of trouble, because the Sea beats against it; and besides, there came such a furious Wave, that I thought it would have carried

carried me away. This Building is so well wrought, and appears so entire, that it seems not to have been 20 Years since it was built. Now, as I was amongst these Ruines, I saw a great Wolf approach towards me, which I thought at first to be an Ass; but after having known what it was, I kept my self still, and let it pass along by me, without stirring a Foot, for I saw that it was looking for Food. Not far from these Ruines I found a Temple, where I enter'd, and it looked like an Azoy, or Mosque, after the *Turkish* manner; yet there is an Altar set up, where sometimes they say Mass.

As I was returning towards *Calix*, I found the Sea mightily risen, so that I was a little wet in repassing the same; and had I stayed but a little longer, I had had a bad Nights Lodging there: At last I passed over, and found in my way a good old Man, who discoursed a great while with me about all these Antiquities; and how that in those Days there was more Men morally Good than now, though they

they had not the Knowledge of the true God; but at present, with all this Knowledge, the Christians were the most inclined to Wickedness of any, not having any thing amongst them but Injustice and Avarice: And hereupon he told me, that he had been one of the chief Men of the City of *Calix*, but that some wicked Varlets, out of meer Envy and Malice, had raised a Suit of Law against him, which had lasted above 30 Years, and had utterly ruined him.

After we had discoursed together of our Fortunes, I left him, and went back to *Calix*; where being come, I went to see the Apothecary of the Army of Don *Louis Fajardo*, who was at the Hospital of the sick and wounded Men, returned from *Barbary*. I was not a little astonished to see this miserable Place; for it was a pitiful House which they had taken near the Wall of the City, there to dispose of the poor wounded Soldiers whilst the Army should be there. I entred then into this dreadful Place, full of the Cries and Complaints of these poor sick Men, who were but ill

ill looked after and dressed, after having taken so much pains to fight against the Infidels: They were very badly and dirtily lodged; and it was a horrible Sight to see so much Blood spilled in Vessels hard by them: Their Beds were like Hamocks, to wit, Quastres, as they call them, which are a sort of Ladders 7 or 8 Foot long, and 4 or 5 in breadth, and are hung with Cords, some high, and others lower, and are fastened one to another. But I was no less astonish'd to see the Apothecary, considering the mean Equipage he was in, and had nothing at all but a few Boxes in a corner badly placed, and worse furnished, as I believe. We discoursed a little together, and he told me, amongst other things, that there was a great deal of Money due to him, which he should never be payed off.

After that, seeing that I could not there find any means of Embarkment, I left *Calix,* and with no small trouble and fatiegue I returned towards *San Luçar* and *Saville*, and passed through *Rote*, a little City, and by an Abbey called *Nostre Segnore de Rhede,*
and

and from thence I came to a Place named *Chipione*, where having gotten some Money by certain Cures, I returned to San *Lucar*, and from thence to *Sevillia*, where I was forced to continue for some time and joined my self with a certain Apothecary, who lived in the *Triane*, or on the other side of the Bridge. This *Triane* is a Suburb on the other side the River of *Qualquiver*, which hath a Castle, where is the *Inquisition*, or *Holy-Office*, as they call it. This Apothecary made Profession of Christianity, but was held for a Jew, as he made it appear to me; for he treated me but scurvily, notwithstanding the Service that I did him in his *Alquitarres*, or *Limbecks*. I endured a great deal of Hardship with him, and became extream sick with a Vomiting, and a Bloody-flux, so that I thought I shou'd have died, and had no small trouble to recover my self; never receiving Help from this *Jew*, or any of his.

Whilst I was there, I remember that they of the Parish of St. *Ann*, or the Suburb of *Triane*, made a Procession on *Palm-Sunday* in the Evening

ing, carrying all lighted Wax-Candles, and sung a Hymn in Honour of the Blessed Virgin, to shew that she was conceived without Original Sin; to which they applied the Words of the Royal Psalmist, *Cœli enarrant gloriam Dei; & in sole posuit tabernaculum suum*, &c. and other such-like things. And hereupon the whole City of *Seville* was in an Uproar, and there were some Priests themselves put into the *Inquisition*, because they had the Boldness to maintain, that the Virgin was conceiv'd in Sin; insomuch that there was likely to be a great Tumult; and my *Jew* was then in such fear, that he durst scarcely stir out of his House, though he was of this same Parish. There was some, who either out of Fear, or Devotion, wore, writ upon their Hatbands in great Letters, these Words, *Sin pecado Original voto a tal*: to shew that they believed, or would have others believe. At the same time they caused to be cut before the great Church in *Seville*, upon a Marble-Table, in golden Letters, **Concebida sin pecado Original.**

Leaving

Leaving then my Apothecary, still sick as I was, having found some Friends who lent me Money, I returned towards *San Lucar,* in Hopes to find Means to embark my self, not for the *Indies,* (of which I had lost all Hopes,) but to return into *France* : But as my bad Fortune would have it, not far from *San Lucar* I was Robbed in the Pinars; and coming to *San Lucar,* I soon found out who it was that had robbed me, but I durst scarce speak thereof for fear of worse; besides there, as in other Places, Justice is very difficult to be had without Money.

Return into France. At last, having found an Opportunity to go for *France,* we parted, (Ten Ships we were in Consort, and held our course far out in the Sea, for fear of the Ships of *Tunis*: The Ship wherein I was, was of *Incuse* in *Holland,* and the Captain was named *Jan Taye.*

Now one Day, when it was a great Calm, this Captain invited on board his Ship the Admiral, and Vice-Admiral, with other Captains, who had treated him before : And after having made good Cheer together, and drunk

plentifully

plentifully of these *Spanish* Wines, they withdrew themselves each one on board his own Ship. In the mean time the Wind began to rise, and we were forced to change the Sails; but all the Mariners, and the Pilot himself, were so drunk, that they knew not what they did: When he who was at the Helm commanded to set to the Larboard, they hal'd to the Starboard, having the Wind in their Faces; one cried this way, another that way, it being the greatest Confusion in the World, not one understanding what another said. When I saw that, I took the Helm my self, and brought the Ship fairly before the Wind; then came a *French* Mariner, who was just come out of Captivity from *Barbary*, and had not drank so much as the rest. I quitted the Bar to him, because I was bid to beware of the Captain, who was in a great Rage against me: Nevertheless that hindred me not from going to find him out upon the Deck, where he was still emptying some Bottles of Wine with his Mariners. As soon as he saw me, he began to mutter something to himself; whereupon

I took

I took up a Cup and drank to him, which pacified him a little, and told me that he was very angry with me; and having asked him the Cause, he shewed me his Arm, scarce being able to speak, meaning to tell me that I had never a Lancet to let Blood. Hereupon I doubted that a wicked *Norman* had told him of that; for in parting from *San Lucar* I had told him how I had been Robb'd, yet I had made Provision of Medicines to cure the Sick when there should be occasion; and I had cured the Captain's own Brother of a certain Pain that he had in his Legs, which was no small Help to me; for ever since that time he was always my Friend against those who had a mind to do me any wrong, and especially this *Norman*, who made it his chief Business to exasperate these People against me, to the end that they might do me Mischief; but God preserved me from them. The next Day they took a poor Boy, a *Fleming*, who was a Passenger, and tied him fast to the great Sail-yard, to duck him into the Sea, because, as they said, he had been drunk;

drunk, and had spoiled the Deck: He was thus hoised up Three times by the Sail-yard, and so duck'd in the Sea, after the Captain had first drank to him, which he pledged. 'Twas a great Pity to hear the Cries and Complaints of this poor Boy, and I was not able to behold a Spectacle so cruel, but withdrew my self below Deck, where in the mean time I heard them murmuring against me, at the Inspiration of this *Norman*, who had been Captain of a Ship in the New-found Lands, and was now a Passenger in this Vessel, having more store of Crowns than Good-nature.

After having sailed thus for some time, we arrived happily, by the Grace of God, at the *Havre*, the 15th. Day of *August*, 1615. and from thence I went straight to *Paris*, which was the Term of all my Voyages, and of this last Peregrination, which was more troublesome and incommodious than long. But God be praised for all, to whom I render infinite Thanks that it hath pleased his Divine Goodness to preserve me from my Infancy to this time, from so many several Misfortunes and

Arrival at Paris.

and Difficulties which I have met withal: For I was but at my Mother's Breasts in the Year 1576. when my Father was Imprisoned at *Meaux* for being Surety for a Debt, which he was obliged to pay; and whilst he had Permission to provide accordingly, it behoved my Mother to supply his Place in the Prison with me; and thus began I betimes to resent the Miseries of the World, which since in greater Age I have experienc'd more fully, and more roughly, in regard of my almost-continual Absence from my native Country, in strange Lands, and remote Places, devoid of all Comfort, and exposed to all sorts of Miseries that could befall any Man; and moreover, since my Return into mine own native Country, I have not been exempted from the like Misfortunes and Calamities, having had but very little Support from Men, assisted only by the Providence of my God, who hath never forsaken me, but hath caused the Afflictions which he hath pleased to send me, to be an Object to several Persons of Honour to exercise towards me their Good and Laudable Charities.

FINIS.

www.ingramcontent.com/pod-product-compliance
Lightning Source LLC
Chambersburg PA
CBHW051732300426
44115CB00007B/520